A LIFE-SAVING
GIVER

A Rescuer of the Perishing

The revelation of the ministry of the Lord Jesus through the parable of the good Samaritan on the platform of Giving

Dominic Adu

A Life-Saving Giver
Copyright © 2023 by Dominic Adu

ISBN: 978-1639459940 (sc)
ISBN: 978-1639459957 (e)

Writers' Branding
(877) 608-6550
www.writersbranding.com
media@writersbranding.com

Table of Contents

Acknowledgment vii

Blurbs ix

Introduction

    Giving Sustains the World xiii

Notable Points xv

CHAPTER ONE: Everyone is Needy 1

    To Survive, Every Creature is Important 2

    Men need Other Men more than other Creatures 3

        The Uniqueness of Eve 6

        Original Condition for the Additional Operation Underlying the Divine Biological formation of ONE-FLESH in Marriage 6

        Men are Mission-Helpers 21

            The Need for Unity Among Men 22

            The Flaw of Some United Men 29

    Significant Notes 33

CHAPTER TWO: The Giver versus The Receiver 36

    Similarities Between Givers and Receivers 37

        Respect for Receivers 38

        Respect for Givers 42

    What makes Givers Differ from Receivers 44

        More Blessed to Give than to Receive 44

        The Sower and the Eater 48

            God's Resources Allocation Plan to Meet Men's Needs 49

        SELFISHNESS – the reason some people cannot become wealthy 53

The Accountability associated to Riches 58

Significant notes.. 67

CHAPTER THREE: How to Give and How to Receive 70

The Proper Basis for Giving... 70

Wrong Ways of Claiming to Receive 73

Men to God Requisition Relationship 74

Absurd Character of Receivers from God.............................. 74

Reasons Some Blessings Delay.................................... 76

A Ceaseless Cause to Show Gratitude to God.................. 86

Past, Present and Future Causes to Thank God.............. 87

Men to Men Requisition Relationship............................ 100

Wrong Approach for Requesting from Men.................... 100

Summary points to note 107

CHAPTER FOUR: Overcoming Barriers to Giving 111

Ungratefulness 111

To the Betrayed Giver having trust issues 117

Fear 119

To the Potential Giver gripped by Fear 123

Discrimination 124

First Root of Discrimination - History 127

To the Historically discriminatory Giver........................ 128

Second Root of Discrimination - Contempt 135

To the Despising Discriminatory Giver........................... 136

Notable Points.. 138

CHAPTER FIVE: The Necessary Queries on Giving Answered 144

Who Must Give?.. 145

What can One Give? 147

The Wrong Gift and Wrong Reception....................................148

Why Must One Give? 152

    Freely Given, Freely Give..153

        Breath of Life was Given 153

        Just Custodians, not Full Owners..................................156

    Reflecting Increase in one's Divine Accounts......................165

    Former Experience 169

Notable Points..170

CHAPTER SIX: A Life-saving Giver 175

    LESSONS FROM THE GOOD SAMARITAN 177

    Characteristics of a Life-saving Giver. 177

        Is Eternal Life Conscious 177

        Qualifies to be called a Neighbour 187

        Is Spirit-led 192

        Stands in the gap 197

        Overcomes all Barriers to Giving...................................202

        Is Godly but Not Religious...212

        Gives not on Condition 215

    Points to note 217

CHAPTER SEVEN: The Theme Centred on Jesus Christ
The Ultimate Life-Saviour..220

    JESUS EQUATED TO THE GOOD SAMARITAN.............221

    Jesus was Eternal-life Conscious 221

    Jesus was a True Neighbour 223

    Jesus was Spirit-led 224

    Jesus stood in the gap 226

    Jesus was Godly but not religious 229

    Jesus gave His life unconditionally 231

Jesus is Coming Back Again 232

The Assurance of the company of the Holy Spirit 233

Revealing the current Ministry of Jesus from the
Good Samaritan Parable 234

The Work of the Evangelist/Apostle........................... 234

The work of Pastors, Teachers and Prophets 236

Back Again with his Reward... 238

Back Again to take God's children Home............................. 240

Uncertainty of His coming 241

A call to become a Life-saving Giver.................................... 242

Notable bullets 243

Acknowledgment

Where are the friends of a person who is at the verge of failing? Whoops! Hardly can any of such be found. Though many stand by a man when everything goes well with him; yet, it is difficult to find any by him when he is forced to descend the mountain top to the valley by the waves that oppose destiny. Many can easily identify themselves with the successful. When one triumphs in life, even his enemies become his lovers and his accusers become his supporters. That is one of the dilemmas of life that is hard to explain but has been accepted as it is.

It happened to the Lord Jesus along His mission on earth. At the point where He was at the brink of offering Himself to be sacrificed as the lamb of God; when he was caught up, bound and being buffeted, in what seemed like a failure in life, men of all sorts rejected Him. Yet He was the mission of God at play as it had been inscribed in divine scrolls before the foundation of the earth. Jesus cannot fail; He snatched victory out of the jaws of defeat! When He had done that being witnessed by Heaven and earth as the Risen Christ, all who rejected Him came back to Him.

It is God our everlasting Father who never forsakes and unto Him be the glory forever and ever. Just as Christ spoke through His anointed king David about Himself that 'For You will not leave my soul in Shoel, nor will You allow Your Holy One to see corruption,' Christ did not remain in Shoel, He was raised back by the Spirit of the Father. Even up to the deepest pit, God shows up to those who trust in His mercy to keep them back standing tall again. Unto the faithful God, never disappointing God, and the Good Shepherd of my life who owns the glory of my life be honour forever and ever.

Blessed is he who supports God's mission; for a mission of God cannot fail. Him whom God has not taken out cannot be taken out by any abstract or tangible force. God bless everyone who saw what God had envisioned for my life and supported me; prayed with me and for me. Worthy are they to be labelled among Life Saving Givers who always focus on what God can make out of what is generally seen as nothing. Forever am I in their hearts and forever are they in mine. God bless them all. My appreciation goes to the great men and women of God who, having read excerpts of this book, gave me their reviews to add to the Blurb, and encouraged me. Jill and John Pauling whom I got introduced to by Rev. Kina Robertshaw did an exceptional work with proofreading the book, God bless you all.

Get a peep through this manuscript; along the line as you read, you will hear God speak His mind. Let the ready ear grasp what the Spirit has for God's children. God bless you!

<u>Blurbs</u>

"Life Saving Giver is an excellent book that will strengthen the revelatory flow on giving. Whether, a one off read, or utilised as a devotional for small group purpose, all who engage will grow as Kingdom Givers"

Rev. Alan Ross (Scottish)
Associate Pastor, Gateway Church
Glasgow, Scotland, United Kingdom

The author's reflection of the ministry of the Lord Jesus through the parable of the good Samaritan is true. That's a wonderful explanation for His divine missionary work and how His believers ought to conduct themselves. This is highly an inspired message from Jesus and the author has gotten it right by the grace of God and the act of the Holy Spirit.

Rev. Edward Kwarteng (Ghanaian)
Published Author in the USA
Ghana

A Life-Saving Giver by Dominic Adu reflects on the important parable of the Good Samaritan in the Bible. He weaves creative imaginations through this biblical concept and connects it to contemporary life issues. Dominic draws very vital lessons that are relevant to our everyday lives from this story. Dominic reminds all believers in Jesus Christ, not minding titles or offices held, of the importance of spending time with the Word of God and being led by the Spirit. He further admonishes believers to show genuine compassion to people around us, connect with their needs – physical, spiritual, material, or in any way, and do all we can to meet these. Where we don't have what it takes to practically meet these, he recommends seeking God for a solution and not leaving the needy in their needy state. "A Life-Saving Giver" is a thought-provoking piece of work.

Dr. Yinka Somorin (Nigerian)
Researcher, Research Consultant
Scientific Writing and Editor
Ajayi Crowther University
Glasgow, Scotland, UK

This book provides a profound and enlightening perspective on the interconnectedness of giving and receiving, shedding light on the inherent value and necessity of both roles within any community. The emphasis on respect for receivers is a refreshing take that highlights the dignity inherent in receiving. It compels readers to reevaluate societal attitudes towards giving and receiving, urging a move away from viewing receivers merely as beneficiaries to acknowledging them as integral to the process that allows givers to realize the actual worth of their possessions or wealth. Furthermore, the book serves as a revelation on the true value of possessions, which is not in their mere existence but in their ability to effect positive change in the lives of others. This insight encourages a shift from accumulating wealth for its own sake to viewing wealth as a tool for fostering wellbeing and happiness. This is a truly inspiring book that will revolutionise Christians views on giving and receiving.

> Dr. Bla J. Charlotte Eba (Ivorian)
> Lecturer & Module Coordinator,
> Economics Principles for Business
> Member of the Centre for African
> Research on Enterprise and Economic
> Development

This book is absolutely unputdownable. It is the antidote of life's current grimness. Are you ready to find the purpose of God for your life? Then I recommend that you get a copy of .... and start turning the pages. Reading this book reminded me of this declaration from St Augustine 'You have made us for yourself, O Lord, and our heart is restless until it rests in you.'

> Asongacha E. Leke (Cameroonian)
> Teacher of philosophy
> Postgraduate diploma in education
> Business Analyst.

'Dominic has sincerely tried to tease out the work of the Holy Spirit in the acts of 'Giving and Receiving'. His exposition of the parable of the Good Samaritan presents us with a challenging model for our own lives. This culminates in the examination of the ongoing work of the Holy Spirit in Jesus Christ's earthly ministry. No stone has been left unturned.'

Jill and John Pauling (English)
Retired Headteachers

Introduction

Giving Sustains the World

It is essential for every being to give as far as living is concerned. This is because every aspect of life is one way or the other supported by giving. One creature gives out to support the life of others and in turn receives from others to survive. The life cycle of plants as well as that of animals depict the very fact that a living creature alone cannot provide the supporting elements of its life all by itself. Plants depend on almost all the excretory products that result from the metabolic reactions that take place in animals. Part goes to them directly through absorption (carbon dioxide, a necessary raw material for photosynthesis) and the rest indirectly by enriching the soil which ensures a proper medium for growth and development of the plants. Conversely, humans and other animals depend on glucose as an energy source, but they are unable to produce it on their own and must rely ultimately on the glucose produced by plants. Moreover, the oxygen humans and other animals breathe is the oxygen released during photosynthesis, the biochemical process through which plants prepare their food. Thus, animals give to plants while plants also give to animals in order for each to survive. Such is the established interdependence between and among living beings.

The water cycle is another good example which portrays the interdependence of the atmospheres and the earth. Water falling from the atmosphere forms pools, lakes, rivers and streams which join to the sea. Other part of the rainfall is imbibed by the earth to provide it with the suitable moisture necessary for plant growth. Notwithstanding, the rest of the rainfall settles at bed rocks deep down the earth from where wells are drawn to quench the thirst of man and also for other domestic activities. The earth does not play selfishly after receiving from the atmosphere. All human activities resulting in gases go to the atmosphere. The seas, rivers, lagoons, lakes and other water bodies also give back water to the atmosphere through evaporation as the sun directs its beam of rays on them. The plants also lose water to the atmosphere through transpiration. Some of this water taken by the atmosphere is used to ensure a humid and environmentally friendly air that makes it possible for man and animals to survive. The rest of the water taken up together with the gases is used by the atmosphere to form clouds from which rain is formed and brought back to earth. Look at how the display of giving here is ensuring the sustenance of animate and inanimate together with the whole world.

No party among the elements of nature plays stingy when it gets to its turn to give. They automatically release out what is in their custody when the appropriate season and time comes for them to give. In fact, God who created them is very wise. He has made it in such a way that the provision, in other words products, of the individual parties serves as raw materials to the agent of the subsequent activity so as to ensure the smooth execution of the next process in time by the other parties. For that matter, the sessions for the display of the output of each element of nature is not curtailed. Every element gets the sufficient essentials at its disposal when it must begin its process. All because the others would have already given out what they ought to give. By this the earth and the world is sustained. The elements of the world understand each other. They do not hesitate to extend their possession from one another. As a result, the four seasons are kept in place and each comes at its appointed time. The reason being that the elements of nature, which God has compounded the world with, understands giving.

Notable Points

➤ Every aspect of life is one way or the other supported by giving

➤ Animals give to plants while plants also give to animals in order for each to survive. Such is the established interdependence between and among living beings.

➤ Every element of the world gets the sufficient essentials at its disposal the time it must begin its process. All because the others would have already given out what they ought to give. By this the earth and the world is sustained

➤ The elements of the world understand the necessity of giving. They do not hesitate to extend their possession from one another.

CHAPTER ONE

Everyone is Needy

Each organism on earth depends on whatever its neighbour has to offer in order to get in full measure of that which will keep it strong and help it to thrive successfully as a living being. That is exactly how the Creator of the creatures has designed existence to be. No being can go away from this manner of interdependence and continue in life and survive the systems of this natural ecosystem. Thus, if any being decides not to receive any gift from any other, then that being is likely only to exist for a very short time interval of life. Conversely, if every being decides to hoard what he has in his possession and decides not to give it out to any other, then each being will be lacking a fraction of the needed essentials of life; and as a result, all beings will fail to survive. **Therefore, everyone is needy in the sense that each living being is in need of some part of the possessions of his neighbour in order to make a complete life meal**. (Only God is self-sufficient and in fact, only He is not needy)

It therefore implies that the inability of one to give puts some other neighbour of his who needs some part of his possession to survive into a critical situation which can terminate the victim's life. So, life should not be about always receiving but rather about giving out and taking in. At a certain time, one must receive and at another time one must give. Yes, it is because according to the ecclesiastical times and seasons, it has been written that there is a 'Time to cast away stones, and a time to gather stones; A time to embrace, and a time to refrain from embracing; A time to gain and a time to lose; A time to keep and a time to throw away.' (Eccl 3:5,6) It is important to maintain an equilibrium between giving and receiving. An imbalance either way, especially giving, could be very dangerous.

To Survive, Every Creature is Important

Yes, you need me and I need you. We need them and they need us. To survive we need one another. As a matter of fact, every living or non-living thing around us is one way or the other beneficial to us. Whether directly or indirectly, they form part of the overall constitution of the environment that makes life meaningful and survivable. All kinds of trees are of great benefit to humanity. Water bodies around us cannot be underemphasised with regards to their immense significance towards survival of human beings. Animals on the other hand serve different purposes such as pets, food, work force, travelling media, etc.

Even animals we might not like are still important as far as successful existence in the environment is concerned. Taking for instance biodegradable organisms which help in the decomposition of organic matter. Those microorganisms such as bacteria, fungi, etc. are not nice to look upon. Some people will even vomit seeing them. Nevertheless, we must doubtlessly admit that without their action the world would have turned into a difficult place to live. This is because, without them, the management of the organic waste produced by human beings would be a burden for us. Even the cockroach and the mice you are fighting everyday have some importance. Biologically, every living thing has some economic importance that affects the natural ecosystem.

It will surprise you to know that the mosquito, that sucks human blood and in turn causes malaria, is of importance. Bear with me here because I know that the negative actions of some insects and organisms have caused some people to generate a great hatred against them. To identify whether these organisms are actually beneficial or not depends on the angle you view them from. Maybe you only centre your conclusion on the negative effects they might have caused you, your loved ones and your properties. But the truth is they are of use in the other waysides. Unless you are told, you might never know how useful they are in other fields.

Mosquitoes for example play a very important role in pollination of plants. Even with the species which suck human blood, the anopheles, only the females do so. The males serve a great purpose in plant pollination. Someone would say, 'Why not wipe out all the females who suck human blood from the world?'. If that is done, how would the males then be produced. Mind you, the action of the males which is plant pollination goes a long way to help in the production of fruits and food that we human beings feed on.

You see, the organism you might detest and even see as a menace might be the one which is, in the long run, feeding you. So, in conclusion, the chimpanzee is useful, the millipedes and centipedes are of great importance, and so does the little ant have a great value of significance in the environment around us. If you doubt it, enquire about them from a zoologist. Or better research the one you strongly believe is never of use and that, left to you alone, it must be eliminated from the world. Therefore, we need the animals around us to survive.

Men need Other Men more than other Creatures

If that conclusion is established that we need even the animals around us to survive, how much more other human beings. The most complex formulated organism God created is the human being. God fearfully and wonderfully made him. A human being therefore surpasses all the other creatures in every sort of quality. No matter the kind, colour, race, strength, etc. that a particular human is made up of, no other non-human creature of the world can be compared to that human being. All because a human being is a replica of God's image while other beings are not. It is awesome and also awful that a human being will reject another human being for an animal; giving respect to the animal more than the other human being who is made in the likeness of God. That is a deceptive brainwashing mind-set attributable to the devices of Satan to create discrimination and separation.

Other creatures, especially animals, provide companionship and other importance which cannot be underemphasised; yet, the significance of animals' help is way below that of a human being. I read a caption from a label just at the front of a pet's servicing shop in Scotland. It read, 'Give a dog a bone, and give an animal a home'. Very touching as I thought about it. All because, animals deserve to be treated naturally as they are created so that they fit well in our environment. So, I thought as much that animals are worthy to be given homes so as to explore all the positive impacts within them that they could have in the community which would in turn affect human beings. Now, the other thought that dawned on me while thinking about it was the question, 'If animals need to be given a home, then what would a human being need to be given? If an animal needs to be given a home, then a human being needs to be given more than a home around us. Yes, because a man needs another man more than an animal per the divine designation of God.

Let me draw your attention back to the Garden of Eden. God created whatever a man will need to survive before creating the man himself. God is good. He thinks about His children far ahead before His children get to any point. Before sending the people of Israel to the promised land, He made sure the place had already been developed such that it was qualified as a land flowing with milk and honey. God never leads us to doom. Whoever will follow God obediently would indeed end up in peace. That's what Eden was made up of. A garden of peace. Whatever would give man happiness and a sense of quality life was available. All what God created from the first to fifth day, with animals inclusive, was because of the subsequent creation, man.

The essence behind the need of the presence of an animal or other creatures is to positively impact a human being. So, God had placed all of them there before creating His image, Adam. With all their importance, how helpful they were to Adam in Eden had a limit. All because, though they were in their right positions, when God, being caring still thought of man, He identified that man needed another being for his successful survival to accomplish the mission He had given him. Let's consider His concern from the word of God.

"Then the LORD God took man and put him in the garden of Eden **to tend and keep it**. ...... And the LORD God said, '**It is not good that man should be alone**; I will make him a helper **comparable to him**.'" (Gen 2:15,18)

Considering carefully, God placed man into his furnished abode and then gave him something to do. He gave man a mission to accomplish. That was to tend and keep the place. The man, our foremost grandfather, Adam accepted his work in good faith believing that he had all it takes to do it. Looking at his surroundings he imagined everything for him was intact and he would not be in need of any other thing. Yet, God being so wise and all-knowing identified that man still needed something else. He reasoned, 'It is not good that man should be alone'. God Himself saying something is not good means that it was really not good. This implies what was missing was indeed a necessity for man, not a want. Man needed a helper which made him needy. That helper, God affirmed, was one comparable to him not the other creatures.

In addition, it stands to mean that a man without other men is alone, no matter how many other creatures he/she is surrounded with. Adam was surrounded by a greater number of 'obedient' animals than any man can afford today; yet, God confirmed that Adam was alone. Yes, 'It is not good that you should be alone'; thus says the Lord to he/she who has rejected the company of other men for that of animals. Let it be categorically affirmed beyond a shadow of doubt that if the other animals were worthy to help man for the particular said mission, God wouldn't have brought Eve to the scene.

The Uniqueness of Eve

The helper God envisioned was one comparable to the man but not as the animals. Additionally, the qualities, fashion and makeup of that helper was unique. The characteristics of this helper were to meet the missing element in the originally existing man to help him accomplish his given missions. The first most important among the conditions to facilitate those missions was procreation and therefore the next to Adam needed to be a female. Eve had got to have some qualities that would help Adam to procreate so that many other men would be produced as helpers to Adam's other visions and missions. There was already a lot of work for Adam to do and for his plight, he was alone. Hence, for the purpose of procreation, God instituted marriage that day so that other men would be produced. 'Therefore, a man shall leave his father and mother and be joined to his wife, and they shall become one flesh' (Genesis 2:24).

Thus, the law for the institution of marriage was enacted right from the onset. Whoever regards the constitution of God which is His word would honour such and not violate it. Honouring the word of God would produce the right results God intended for the two becoming one flesh. Therefore, any man who plans to marry must get the opposite sex in order to fulfil the divine mathematical theory of adding two people to become one flesh which was instituted by God Himself from the beginning. Apart from satisfying the conditions of the two terms of the divine additional operation which is man plus woman, the result will not and cannot be one. Detailed explanation is illustrated below:

Original Condition for the Additional Operation Underlying the Divine Biological formation of ONE-FLESH in Marriage

Man + Woman = One Flesh with paralleled visions from two
mended personalities (Satisfied)

Man + Man = Two people with unparalleled visions from two
distinct personalities (Undefined)

Woman + woman = Two people with unparalleled visions from
two far diverse persons (Undefined)

Thus, to satisfy the original instituted equation of producing one flesh in marriage to tackle the mission that God has given to man, the different arguments of the divine additional operation should be a man and a woman. The one flesh produced has an urge towards a common vision such that the two constituents which are the man and the woman come to easily understand each other towards the will God has for them. In other words, this correct biological combination will produce the right inward chemistry among the couple thereby ensuring the proper outward physics in their lives. Achieving the aim God has for the couple then becomes easier since spiritually, emotionally and physically, the two are driven towards the same or similar direction. Thus, they become one flesh with paralleled visions. The products of the visions of the female end up as a support for the male to successfully achieve his God-mandated vision. Likewise, the male acts as a support to help the female achieve all her Spirit-led yearnings which are divinely committed to her. Together with that common urge and understanding, they are not far from accomplishing the desire of God upon their lives.

Notwithstanding, we should not be unaware that there could still be correct understanding between two people coming together in such respect, as it is today, but do not fall into the original plan of God: thus, a man with another man or a woman with another woman. Certainly, such instances can occur where two people with the same sex intending to forgo the plan of God and to marry, have common aspirations, desires, etc. yet; note that their vision to achieve will be way meandered from what God designed for them individually. They can achieve something great in the perspective of the world but not before God. In that way they would have pleased themselves and the world around them but would have missed the purpose of God for their lives in which lies the salvation of their souls. In effect, the act of those trying to reject the original plan of God concerning establishing marriage would not benefit them in the long run. All because the one flesh composition wouldn't be achieved in their marriages; that act would amount to despising and rebelling against God; and as a result, they would be separated from God forever which means loss of salvation.

The one flesh composition was God's original intention about marriage when He thought of man's immediate companion of help before other external companions. It is beyond doubt that God could have created another human being from scratch if He desired to do so. The important question is why He didn't do that but took away a rib from the existing man to model another and afterwards called two of them one. It is better to explore the intentions of God than to just accept some unjustified ideologies which we might think would be best for us; all because it falls within our fleshly desires. I believe every person would want to enjoy his/her rights and live happily as possible as he/she can. Nevertheless, we cannot deny how procreation began with regards to the original plan of God. Therefore, as we concentrate on our rights and freedoms the systems of this world make available for us, the will of God from the beginning cannot be underemphasised. In the divine view, some of the acts we assume today as our rights are wrong; only within God would we identify what is rightly right among our present rights.

God created the path through which the process of procreation must occur among men. It is therefore unjustified before God for man to develop some other paths to procreate different from that of God and therefore obtain the desire for same sex marriage. God's way of getting children or bringing human beings into the world is the right and justified path rather than the other numerous paths that can be suggested by the world today. Trials that could be done on trees and animals should never be tempted on the images of God, men!

What about if someone does not have the desire to procreate and hence would want to reject the thought of having children, and as a result, resort to same sex marriage? I believe that man, so far as he was born, must reconsider his position, think about how he himself came into being and desist from reasoning that way. That person wouldn't have lived and gotten such wisdom operating from a-God-made brain if he was not procreated. Before one concludes that people are becoming too many and for that matter there is overpopulation and hence think to develop devices and measures to curb it, take time when making such a consideration. Don't be too much in a hurry, lest your miscalculations would land you into concluding wrongly. Had your grandfather's generation thought of these and hence decided not to produce your fathers, where would you have been? Or even not that far, if your parents' generation decided not to need any more men and hence employed weapons to battle procreation, I believe you wouldn't have existed to have a deep-developed brain that reasons the way you are reasoning now. A man must take time to think through what he intends to do whether his action will be in line with the original plan of God.

Inventions are good, new things are better and innovations are excellent, but nothing can succeed wiping off or altering the original intention of God from existence as it was from the beginning. Though there could be some trials in the aim of trying to attack the divine institution, such trials are temporal; they just evaporate and vanish with time. Anti-God-institutions cannot ever be established and last on the already founded foundation God has made. Those rebelling institutions that seem prevailing today have been allowed by God for His wrath to consume them at the day of judgement.

God is always new, so are His ways and His intentions. His words cannot be outmoded; everything can pass away but not a word that has come out from God's mouth. So, the king Solomon in his wisdom said, 'That which has been is what will be, that which is done is what will be done, and there is no new thing under the sun.' (Ecclesiastes 1:9) The original plan of God shall always be and must always be because God knows the best. In the pursuit to alter God's plan, men fail in their own strength because the source of men's strength is God. The power behind the constitution of our wisdom is from God and God is the author of our understanding. To slip off our divine cognitive foundation is to fall into the pit nearby – Satan's bosom.

If it was not that men have rejected God and His council, why would one want to obstruct other men from coming into existence with the reason that the earth is becoming full, and that resource sharing will be difficult. God who measured the layout of this earth, dug the foundation and built it understands how the earth could contain the number of men that would inhabit it. And He who causes flowers to blossom so that seeds and fruits will be produced to feed men on earth knows very well how He would feed the numerous men inhabiting the earth through birth. The innumerable birds and other terrestrial animals are not a nuisance to the earth, the sea, oceans, etc. Other water bodies have not complained of lack of space for the innumerable fishes they provide shelter for; why are men complaining about overpopulation of men? The problem to tackle is not the number of people but the character of already existing persons which causes inconvenience to their fellows and other humans yet to be born. Hence combating overpopulation through reduction in birth rate to reduce inconvenience is a miss of target.

It is beyond doubt that a man is the most important of all other creatures; yet these other creatures do not have anything like birth control. Different greater numbers of different creatures enter existence every now and then. The sad thing is that the man who is supposed to have dominion over these creatures is being restricted to come into existence; all in the name of controlling overpopulation. It wouldn't be surprising that the other creatures would grow and outnumber men and then rather take dominion over men; except God intervenes. Why would a man want to block his own seeds from coming out of him into existence?

We never know the stars upon the seeds we contain as men. Unless children grow up and unleash the potential within them, sometimes no one would even know that a particular man had some valuable gift inside him. All because those potentials are latently hidden by the God who forms them from scratch through the supernatural combination of sperm and egg upon the unseen medium of dust. So, it will be better to give these stars the opportunity to live to deliver what the creator has placed in them.

You will agree with me that there are a lot of generals of God, great leaders, celebrities and stars that have made impact and are currently making impact on the earth who were 5th born, 6th born, 9th born and even beyond that. Supposing their parents blocked them from coming into existence, imagine how much the world would have missed. Don't forget about these remarkable figures in the bible: Joseph was the eleventh among the sons of Jacob, David was the eighth and youngest son of his father Jesse, etc. This is to acknowledge that aside from God using first, second and third borns, He also uses those beyond that number of births to do extraordinary things. So why then are we seeking to deny such borns entry and hence serving as restriction to what God might have intended to use them for. It would be extremely sad for God to have had a purpose for your fifth child, but you stopped at two.

Even hell has opened its mouth wide to receive men into death, why wouldn't the earth accept men into life through birth. Hardships of this current world could deter us from attaining many rich possibilities in God, beware! When we put our trust and confidence in God, all heights become reachable. The desire and decision of man to restrict the entry of other men into the earth must be carefully reconsidered and one of those methods of birth control which is same sex marriage be shun completely.

Now, what about those who do not have the ability to procreate because it is well acknowledged that some people are barren. Yes, there is the possibility of having people like that. It should be understood, that it is not compulsory for a married couple to have a child if they sincerely do not have the ability to do so. In God's own wisdom, some people can be barren their whole lifetime. The explanation of that is up to God alone who knows all things. All because there are many who have remained barren their whole lives though they were married correctly as the original marriage God established in the beginning, thus male-female marriage. Some of such people eventually get healed from infertility either by divine intervention or by the ministry of medicine; yet most others remain infertile their lifetimes. There is therefore the possibility for some people to find themselves barren and that they cannot produce offspring their whole lifetime.

Today there are technological diagnostic systems such as ultrasonography, sonohysterography, etc. used in the health sector that can make people aware of one's fertility status. They are doubtless a plus for our advancement in technology and hence making great impact; yet that does not call for a reason for same sex marriage. The inability to reproduce is not a justification for bumping into same sex marriage. All because the companionship and complements to be satisfied in God's own wisdom for the institution of marriage demands the opposite sex as it is from beginning. Everyone is needy and some needs are unique and hence such needs require unique help from unique givers. God gave that specific need to Adam.

The institution of marriage God created right from the beginning was in such a way that the specific deficiencies of affection in Adam as a man would be met through Eve; and the other way round, Eve would also be satisfied the same way. It is within this phenomenon of chemistry that the one flesh nature is created from the two different personalities. Indeed, a woman in her own assessment will know better what womanhood needs but does not have what it takes to provide it; so is a man. By divine order the elements of need in the flesh with regards to marriage for one sex is built within the opposite sex. It is also therefore unjustified before God for men to look for other media to satisfy themselves other than the original plan of God which is right from the beginning. Every spot demands a perfect fit; not just anything at all to fill the space!

When you look at how Eve came into being through the Creator's wisdom of fashioning her, it is worthy for men to get into the original plan of God with regards to marriage. Get a closer look now:

And the Lord God caused a deep sleep to fall on Adam, and he slept; and He took **one of his ribs**, and closed up the flesh **in its place**. Then the rib which the Lord God had taken from man He made into a woman, and He brought her to the man. And Adam said: "This is now bone of my bones and flesh of my flesh; she shall be called Woman, because she was taken out of Man." (Genesis 2:21-23)

This is the genesis of the two shall become one flesh. All because he was one, and one rib was taken away to provide another help of his similitude. Adam was made incomplete because of Eve. The manifestation of Eve made it necessary for a space to be created in Adam which occurred as a result of God taking out one of his ribs. A woman therefore is the cause of the more incompleteness of man. The product thereof in return became beneficial to man because the woman created out of his rib became the help offering services beyond what the inward rib could do. The new being created out of the rib, modelled into a fashionable form and named woman was a package containing a lot more than the single rib that Adam had in him. Adam was perplexed at the scene when he was enjoying the spectacle of the view of the new model which is a product from himself; hence, the God-factor in him aroused for him to name her Woman, a modelled product taken out of man.

Per the consideration and wise thought of God, the emergence of a woman would be of a greater help to the existing man, Adam. Eve had thus become composed of the same divine DNA as it is in Adam that bears the divine assignment of God. All because it was a duplicate of the chromosome arrangement on the rib taken from Adam that was expanded, divided and multiplied by divine creative ability to form Eve. So, in the external view of flesh, men would consider them two but in the sight of God, the two are one because they bear the same purpose. Their inner composition is aligned to accomplish the same unique mission set by God. It was for that reason that He took a portion from the existing man to create another being so that they would become two but one in the accomplishment of the mission at stake for Adam. In fact, God is wise! This is the beginning of the institution of marriage. Yes, the underlying reasons in the thought of God for creating Eve for Adam forms the foundation for marriage, and in fact, a divine marriage for that matter.

As a result, forsaking the foundation laid by God from the beginning would not help if a man seeks to find a wife or partner. All because finding a wife means finding a perfect fit for the space that has been created in man. If the one found is shorter than normal to fill the space, there would be uneasiness in the life of the man. If the one found is also longer than normal to fill the space, that would also cause an upset; this is where it is usually said 'she is a thorn in my flesh'. All because, since it is an imperfect fit, there is an imbalance created in the divine combination of the two becoming one flesh; hence there is an instance of piercing into the flesh causing uneasiness in the life of the two different parties because of an incomplete formation of the one flesh. Any of the two; either shorter than normal or longer than normal negatively affects the accomplishments of the mission set before the man.

Though there is very low probability of getting an ideal marriage; yet a wrong fit would cause a very tough time for both man and woman with regards to the mission set for them. The marriage which is hundred percent ideal and cannot be altered is the one between Christ and His bride, the church. Other godly marriages under the supervision of the Spirit of God also work very successfully well. Yet, a wrong match in choice of spouse would always affect how a man would match towards his mission. It either slows the accomplishment of a set task or destroys the vision and mission altogether. The intervention of God alone could cause a rescue in such an instance. Only God can make the impossible possible if this has already occurred; yet, it is worth embracing the will and original plan for the one who is yet to enter into the institution of marriage.

Every man has got a task at hand to accomplish; and that task is discovered at Eden, a delightful spot. A spot where God associates and communes with man and ushers the man into the divine mission which is predestined for the man before he was created into being. That calls for all men to seek God before planning to do anything in life. The reason is that God planned about you before bringing you into existence. God had started planning about your life long before you came into being; yes even before you yourself started thinking of planning. That means there is already a foreordained plan about man known to God but unknown to man; yet, searchable. The plan of God about a man can be sought for and found. Forsaking God to do our own things would rather be disastrous because God knows our end from our beginning. It is better for every man to search for that spot where he would have fellowship with God; so God will reveal to him what he is meant to do in this life. The reason is because life is really beyond what we see.

This life we see is about what God has got for us to do within our limit of available time. Time will be up soon for everyone. Whether one likes it or not, he would have to leave when his divinely appointed time is up; and the second, minute and hour hand of the clock keeps ticking. Thus, time waits for no one. So then, if a man is designed for marriage, then he ought to find the woman who divinely fits into the space created in him. I say a man designed for marriage because there are men who do not marry and yet can accomplish their set mission per the will of God. There is the possibility of that. The Lord Jesus Christ spoke about that when He was describing the reasons by which some men do not marry whom He referred to as eunuchs.

For there are eunuchs who were born thus from their mother's womb, and there are eunuchs who were made eunuchs by men, and there are eunuchs who have made themselves eunuchs for the kingdom of heaven's sake. He who is able to accept it, let him accept it. (Matthew 19:12)

This implies that there is the possibility of a man finding himself among such categories of eunuchs based on the ability of acceptance. Yet if a man would need a woman to accomplish a mission set for him, then obtaining the right woman is paramount with regards to the success in accomplishing given assignments. He who finds a wife has found a good thing (Prov. 18:22). So, the specific one to fill the gap in every man needs to be searched and found; and when found, life would be good. Good in the sense that there would be smooth progress towards the accomplishment of one's missions and visions.

So, the picture becomes clear now that for even a man to marry, it is not any woman that a man can choose that would help him to honour divine responsibilities assigned for him. How much more going over the boundary for same sex marriage? That would be worse with regards to the associated honour that must be given to our creator; and that would also totally deter one from attaining divine accomplishments through executing divine responsibilities. All because the services the opposite sex provides to cushion each other towards the progress of a set mission is deemed it with regards to how the creator made it from the beginning.

The company, affection and other services the opposite sex offers in marriage result in a product that accelerates the process of a God-given mission. All because the conditions of the chemistry for divine combination into one flesh would have been met and as a result a perfect bond of oneness, coded by the same divine DNA, would have been created. This bond becomes greater than the individual personalities' abilities. From divine perspective therefore, it is worthy, as it was instituted from the beginning, for a person who seeks to marry to go for the opposite sex. If the search for a spouse is browsed on the word of God with the Spirit of God being the search engine, the right search result which is the right spouse who fits perfectly into the created space in man would be found. This would help us not to stand against the instituted word of God and we would also not be far from successfully accomplishing our missions set for us by God.

There is the possibility of the infusion of inordinate affection into the world arising from lust of the flesh brought about by the ancient deceiver to enslave men. Satan got his way around the disobedience of man at the garden of Eden; therefore, man lost his heritage God had given him. Satan has not stopped working. The bible describes the agents of Satan as serious hunters always seeking any man they come across to beguile: 'For they do not sleep unless they have done evil; and their sleep is taken away unless they make someone fall' (Prov. 4:16) And particularly for our era in which the end of all things is near, the Apostle Peter warned us through the Holy Spirit that 'Be sober, be vigilant; because your adversary the devil walks about like a roaring lion, seeking whom he may devour' (1 Peter 5:8)

This calls the attention of all men to be alert, lest we be deceived. The fact that we felt like doing something doesn't mean that it is right. One's desire must match the desire of God for it to be justified in the presence of God. Once there are innovations of electronic devices for creating sexual sensations other than what God designed for man doesn't mean you should follow up. These inventions can never meet the same need men desire per how God's original design is. No artificial combinations can match the natural use of the members of the body of man. Hence those inventions are not just man-made but devil-invented to derail men from the purpose and desire of God.

No matter how sophisticated men become in their innovations, they cannot get near what God naturally established. Those inventions are not of God but of the world and they aim to drive man to stand against God. Beware! Certain inventions are not to be upheld as a child of God who wants to please God knowing that following them positions you against the original plan of God for your life. The fact that many people have adopted it does not give one a justified ground for him/her to also to go for it. 'You shall not follow a crowd to do evil' (Exodus 23:2a), that's how God warns us.

The devil is so cunning and deceitful, and he only leads people to doom even, most at times, through what the society has accepted to be a right. Don't adhere to a right before men and become wrong before God. That societal right then would have rather been wrong in the sight of God. Our rights and freedoms should find their place within the will of God to be well labelled as being really right. The former right refers to the power to claim what is lawful in the systems of our society while the latter right refers to standing morally proper with God. Follow the devil and his schemes and later find yourself doomed. The only way to find whether he has deceived you or not is to measure what you desire to do every day with the original plan of God for you through the word of God. The devil might be leading you through your fleshly desire to cause you to dwell in the abominations of God; and yet deceive you to see it not to be a big deal.

In fact, men must be extremely vigilant with regards to this issue because Satan can be so cunning working around how advanced we humans become to cause us to fall away. Under the influence of Satan, it is very easy to rebel against God without knowing we are doing so. Losing the knowledge of the spot where we could meet God for a communion between Him and our souls, we indirectly forsake His intentions for our lives. Sometimes it becomes difficult for some people to realise that they have rebelled against their creator; and for that matter they cannot fathom the need for them to get back to do the appropriate restitutions in order to reconcile with Him.

There was once a time in the bible, in the book of Malachi, that God notified His people that they had forsaken Him and gone away from His ordinances. The bible declares that the people, looking surprised with the caution from God, answered back with a question to God that 'In what way shall we return'. Meaning they thought to have done all things right in their own points of view. To them they have got no problem with God, and life was normal for them; only to hear the opposite from the voice of God breaking through the silence of the fleshly influence via the vessel of God, Prophet Malachi. It is always very good to hear the voice of God. The voice of God contains the light of God that brings the reality of our life into proper view at a particular time in our era of walk with God. Unless we get the view of God about what we are doing now, we might have been out of the right path without knowing. That is the reason men must include God before we conclude!

Have you come to think about why God spoke through the prophet Isaiah this way;

> Hear, O heavens, and give ear, O earth! For the LORD has spoken: "I have nourished and brought up children, and they have rebelled against Me; the ox knows its owner and the donkey its master's crib; but Israel does not know, My people do not consider." (Isaiah 1:2,3)

Through the prophecy of the prophet Isaiah captured in the text above, we are informed God's people had rebelled against Him. The reason for their rebellion was the inability to know and consider where to link with God for the safety of their souls and divine direction of their lives. Now, it is sad here, because the weight of this prophecy reveals the level of how unreasonable men who rebel against God are. The ox and donkey, being animals, know when and where to contact and associate with their owner and master. Why do they do so? All because they consider and know! They get to realise in their consideration that their master and owner is the one who can give them better shelter and feed. They also know that the next journey of their life would be better directed by their master and owner. They can choose to find shelter and feed their own way; they can choose to continue their journey in any direction; yet their consideration from their infancy proves to them it is better always going back to the owner and master.

The dangers that await them when they go their own ways deters them from following up whatever other attractions they get along their path. As a result, they choose, out of the numerous options that life gives to them, to return to have an association and direction from their master and owner. By that way they are able to survive and thrive successfully for the length of days they have to spend on the earth with meaning. Again, how are they able to do all these? They consider and know. Now, if animals are able to do this but men who rebel against God cannot, then those men become more animals than animals!

That's the plight of the modern man in our era today. Our advancement in technology and things we claim to have put in place that ensures our safety of life are denying us the ample time and privilege to consider and know. If men would really have time to consider, they would really know. Even animals consider and get to know where to get real safety and direction, how much more human beings. Made higher in the capacity of reasoning than all other creatures, a man is expected to know better than all other creatures through proper consideration with his divine intellect. The problem that comes into play is when we have got the wrong target of consideration; thus, when our mission to accomplish falls out of the divine goals set for us. It is then that we begin to be influenced to consider not about how to get back to our owner, master and maker, but to focus on other things.

Men of today have got different agendas to attain with their IQs apart from seeking to please the will of God Most High. In effect, we decline in the ability to properly consider and to attain the right knowledge to the point that even animals become better off when we are put on the same scale. How sad! That should not be the case. That was not what we are meant for. We are entitled to obtain the right knowledge that would set us above Satan and all other creation according to the in-depth mystery of being made in the image and likeness of the Most High God.

One question we might want to ask to help us is, 'Would Satan ever wish that men had rulership over him?' Satan would not easily allow you to become above him; that's what we need not to be ignorant of. It is also because of this that we need to know that Satan has put all sorts of devices in place to keep men from attaining the right knowledge about our creator, master and maker. The right knowledge worth knowing about God for humanity that sets men above Satan and creation is the knowledge of the totality of Christ Jesus.

The fact we have become modernised and well sophisticated does not mean men must reject the will of God. Discovery and innovations must rather produce an awe for giving reverence unto our God who placed all things into existence. When you discover, honour Him the more. Yes, the more we get to know a lot of things with the intellect God has given us, we should be driven to give much glory to God who fashioned them into being.

Whatever piece of item we take from anywhere to manufacture anything is among His creations. We ourselves with our intellects are His creation. The problem we ought to deal with is how to properly direct all that we discover into the will of God. Whatever products from our intellects must glorify God and not tend to stand against the word of God. What is happening today was prophesied by the Prophet Daniel that in the end of time, knowledge would be increased. So, it is not surprising to witness diverse levels of knowledge in engineering, medicine, religion, etc. Yet in the same prophecy of the Prophet Daniel where it is said knowledge shall increase, it is also written that those who are wise shall shine. So, in this era of the end time, it is better to shine than to follow the multitude to doom. It is possible we are going to see much more than what we are seeing now; yet the wise among us shall shine.

Shine with the knowledge of Christ. Shine being led by the Spirit of God as to how to obey God but not man. Shine not to be a delight to men and your own self ego whereas being abomination unto God who created those men and yourself. God bless you that you would shine and not glow dim. Our source of light is Christ who illuminates us to shine when He is allowed to have a place in our hearts and a rule over our lives. With Christ living in us, the influence of Satan, the world and the flesh can never overrule us into switching off from the will of God who made us and has a purpose for us.

Men are Mission-Helpers

What a man can do, an animal or other creatures cannot do exactly the same. God intended bringing into existence more species of men who possess special abilities to complement the strengths of the already existing man. So, the next man in the pipeline is designed to be of benefit to the originally existing man. The next child to be born will be of benefit to the others already alive. What does this mean? God has in His own wisdom designed men that the very needed help for one man to accomplish a given task is placed in the other close or rear man. Thus, a man himself is never self-sufficient. Self-sufficiency is attributable to God alone.

It is God who will not need the help of any other to accomplish His mission. And with even God Himself, He is three in one – God the Father, God the Son and God the Holy Spirit. The three are one as the man has a soul with a spirit living in a body. God made man exactly as Himself. In His own image and likeness, He created man, that's what the bible confirms. The prime agenda from the Father forms the word (Son) to be executed by His Spirit. So, the Holy trinity reason together making the totality of the self-sufficient God. Contrastingly, the tripartite nature of man, thus the soul, spirit and body combine to produce an insufficient figure needing the help of God directly or indirectly through other creatures. That's what differenciates man from God. God is God, self-sufficient. A man is a man, a needy person. God's help through other beings completes and corrects the insufficiency of man. A man must therefore rely on God and His help through other men.

The Need for Unity Among Men

There is therefore the need for a man to consult his fellow for other possessing qualities that are not available to him. That's not self-inferiority, neither is it shameful begging. There is no negative stigma that must be attached to the act of seeking for sincere help if only it is not meant for evil. If a needy person would not require some need to do a negative thing, then nothing is wrong for him/her to make a request. It is factual that no man has it all. No group has all that it needs. And indeed, no nation can boast that she never needs anything from any other nation; thereby claiming not to require or negotiate to receive even a pin from any other nation. I'm yet to discover that nation. I'm sure that nation would be the new Jerusalem yet to descend from the bosom of the Father of all Spirits. A man needs the help of another close or rear man. No matter how isolated one would be, there would always be a time you require a company. **Those living on the island occasionally visit the mainland. Why? It is because of some need**.

Therefore, do not shun the next man you encounter just because he is not a calibre you think you can associate yourself with. For all you know, that man you are rejecting possesses some beneficial quality you will need to accomplish your mission. Maybe what you could have been struggling to do alone for years yourself; with the help of some other man, you can complete it in a few weeks. The right and the left hand combined could accomplish a great deal of work that only the left or right alone would not be able to do for ages. There are other dimensions of God that have never occurred to you to even think of; yet another man might have been made well equipped in that sector. It is not a flaw or deficiency for a man to lack knowledge about certain dimensions of God. It is just that it is God who is all knowing and therefore attributable to be in custody of all knowledge. This is what keeps all men humbled before God and with other men. All because no matter your office of designation in authority, you still lack with regards to other important things you don't know. A man is limited to a fraction of the knowledge of God per the extent that man is authorised to know.

Unless it is given from above, no man is divinely legalised to attain a certain level of knowledge with regards to the mysteries of the kingdom of God. More often, men get to know something about a particular subject within the knowledge of God but not the fullness of it. Responsibility is then laid on them to dig deeper through deeper relationships with God for deeper revelations. Knowledge builds up with time, where levels of maturity are attained through experience of intimacy with the Spirit of God.

The secrets of God are not easily made available to toddlers. The subjects on which men are given the ability to know about are also ones that are in relation to their assignments. Therefore, it is not common and possible for a particular man to be knowledgeable in all things. I wonder how a man with such knowledge about everything would be and the effects that it would bring upon him. It is just impossible.

Even the world at large could never contain the books that could capture the works of Jesus if they were all recorded per the testimony of Apostle John. That's only to talk about the works of Jesus while on earth. What about the others before Him and after Him together with the mysteries of God about the future of man? How could one man keep all this knowledge? The memory space of one man is limited with regards to such a great size of information. All that being aside, the tendency for arrogance to take over such a man who has such knowledge is very high.

As a result, a particular man would speak only with regards to the level of his knowledge and to the best of his understanding. That's the reason one should be careful how he tackles topics on subjects that he is not conversant with or has not been divinely authorised into attaining the deep knowledge required of him to deliver on such a subject. It is always better for him to balance his speech to leave room for the complement of God on the parts he is not well informed. When that space of ignorance is humbly left, God fills it Himself by revelation or through another endowed man so that there would be no error of passing on wrong information. Passing on wrong information is as dangerous as giving poison to the audience; hence, all information carriers will diligently be held accountable for the right or wrong passage of information.

It is not unprofessional, in the divine sense, to admit that you lack knowledge about areas where you have not specialised; but rather, it is humility. Failing to admit that you are short of knowledge in certain fields would compel you to try and give explanations on topics you are not capable of tackling; and that amounts to arrogance which leads to a great fall. The disgrace and consequences that are attached to getting it wrong in tackling topics of which you are less knowledgeable is far greater than to sincerely admitting that you are incapable of tackling such a subject. The humility that comes at play here is when the man who is short of knowledge in a particular field admits so and invites another man who knows better to come and express his knowledge acquired in that field. When that happens the best of knowledge is attained in every sector of what is at stake and hence proper results are guaranteed. Proper delivery by appropriate personalities ensures that the audience imbibe balanced knowledge which ensures the optimum preparations of their hearts and minds towards the will of God for their lives.

The common but significant mistake witnessed in our generation even among ministers is when one person, in a particular office, slips into the other offices of divine ministry to expound on topics which, in actual fact, he is not fit to tackle. The result of this is partial tackling of issues or unbalanced assessment of topics on board which in turn affects the audience. All because the one tackling it is not equipped enough with the knowledge required on such a topic. It isn't that the person is completely not knowledgeable; no, but the knowledge he has attained has nothing to do with what he wants to tackle.

Every tool is job-specific; exactly so it is with knowledge. Knowledge is akin to different formulae in equation forms which are individually used to tackle peculiar problems in mathematics or science. To employ the wrong formula for a particular problem is to be getting a wrong solution for it. It therefore remains reasonably helpful that men leave topics which are not in their field of knowledge untouched for others who are well versed in those fields. Sincerely practising this would bring into manifestation the need to request for a helping hand from others who are more equipped in certain fields. That would in turn bring to light that every man, no matter what he knows, is still needy in terms of knowledge of other matters he is not conversant with but are important for his survival.

The rich are needy just as the poor. The royal is needy just as the slave. Let the royal and the slave quarrel and say they do not need each other. Let the royal and the slave be separated and let's see what will happen. Who is bound to suffer? Everyone will get a choice here as to whether it is the royal who would suffer or the slave. But I strongly believe both are bound to suffer. It doesn't matter who is suffering the most. As long as any of them are suffering, whether little or more, they are both not alright. And that is what will happen to both the royal and the slave if they now think they do not need each other. This is because the slave will ever need the provisions of the royal; and exactly so would the royal ever need the service of the slave. That is what shows the reason each needs the other and likewise the reason one group of people must never despise the other. For all the boasting a particular group would boast of, without the other group they would lack.

For that matter, the cleaner is as important as the Managing Director. This is because each of them is affected by the service of each other before the firm would do well on the market for them also to get paid. The landlord needs the security man's service, and the security man needs the landlord's provisions. The gateman is useful because the house owner would have to open his gate on his own, attend to visitors, etc. without the gateman. And maybe if the house owner resorts to those services the gateman does, he would be lagging with punctuality to work and doing other 'important' things. If the gateman also complains he is tired of opening gates and other stuff and stops work, he would be denied the pay, food, accommodation, etc. he receives from the house owner. Therefore, everyone needs everyone and for that matter everyone is needy.

The abundance of skill or substance a particular group does not even value is a lack at some other place. Therefore, that compelled men to introduce barter trade as recorded in history. So that which is very common to one person, and he does not need it the more will be given out to some other person who needs it the most and in return the one who gave will be given back what he too lacked. Hence, as stated above, to prepare a complete life meal a little possession from different people must come together. More meaning comes into play with regards to the need for coming together for individual achievements as well as corporate achievements. For even one person himself to accomplish his own planned visions, he is bound to need help from others.

No king conquered other kingdoms alone. Most of the time, the leader's name is what is trumpeted for the world to know. Yet the victory kings have obtained in ages past were due to their supporting subordinates who gave the kings their commitment and service. In fact, without these subordinates, no renowned conqueror who has ever arisen could have ever done so to the extent history attributes to him. A man must therefore be willing to accept help from others to help him bring into fruition his intentions and visions. Equally so must every man be ready to give a helping hand to someone who needs his help to come up with something worthy.

Corporate visions are also best achieved by the selfless contribution of the individual members. A team working spirit is a necessity for hitting the target when it comes to cooperative visions. Here, every individual that forms part of the group gives out their best to ensure the right thing is done at the right time within the stipulated deadline. It is often seen in practical group missions where a member gives a helping hand to another member to speed up and facilitate the group target at stake. That's a good signal of how we need each other!

You might want to remain as much independent as you can; yet there would be a point that you will need to share with others to survive. Not others sharing with your resources; no, but you going to share with them their own resources to keep you thriving on. That's the reality of life that must be accepted whether it seems good to hear or not. At other points where adversity strikes a man or when age catches up with him, he would realise that he needs help from another hand. Such helping hands are sometimes those the man would have never allowed to be touched or associated with if not the adversity or old age; yet, he wouldn't have choice because of the point he has reached. A man is bound to need help from another man.

This keeps every man longing to receive the help of God that He provides through other men. Else, some people becoming independent would be too proud to enter the realm of arrogance; all because they can achieve all things by themselves. So now, for someone to reach the next level of life, he's got to contact another man for help. Therefore, the next level reached is attained not all by oneself. The notable fact is that God is self-sufficient. He does what He does by Himself. The instruments He employs to execute His mission are all His. Thus, the media and channels through which God accomplishes something are all His creation. God can use anything and everything. He sometimes uses men, animals, angels and even the devil for His purpose. And the honour of all those vessels goes back to Him because they all belong to Him. God does not dip into the possessions of any other for His mission. He uses His own subjects whom He owns by right of creation.

Yes, a pot is at the mercy of the potter. So, no entity can claim that He helped God because the existing foundation of that entity belongs to God. God can use and control Satan, but Satan cannot use or control God. The only asset Satan employs is deception against the children of God. Even in that regard all things work together into the will and plan of God at the end of the day. God therefore owns every creature and as a result could decide to use any of His creations as it deems fit to Him. Nevertheless, when it comes to men, no man owns his other fellow man; so, the help received from other men cannot be attributed to self no matter the status and identity of the helper. Once you receive support from other people, you must accept and count yourself a needy person who requires the help of God through other men for your accomplishments.

What Satan does is to cause separation so men cannot live and do up to expectation on what they plan. Satan sets men against men to obstruct both individual and corporate accomplishment of visions. With separation and disunity, men become less powerful to stand the attack of Satan. Gaining that opportunity, Satan would then use men to stop the visions of other men. Hence men would deny helping others to come up with what they have envisioned because of competition resulting from strife and jealousy. But that is not the mind of God who created men. God desires us to be together as one people helping one another generously for His will He placed in individuals and corporate bodies to be fulfilled. Satan's agenda is to stand against God's will; yet any individual or group who rejects satanic influence and helps one another would surely achieve their set missions.

The Flaw of Some United Men

When men came together in Genesis, the eleventh chapter to build a tower, they could start well and make progress because they were together yet different individually. I mean they were individually different, but the power of togetherness and unity was the fuel of their strength. Until God divided them by altering their language, they were doing marvellously well. That's the power of unity. They couldn't finish well. Before you ask why they were together but still couldn't achieve their goal, let's help ourselves to better understand this. They were together though; yet their mission was not to the glory of God but to gain a name for themselves. Most importantly, it was against the word and the will of God as He spoke to Noah after the flood was over in Genesis, the ninth chapter. Let's take a close look at it here.

"So, God blessed Noah and his sons, and said to them 'Be fruitful and multiply, and **fill the earth**'" (Genesis 9:1)

I hope you get this commandment of God to Noah. Take note of the words in bold 'fill the earth'. We will consider it in a moment as we move on. Let us also look at what happened in Genesis chapter eleven.

Now the whole world had one language and one speech. And it came to pass, as they journeyed from the east, that they found a plain in the land of Shinar, and they dwelt there. Then they said to one another, "Come, let us make bricks and bake them thoroughly.... Come, let us build ourselves a city, and a tower whose top is in the heavens; **let us make a name for ourselves, lest we be scattered above over the face of the whole earth.**"

But the LORD came down to see the city and the tower which the sons of men had built. And the LORD said, "Indeed the people are one and they all have one language, and this is what they begin to do; now nothing that they propose to do will be withheld from them. Come let Us go down and there confuse their language, that they may not understand one another's speech." **So, the LORD scattered them abroad from there over the face of all the earth**, and they ceased building the city. (Gen 11:1-8)

Just look carefully at what the people said, 'let us make a name for ourselves, lest we be scattered over the surface of the whole earth'. From their speech, they were doing that to glorify themselves and not God. And that is a big error for a man or men to try. All tentative actions and decisions of men must end up glorifying God not themselves. That is why if men should come together, that unity should be unto the glory of God, not any other man or deity. It is a proven fact that all missions or togetherness that will not end up glorifying God will not last. The city of Babel in Genesis, the eleventh chapter is a concrete example as you can see from above. Again, comparing their speech with the commandment God gave to Noah that 'multiply and fill the earth', their ideology was against the will of God. God says, 'Fill the earth', the people said we don't want to fill the earth. So, who is superior to whom, and whose word must stand?

It's not that the people didn't know this; they knew very well because they were descendants of Noah and his sons to whom God gave the command. They were very aware. Yet they had gotten to a point where they wanted to challenge the idea of the God who created them. That's exactly what is happening in this era of ours. People want to create their own world and live in it as they envision it to be but not according to the will of God who created them. How impossible! The result is what eventually happened, confusion! Those who thought they were very wise, reasoning in their high intelligence, eventually got confused. The wisdom of the wise amongst them got limited and the understanding of the prudent within them couldn't operate anymore. They couldn't fathom how to continue from where they had gotten to. Their bond of unity got broken because the foundation of their plan thereof was not of the will of God.

The unity of the world must be appropriated in the will of God; else, any mission which is opposite to God's intention will collapse as did the tower of Babel. God proved to them that He is God, and His will alone must be done in all things. Before they knew, they had scattered and filled the earth because that was the original plan of God. That is the very commandment He gave them.

Dear reader, please wait here. Don't miss it. Are you in the original plan of God or have you taken your own path? Have you departed from the commandment of God, or are you abiding by the word of the God who owns your breath? Beware, lest you waste your resources and all your toils become vain. If anyone is not in the will of God or has rejected the commandment of God, he cannot achieve his mission. You might start very well and even progress as did the Tower of Babel, yet you will fall just as it fell, and the will of God which you rejected shall come into play. The reason is because God is God, our creator and man is man, His creation. Whatever source man thinks he operates from and whatever strength that pushes a man, if it is devoid of the will of God, it shall come to nought. Man should not challenge himself against the will of God. It would be better to call the men of Babel from the dead and enquire from them. They would tell you how confident they were to complete their mission; nevertheless, the bible says they eventually ceased building the city. It doesn't matter what a man relies upon and the confidence he finds in himself, if God's will be denied, so also are completion and success denied, period!

A man must therefore surrender to the will of God because, come what may, it is this will of God that will be done. To be on the safer and winning side is to be on the side and in the will of God who began the universe. In fact, everyone must know that whatever anyone sets up to do, he is not beginning. Someone began in the beginning and for that matter He has already set how things must end. That Person is God. He declares the end from the beginning. Hence the ending of everything is already determined. Don't worry yourself therefore to change anything. A man must forsake self-wills and other wills that are against the will of God because they can never outlive what has already been determined by the Alpha and Omega, God Most High.

The only thing worthwhile men can do is to humble themselves, forsake arrogance against the supremacy of God, and factor their missions and achievements to be in line with the will of God and to glorify God. That is safety and that yields successful endings and completion of missions. Yes, if any individuals, groups, etc. of men could come together on a purpose that glorifies God, then surely that mission will succeed. Why? It's because they would be strong due to their unity, they would be ready to provide for each other, and God will also be their leader to ensure the successful ending of their mission. For God is the Alpha and Omega of every good mission. Now I'm sure we have understood why the coming together of those in Genesis chapter eleven was not fruitful.

So, in conclusion we need ourselves to survive. A man must not reject the immediate needy person whom he comes across. It might be God's will for you to help that needy person to become successful unto His glory. The needy whom you will obediently help would also in turn help other needy people to stand up to their feet. By that way God has passed through you to solve the situation of many and the visions God placed in such people would not be curtailed. Surely in addition to that, because you are obediently serving others by God's will, when the time of your need comes, God would also provide a unique helper in the field you are also in need to give you a helping hand. So, all your intended visions will come into fruition because you regarded the heart desire of God to extend a helping hand to your other neighbour.

Everyone is needy. If even any would challenge that he has never received from any other man before, still it is God who gave him whatever he has. No man can deny receiving from God, right from the gift of breath to whatever material possession. So, that's what makes the person who claims not to have received from any man still a receiver and hence a needy person. It must be accepted by all that as far as surviving in life is concerned, every individual is needy. That is how God made it. So that no one would magnify himself above all other men. Let us therefore humbly seek help when our need arises and be ever ready to also extend the needed help to others who require from us. So that we will love one another and together, we all would love God as the creator of all creatures who satisfies all our needs through one another.

Significant Notes

❖ If any being decides not to receive any gift from any other, then that being is likely to exist but for a very short time interval of life.

❖ Everyone is needy in the sense that each living being needs some fraction of the possessions of his neighbour in order to make a complete life meal. Only God is self-sufficient and in fact, only He is not a needy

❖ The inability of one to give puts some other neighbour of his who needs some fraction of his possession to survive into a critical situation which can terminate the victim's life

❖ Equilibrium balance of attention on giving and receiving is very important and an imbalance in either way, especially giving, could be very dangerous

❖ The organism you might detest and even see as a menace might be, on the other way round, feeding you.

❖ Different greater numbers of different creatures enter existence every now and then. The sad thing is that the man who is supposed to have dominion over these creatures is being restricted to come into existence; all in the name of controlling overpopulation. It wouldn't be surprising that the other creatures would grow and outnumber men and then rather take dominion over men; except God intervenes.

❖ The significance of animals' help is way below that of a human being. A man needs another man more than an animal per the divine designation of God.

❖ To satisfy the original instituted equation of producing one flesh in marriage, the different arguments of the divine additional operation must be a man and a woman.

❖ As we concentrate on our rights and freedoms the systems of this world make available for us, the will of God from the beginning must not be overemphasised.

❖ Anti-God-institutions can never last on the already established foundation God has made.

❖ The institution of marriage God created right from the beginning was in such a way that the specific deficiencies of affection in Adam as a man would be met through Eve; and the other way round, Eve would be satisfied the same way. It is within this phenomenon of chemistry that the one flesh nature is created from the two different personalities.

❖ Every spot demands a perfect fit; not just anything at all to fill the space!

❖ Until we get the view of God about what we are doing now, we might have been out of the right path without knowing. That's the reason men must include God before we conclude!

❖ The next man in the pipeline is designed to be of benefit to the originally existing man.

❖ The Holy trinity reason together making the totality of the self-sufficient God. Contrastingly, the tripartite nature of man, thus the soul, spirit and body combine to produce an insufficient figure needing the help of God through other creatures.

❖ No matter how isolated one would be, there would always be a time to require a company. Those living on the island occasionally visit the mainland. Why? It is because of some need.

❖ All tentative actions and decisions of men must end up glorifying God not themselves

❖ It is a proven fact that all missions or togetherness that will not end up glorifying God will not last.

❖ God is God, our creator and man is man, His creation. Whatever source man thinks he operates from and whatever strength that pushes a man, if it is devoid of the will of God, it shall come to nought. If God's will be denied, completion and success are denied, period!

❖ God is the Alpha and Omega of every good mission.

CHAPTER TWO

The Giver versus The Receiver

We have just found out from the previous chapter that everyone is needy. That underlies the fact that everyone receives some sort of help from somewhere directly or indirectly. This is because every needy person is a ready receiver. We might also want to discover whether everyone gives. Everyone in one way or another receives; but does everyone give? If even so, what do givers have in common with receivers? It is worth noting the similarities and differences between givers and receivers. Let's keep the ball rolling.

A giver, in respect of the subject under discussion, is someone who offers what he owns to another person, - called a receiver, - so that the receiver becomes the owner of that possession. Givers lose what they legitimately own to others without claiming ownership over what they have given out. So, **giving is disowning your possession for it to become the possession of another person**. This insinuates that the giver loses the right of ownership of a belonging to the receiver after giving it to him. Yes, the giver ceases to have authority over the possession he has given away and cannot exercise authority on it as he used to when it was once his bona fide property. Unless the giver does so on the terms of lending, a wholly given item is fully owned by the new owner, the receiver. Even when lending, the terms and conditions between the giver and receiver ought to be honoured by the giver. Anyone who offers some kind of possession or service out to others in this respect can be termed a giver. Yes, simply, a giver gives. Their coffers, properties and wealth diminish in their action of giving so that the needs of some others would be met. Other references that can replace a giver are the following: donor, contributor, benefactor/benefactress, provider, supporter, backer, subsidiser, patron, sponsor, subscriber, philanthropist, well-wisher, helper.

Conversely, a receiver is someone who receives some offer from others termed as givers so that his need would be met. Receivers benefit from the donation they receive from givers. Their coffers, properties and wealth increases in their action of receiving thereby getting their problems resolved. Anyone who accepts an offer or service from any other person is a receiver. Certainly, and simply as explained, every receiver receives. Other names that could be given to a receiver are as follows: recipient, beneficiary, acceptor, collector, etc.

Similarities Between Giver and Receiver

Without a receiver, there will be no giver; so, must there be a giver before there would be a receiver. **If the world were full of only givers, no one would give; likewise, if the world were full of only receivers, no one would receive**. Therefore, the level of the importance of the existence of these two parties is the same with regards to giving and receiving. This is because one party is termed a giver owing to the presence of another party called a receiver to receive from him. Exactly so, the other is termed a receiver because of the existence of the other party called a giver to give to him. That establishes the fact that the receiver makes the giver, a giver; and the giver makes the receiver, a receiver. In the absence of either party, the other present party has no reference and no recognition. In this respect therefore, the giver is as important as the receiver. Despising either party would be wrong because without the existence of one group, the action of giving or receiving cannot occur. The givers must therefore give the respect due to the receivers who made their work of giving possible. Also, the receivers must respect the existence and the action of givers and present to them their necessary appreciation.

Consequently, givers are to respect and love receivers when giving to them; while receivers are to respect and appreciate givers for their offer of giving. Whether love and respect from the giver or respect and appreciation from the receiver, they all must do well to honour their part in order to ensure effective and successful giving and receiving. The joy that comes out of effective giving and receiving is unspeakable. That joy only comes into play when both givers and receivers are able to honour their part with regards to the conditions of giving and receiving explained above. Now let's get into it further.

Respect for Receivers

Since giving and receiving cannot be possible without receivers, the respect due receivers must not be denied them by givers. Though receivers are at the receiving end, thus they are the beneficiaries who need the service of givers to survive; yet they too must be respected. Though not in all cases, most receivers are denied the respect due them. Some givers do not regard their corresponding receivers all because they think without their giving those receivers wouldn't have survived. It's true that the giving of givers makes receivers survive. Fairly, it's also true that receivers are in dire need of the services and possessions of givers. Yet, let's try to ask those givers who do not respect their corresponding receivers what would have become of those possessions they gave out supposing the receivers had not come for them. Maybe they would have consumed it themselves. Maybe they believe they would have not lost anything. It must consciously be made known to them that they would have missed something great. A person who owns a lot and has not given out is never equal to a person who owns and has given out. The state of being of these two people is never the same.

There is the presence of this sense of worthiness that comes along with giving. There is this satisfaction of heart that occurs to anyone who gives wholeheartedly. That's the joy unspeakable mentioned above. It occurs within the heart and gives a clear conscience to the giver thereby enriching the individual's relationship with God as well as with other people. In fact, worthiness of possession comes in two folds: potential worthiness and actual worthiness. Let's give some examples.

The worth of money is not in the currency itself, whether the coin or paper note. The potential worth of money is seen in what the money can be used for; whereas the actual worth of it is what it has actually been used for. What the amount of 100, 000 (in your currency) can do is what declares its potential worth. Its actual worth is evident when it has actually been used to do that which was envisioned for it. Holding that amount in hand without putting it into use is worthless in the actual sense just as it was not. Unless it has been used to purchase something or used for other transactions, the holder of the money is just as equal as the one with no money. If your wealth cannot change your status positively, then what's the worth of your wealth?

Exactly so it is for any form of service or possession that is given out. The possession itself is worthless in the actual viewpoint when it has not been offered for it to be useful. For instance, if one has a very nice house which was built with no one living in it for years. That house is of no actual value. Neither the beauty of the house nor the cost the person incurred in putting it up means anything actually worthy. Though the actual value of the money used for building the house has now been evident since the house has been built; yet, so far as the house remains uninhabited, the actual value of the house itself is zero. This proposition is coming from divine analysis, not human calculation and consideration. The house becomes actually worthy only if the owner allows access for people to start living in it, then it now starts serving the purpose of its being.

Let's consider yet another common example that could bring clarification on this. This is the incidence of throwing unwanted food away. Virtually almost everyone might have done this. It is not throwing it away because the food is stale or spoiled; but one point when we thought we've had enough of it, and we didn't want the food anymore and probably there was no one else around us to whom we could give it. Imagine the feeling of discarding that proper food all because of excess or having too much of it. Now, look at the other instance when you had excess food the same way but now you had someone in need of your excess and hence you gave it to him and the person became very happy for your provision that would solve his hunger.

Sincerely judge from the afterwards feeling you had or would have (if it has not happened to you before) for the two instances. Thus, having more than enough food, throwing the excess into the bin; and two, having more than enough food and giving the excess to someone hungry who appreciated it with all happiness. If you have really judged sincerely and known the differences of the resultant feeling in both instances, then that's the point being put across here. One's possession becomes actually worthy when that possession has caused someone to laugh, feel safe and at peace. It is the impact your service or giving makes in the lives of others that makes your possessions actually worthy.

Now, without the lives which your possession impacts, where actually would be the worthiness of your possession which you gave out? Hence it stands to mean that it is important respecting those whom you offered your service or possession. All because they revealed the actual worth of those possessions. Don't let your receivers feel bad after receiving from you in such a way that they even regret having received your offer. God loves and respects men whom He always gives to. God does not despise us. He gives to the wicked so as to the righteous. The generosity of God is in such a way that He also has respect for those whom He gives to. This is how the Bible puts it.

If anyone of you lacks wisdom, let him ask of God, **who gives to all liberally and without reproach**, and it will be given to him. (James 1:5)

Check out the giving of God. He gives to men liberally and also without reproach. Givers are not to reproach their corresponding receivers. Givers must not render their giving unsuccessful by backing it with reproachful speeches that put the receivers to shame. That's not godliness. Announcing to the whole world about receivers whom you have given to in order to portray how lacking those receivers are does not portray the character of God. Letting receivers feel downtrodden or inferior because we think we are their saviours is beyond kindness. That's trying to 'lord it' over them than trying to help them come out from their state of anguish and hardship. To think that another man's survival depended fully on you and that without you the person would have not made it, is an error. This is because God has got many options for His work of salvation. The reason being that He has already made it clear in the bible that "For the needy shall not always be forgotten; the expectation of the poor shall not perish forever" (Psalm 9:18)

How God will work it out depends on Himself alone. He knows how He would feed the hungry, cover the homeless and help the helpless. Excuse your task of giving and see what happens in the next minute. It will shock you how God's going to provide through other quarters. You will just be marvelled at the way God will provide from elsewhere for the accomplishment of that same purpose. When this happens, the need would be met, God would be glorified but the one who excused that mission would be left to face the judgement of God. Instead of despising the receiver, the giver ought to give glory to God for being found by God as a worthy vessel to save the receiver through giving.

The opportunity to give is a key to greater doors ahead of any capable giver. So, if one misses that opportunity, he does no harm to the needy but to himself. All because, come what may, God would provide for His children. Surely, the sheep of the Lord shall not want (Psalm 23:1). Yet God must get a legitimate account about someone based on which He can release His supernatural blessing upon him. To be eligible to be called the father of many nations, Patriarch Abraham had to show his commitment of being ready to offer his only son. Sometimes some people expect uncommon blessings; yet uncommon blessings are not given to common people. Unless one demonstrates an uncommon faith, he is not eligible for such blessings.

Some commitments are beyond the lay man's point of view. Some actions of faith are not understandable to the common man; yet those kinds trigger the reaction of God to also respond in an uncommon way to man. Science says action and reaction are opposite but equal. You cannot stay in the realm of common people and receive uncommon promotions. Sometimes you must seem foolish in the eyes of men in order to touch the heart of God based on the burden God has laid on your heart to accomplish.

So, givers must develop the habit of respectfully regarding their corresponding receivers. The act of giving is aimed at healing the broken hearted; hence, a giver must not afterwards break the heart of the receiver by despising him. Love and respect are expected from the giver so that the receiver would have a sense of belonging which would complete the satisfaction of the need. After that joy the receiver obtains out of all his troubles, God would also instil this unspeakable joy also in the giver's heart which provides a sense of worthiness for his obedience to the honourable act of giving.

Respect for Givers

Most often the respect needed to be given to givers is not denied them. All because those at the receiving end always must show appreciation for receiving from them. Notwithstanding, there are few cases where we can find receivers denying the necessary respect to givers whom they received from. That's what makes the world imperfect. What is clearly right that must be testified by all to be right can receive a different judgement in the eyes of some other people whether intentionally or being influenced by other factors. So, it's unfortunate that some givers receive unexpected disrespect from some receivers.

That can cause a great sense of discouragement in some givers to the extent of resulting in a negative response in the next-giving-time. Although there are some kind of givers who are very determined and would never be discouraged by any sort character. Nevertheless, for other givers, if they encounter such a sense of ungratefulness, they eventually quit. It is indeed a bad characteristic on the part of some receivers to disregard the action of giving by denying respect to their corresponding givers. All because giving out what one possesses is not that easy for everyone. **It is easier to receive than to give**. So, if anyone has been able to overcome the barriers in his conscience to be able to release out from his coffers to bless a receiver, that receiver must find it reasonably a need to properly react back accordingly. Sincerely, the impact of the disrespect of receivers to givers is much greater than that of givers to receivers. For that matter the needed respect that must be given to any giver should not be ignored by any receiver. Givers must be given their respect and appreciation.

If even you cannot give anything of yours as a receiver, respect and appreciation should be cheap enough for you to give after receiving. This is the problem men have generated between themselves and other men as well as with God. Men are ready receivers from God, yet we forget to give back the respect and appreciation due Him. It is only when we are in need that we remember God and stretch our hands to Him to receive. Every day, every hour, every minute, etc. some hands of men are stretched towards heaven to receive from our generous Heavenly Father. The moment we are filled and satisfied we leave Him as if He is not worthy. It is heart-breaking; yet that's how some men are characteristically fashioned and raised. They are not grateful for anything given to them. I don't know whether they think they deserve too much of what they have received. It is an error also to think that you deserve a privilege shown to you. It is wrong to imagine that what someone willingly gave you is by reason that you deserve it.

God has willingly given us the breath of life, and most people do not appreciate it. He has given the climates, wildlife, waters, etc. altogether supporting our lives, some men do not see any reason to be grateful. Think about Christ Jesus, what a gift of God to the world! God has given us Christ and some human beings still do not appreciate it. What kind of ungrateful creatures are we? The only cause for this is the deception of Satan which has created scales and veils over the eyes of people in order for them not to properly see the goodness of God towards humanity. When those scales fall off and the veils are stripped away, one begins to realise the reality of the message of God that he has been hearing being proclaimed now and then. May that be your story and mine too! Indeed, the truth of the reality of God's love for us is without doubt. God is worthy of our respect and appreciation!

What makes Givers Differ from Receivers

What then, if it is established that both givers and receivers need to be respected, is there no other difference in any aspect concerning givers and receivers? There possibly is. Here lies the difference. Let's explore it here so that doubts can be cleared with regards to whether it is better to become a better giver or a better receiver. On we go!

More Blessed to Give than to Receive

Despite the need of balancing giving and receiving in the lives of the living, there is one aspect of the two which brings a gap between givers and receivers. **The honour given to givers after they have given is greater than the honour given to receivers after they have received**. What this means is that all-time givers and all-time receivers do not reach the same height in their lives in accordance with their respective activities and the respective associated honour accorded to them. For that matter, they are not the same. They all deserve to be respected equally though; yet their blessings differ in the sight of God. That's the judgement of God and as a result that's what has been working from the beginning of the world till now concerning givers and receivers. Let's search it out.

Quoting directly from the Lord Jesus, the Apostle Paul admonished Christians to obtain the kind heart the Lord desires from them with regards to supporting their needy fellows. And this is how the advice goes:

"I have shown you in every way, by laboring like this, that you must support the weak. And remember the words of the Lord Jesus, that He said, **'It is more blessed to give than to receive.'**" (Acts 20:35)

So, the declaration from Jesus Christ, the Word of God, Himself to all people is that 'It is more blessed to give than to receive'. This actually means that the reward due a giver is greater than that which is due a receiver and moreover, a giver is dear to the heart of God more than a receiver is. Therefore, He blesses the giver more than the receiver just as the text above implies. It is always therefore better for anyone who desires to receive more blessing to be in the position to give than to be in the position to receive. It is good to be a receiver but better to be a giver with regards to receiving more blessings from God.

There are spiritual blessings and gifts in the hands of God which He releases to those whom He pleases. Those blessings are beyond what can be attained by human effort. It is that blessings of God that makes one rich without Him adding sorrow. Those who obtain those blessings do not struggle before they can gain them as the natural man would. It is freely given supernaturally to them in the spirit for it to manifest in the physical. Yet, for any man to receive such blessings is dependent only on how God values the individual. Such men who deserve such supernatural blessings are God-validated. Peculiar commitments attract such blessings from God. It is normal for any man to receive a natural blessing from his toils; yet the large supernatural blessings from the large hands of God are not commonly released to common people. It takes some level of commitment to be deserving.

Though the existence of both givers and receivers are of the same importance and they are equally respected; yet their act of commitment varies in the sight of God. Every act of commitment pleasing to God is rewardable with regards to how it is weighed by the word of God. God has said it and He is bound by His word to also bless or reward any act of commitment to which an individual avails himself. So, after considering both actions of givers and receivers, God has declared that it is more blessed to give than to receive. That's the word of God and so is it settled in Heaven. The judgement of God cannot be questioned by any other and for that matter givers are continually being blessed more than receivers are. Once givers can honour such commitment of giving before God, He also becomes committed to bless them according to His own word.

Sometimes one must not waste the strength of his conscience trying to envy another man's blessings. Being envious and jealous about others keeps you regressing while the others whom you are envious of keep on progressing. To some people, they would have wished other people were not blessed as they see them to be. Be warned because the problems of a God-approved and blessed man are inversely proportional to the envy of his enemies. The more you envy divine people the less their problems become. In fact, it would be as if their problems are being transferred to you. Don't do wrong transactions with your envy such that you get credited with problems while the one whom you envy who is beloved of God gets debited with more blessings.

Some get jealous about how God deals well with some others which in turn leads a lot of people to fall away from the faith. But mind you, genuine blessings of God are not under the control of man; yes, it is completely independent of man. No man can bribe God. For there is no partiality with God (Romans 2:11). A man is totally out when it comes to deciding on which man is to be blessed and to which extent of blessing another man deserves. No man can influence God whether to bless or not to bless any other. God holds that overall authority, and in fact He has the final say. This is how the bible puts it:

> Talk no more so very proudly; let no arrogance come from your mouth. For the LORD is the God of knowledge; and by Him actions are weighed…. The LORD makes poor and makes rich; He brings low and lifts up. He raises the poor from the dust; and lifts the beggar form the ash heap, to set them among princes; and make them inherit the throne of glory. (1 Sam 2:3-8)

It is up to God to decide whether to bless someone or not to. He enthrones kings desiring to Him and dethrones others also in whom He has no delight. His decision to bless a particular man is not based on any advice of another man. Therefore, the blessings that you witness in the child of God next to you was not dependent on any man's authority or consent. God alone validated and decided on that.

Therefore, having too much concern whether someone who is blessed deserves his blessing or not is a waste of thinking effort. Stop envying others' blessing because that behaviour could cause you to become an enemy to God who blessed that man.

You see, the act of wrongly anticipating and judging on others' blessing whether they deserve to be blessed or not can get you into a serious problem with God. That can rather attract a curse from God other than getting such of those blessings of God of which you are envious. There is a better path to take than that if one so wishes to receive greater blessings he has heard of or witnessed in the lives of other people. Take time with me and let's receive the inspirations from the Holy Spirit as we go on.

Knowing that it is more blessed to give than to receive, a person desiring to be blessed must, as much as possible, develop the act of giving. Then when it is identified in Heaven that you are a giver, appropriate blessing will be released to you. It is automatic because God cannot deny His word. All because He is His word, and He cannot deny Himself. He is committed to keep His Word just as His position of the King of all kings. He never fails and never disappoints.

Only if we could do our part, God is ever ready to do His. Give and get blessed, that's it. It is more powerful than going for money rituals from other forces of darkness. Indeed, whatever God provides cannot be compared to what Satan gives. Start sharing what you have with others who are lacking. Extend your alms to reach the needy you come across so that they become relieved from their struggles. Let someone laugh because of your giving. As they laugh and bless God for what you have done in their lives, God's attention would come upon you. The reason is because you have drawn others' mind on Him to glorify Him because of your giving; therefore, He would also glorify you with His supernatural blessing. Is this not better than being envious of other peoples' blessings which would eventually attract upon you the wrath of God? It certainly is. Everyone seeking for greater blessing must go by this tested and proven path. The reason God blesses the giver more than the receiver is explained further as we drive on by the enlightenment of the Word of God and the Spirit of God's elucidation.

The Sower and the Eater

God provides seed for the Sower and bread for the eater. God who is the provider for all does so proportionately in order to balance the equation of giving and receiving. Let's catch up with that in the text below.

And God who provides seed for the sower and bread for eating will also provide and multiply your resources for sowing… (2 Corinthians 9:10)

Here is the Apostle Paul commending and blessing the people of Corinth for their sacrifice through giving. He had led them through the mathematical variations of giving that states that sowing sparingly is directly proportional to reaping sparingly and sowing bountifully is directly proportional to reaping bountifully. As a result, he urged them to give cheerfully for such givers are those whom God loves.

Rounding his blessing in prayer, he described the character of God with regards to how He provides to two groups of people: sowers and eaters. To sowers, the Lord gives seed but to eaters He gives bread. And the text above makes it clear that God is going to multiply the resources for sowing. Eaters eat from the produce of sowers. So, God multiplies the resources of sowers so that much would be sowed and for that matter, much would be produced for the consumption of all eaters. We will be relating sowers and eaters to givers and receivers respectively very soon. Just stay concentrated and connected for better illumination.

One thing to note is that all sowers are eaters; but not all eaters are sowers. Thus, everyone eats; but not everyone sows. If they were sets, then the set of sowers would be a subset of the set of eaters. Thus, a fraction of the eaters in the world are sowers. Check out the illustration from the following Venn diagram.

God's Resources Allocation Plan to Meet Men's Needs

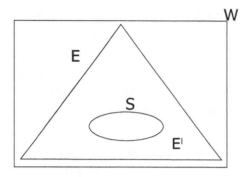

W – World

E – Eaters

S – Sowers

E^I – Eaters only

I hope this diagram helps to make it clearer about the relation between eaters and sowers in the world. You could see that the set S, sowers occupy a portion of the set E, eaters. This establishes the fact that the rest of set E apart from set S are eaters only which part has been labelled, E^I. Therefore, people in the world, set W consists of Eaters, E which also contains two sets: a set of sowers, S and a set of only eaters, E^I. Alright let's continue to look at it with regards to the blessing of God on man.

Now, when God is blessing with bread, He would supply it to all eaters inside which are all sowers; however, when God is blessing with seed, He would supply it to only sowers where the set of only eaters would be out of such an advantage. Meaning that a sower always receives a double portion of God's blessing each time. This is all because the sower has got an extra quality or responsibility laid upon him to accomplish so as to ensure the survival of all the children of God. So, whether to be qualified to receive the double portion of the blessing from God or not would be determined by your position or disposition in the sight of God. Found in the set of S, sowers you are entitled to that right of blessing; but to be found in set E^I, eaters only you would receive some blessing though, yet not equal to those in set S. God blesses those who are only eaters from the products of the sowers. Meaning it is the superfluous or extra blessing of God the sowers receive that feeds the group of people in the set of only eaters.

Exactly so is the case when it comes to givers and receivers. From the above illustration, the in-depth reference of sowers from the Apostle Paul's point of view were givers, and eaters referred to receivers. So, we better understand now that everyone receives but not everyone gives. All givers too are receivers making everyone needy. Now, it is important to notice that it is the blessings which separate givers from receivers. Givers are entitled to a double portion of blessing beyond the blessing of those who are only receivers.

God gives directly to the sowers supernaturally for it to manifest physically on the land of sowing. To only eaters, God gives them their bread through the sowers. God said He would multiply the seed for sowing not the bread for eating. As the seed multiplies the bread also would automatically multiply. Nonetheless, have you asked yourself whose hand gets hold of the first blessing? Obviously as explained above, it is the sower. What about if a sower gets his seed multiplied and hence produces more bread but decides not to give it out. Thus, when the sower who is supposed to extend his extra blessing to the only eater gets a change of mind. What is the fate of the only eater expecting from that 'mind-changed' sower? Only eaters have no choice than to wait on what they shall receive from the sowers' hands. Better will it be for one to be positioned at where he receives first-hand blessings than to be waiting on a man who can change his mind at any time. It is God who gives without reproach, but some men do, and other men would not give at all.

Therefore, one must think through earnestly and decide which blessings he desires; whether one-time which he must wait on other men or double fold which he receives from God directly. Though every man must pass through a point of being a one-portion receiver, thus only eater where he expects to be blessed from the blessing of others. Yet what transports and propels one from such a stage to a point of becoming a double-portion receiver from God is the tendency for the person to be willing to sow. In parallel to giving and receiving, to be a valid candidate for supernatural blessings, you must be a proven giver.

No matter how holy and righteous you would be if you are not a giver, forget about getting that double-fold blessing. One thing I have also noticed about the righteous both in the Bible and outside the Bible is that they are all givers. Only one example to sum it up for us is Father Abraham. By faith he was counted righteous. Most of the works of faith he did was in the act of giving. He gave tithes of all he had obtained from his victorious battle to Melchizedek, king of Salem believing that he was giving to a High Priest. This battle he went for favoured other kings and the bible said Abraham gave all the possessions to them without claiming any though he had the right to. (Genesis 14:12-24)

This proves that Abraham was a giver. He received three angels hospitably and gave his substance to quench the thirst and hunger of these angels. Lastly, he didn't hesitate to give his only son as a sacrifice to God. All these came together to constitute the faith that made God imputed His righteousness on Abraham. So, righteousness and giving cannot be separated. Not every giver is righteous although; but every righteous man is a giver.

Every believer wants to be rich like Abraham became. We also often claim the blessings of Abraham by faith. All because we believe we are heirs of his blessings through faith. We want our descendants to be blessed just as Abraham's. That's all good. But who amongst us are willing to give as Abraham gave? We must be assured that the blessing God swore to bless Abraham was not anything earthly, it was a divine one that could transcend to his generations after him. The bible even confirms that Levi, a descendant of Abraham, gave tithe when Levi was yet in the loins of Abraham as at the time Abraham was giving the tithe to Melchizedek. Yet Levi was the third generation of the descendants of Abraham; Levi's father was Jacob whose father was Isaac whose father was Abraham.

You see, one's giving positively affects his descendants. What does this mean? The blessing that could result from giving through faith wholeheartedly can go a long way to have an impact on your descendants. These types of blessings are not obtained just by chance such that anybody at all can attain it. Not even the one who has inherited great wealth from other relatives. There are people who become very wealthy, yet it ends with them; thus, when they are dead and gone, that's all. You can see the descendants of some wealthy men suffering to a point that you cannot even imagine their fathers or great grandfathers were wealthy people. Natural blessings wither and perish as the beauty of a flower. Yet, supernatural blessings live beyond lifetime. The impact of Abraham's blessing is still felt today. That's the kind of blessing givers obtain that make them unique. People who are only receivers cannot obtain such a blessing. They don't have what it takes to be qualified for it.

Do not dwell on natural blessings that resort from toils and hard work and conclude that you are blessed. Don't consider what you have inherited from other people as a blessing and stay content with it. There is much more than that if you could become a giver, just as Abraham was. Abraham had to leave inheritance behind and follow the call of God. The land and other properties he could have obtained from his father meant nothing to him when he decided to obey the voice of God. Let's forget about what we have obtained from the toils of others and even those we ourselves have gained from our toils. There is this one kind of blessing that goes beyond what nature and human effort can offer. If you are enlightened about it and you get to know what it is, you will no more regard your natural blessings as worthy. I pray God takes us there. May God help you and I who are willing and desiring for His supernatural blessings to develop the act of giving so that we can be good candidates for such blessings.

In fact, God is ever ready to richly bless anyone who proves to be worthy to receive such blessing. I'm speaking of His supernatural blessings in His alms; not just normal blessings because for the normal blessings, God has blessed everyone. To receive such of His supernatural blessings that transcends your own generation is what is special. Those supernatural blessings are reserved for men like you and I. God is not doing anything with it. It is in His hands ready to be offered but to be offered to him who is worthy. Ready-made blessings are up there waiting for us to reach some level of commitment. It is possible for you and I to obtain them. If a human being like you and I have ever obtained such a kind of blessing before, then it is very possible for us to gain it too. It is not a matter of blaming God that He is being biased. It is also not a matter of being envious of the others who have received such blessings that we are witnesses. No, it is a matter of studying their approach to God and how they found favour in the sight of God, making them worthy of such kind of blessings.

Praise the Lord that path and approach has been revealed today. It is the approach of giving. It is the path of touching the lives of other people with our possession in order to deliver them from the chains of suffering. The Bible says, 'Give and it shall be given to you.' I'm happy to announce to you that the very thing that shall be given to you is not equal to what you shall give. A giver gives a natural thing and receives in return a supernatural blessing. It is the supernatural blessing that shall be given to you when you shall have given your possession for the benefit of others. God's word has been fulfilled, it's being fulfilled and shall ever be fulfilled. Glory be to God. Hallelujah!

SELFISHNESS – the reason some people cannot become wealthy

Selfishness is the stinginess resulting from a concern for your own welfare and a disregard of others. In other words, to be selfish is to be concerned chiefly or only with yourself and your advantage to the exclusion of others. When selfish people are satisfied, the day must be over, every chapter must be closed, and everyone must go to sleep. Once they are fine, everybody should be fine regardless of the condition of others. Yet, if they are inconvenienced, everyone must be inconvenienced as well because all others would not be at peace due to their complaints and murmurings. It becomes highly alarming when collective resources that serve many others are put in their care. All because their biassed character would influence them to concentrate their concerns, unbalanced, upon themselves; and hence, they would provide for their quarters more than others. You can witness this in the system of governance and leadership of most current imperfect governments. If care is not taken and a selfish person is elected or enstalled as a leader, woe to the weak populace. Not only leaders in governance exhibit such character; selfish people are generally seen amongst common members in every sector of this world. They are characteristically gluttons who seek to be excessively filled even when other hungry men have not gotten anything to eat. As a result, it also becomes difficult for God to entrust to their care large resources that would benefit them together with others. God has a problem blessing such people with supernatural blessings meant to affect the lives of others.

God gives many resources to those who will also extend their alms to other people who are also in need. This stands to mean that if someone is stingy and selfishly thinks about himself alone, he would receive something from God but not as much as the other who kindly extends his resources to reach others. Why? It is because **God gives out His blessing only to meet human needs,** and since the stingy person thinks about himself alone, he is bound to receive what will meet only his needs; hence, his minimal blessing. That means that a selfish person should be alright with the natural blessings that result from his toils because all other needy people are out of his concern.

Selfishness is a poison that darkens the heart and mind of the victim such that he does not see any reason to care for the nearby fellow. To such people, all positive things must come to their end. They would only let go of the item that is spoiled or of no use to them. So, for a selfish person to release something precious of his for the benefit of others, it becomes almost impossible. They get pain-hearted when they are not the ones enjoying the best; therefore, such character leads them to be jealous sometimes of others. This pain existent in their heart for releasing something good of theirs to meet other people's needs makes it difficult for them to also receive precious gifts from God.

This teaches us that the reason some of us who are expecting to be bountifully blessed and yet have not received anything of such might be because of this character within. We human beings look at the outside but God judges from what is in our hearts. Let's remind ourselves of something. Has it ever occurred to you that there had once been a thought that came to your mind that 'If I get rich, the way I would ...' How would you complete this statement? There could be a lot of complements to this phrase depending on differing individual aspirations and desires. Some would continue with the way they would spend their riches. Some also would complete that statement with the way they would treat some other people. God is aware of all the thoughts of our minds and the decisions of our hearts. So, before God releases His blessings to anyone, all these screenings and inner interviews would have been spiritually conducted on that said man. If you are qualified, you are granted your visa to live in the realm of supernatural blessings on this natural earth. Yet if due to your selfishness, you fail upon a series of tests and interrogations, then you remain with the strugglers to compete for the natural blessings on the natural earth that deals with the survival of the fittest.

In fact, the way you have envisioned in your heart to misuse God's blessing alone can disqualify you of being granted the blessing. God identifies people's urge to release what is in their coffers for others' wellbeing before handing to them greater resources. If resources meant to satisfy a greater number of people fall in the wrong hands, you can imagine the consequences. Therefore, the all-knowing God knows perfectly how He positions people on the throne of wealth and whom to give the appropriate authority of wealth so that it could be of benefit to all His children.

That's the very reason for the fate of most of the people who remain poor till death. Note, it is 'most of them'; not 'all of them' because some people can be poor while such poverty is not as a result of them being selfish. Yes, that point must be clarified. There is a reason behind every happening, and except digging into the will of God to inspect the cause, sharp conclusions might be wrong. Some issues are even existing just to reveal the glory of God in an acceptable time. Some people can continue to remain poor, not because of selfishness, but due to other factors beyond their strength. Some people also have their wealth in the pipeline yet to be revealed in God's own divine timing; hence their state now is not very encouraging. That's also possible. Yet the subject we are dealing with now has to do with the group who remain impoverished due to their character of selfishness witnessed by Heaven. Packages of blessings are ever ready in the hands of God to be given out; yet their selfish character does not make them fit as valid carriers of such blessings. Hence some peoples' blessings get delayed so far as their change of mind and their tendency to avoid the character of selfishness also delays. Some even end up exiting the world without obtaining their designated blessing due to this very character of selfishness. God does not want to be your story as His dear child.

As a result, before we complain that our answers to prayer requests concerning being blessed bountifully are delayed, let's examine our own selves. Before you place yourself in the wrong position, scrutinise your past life and help yourself. Don't jump to the conclusion that you are among those whose blessings are in the pipeline, so God knows the best time for you. Check yourself first. Yes, it counts a lot for one to examine himself in such cases as this. Let's take some small examination of the mind. When was the last time you gave? When was the last time someone laughed because you provided him something out of your possession without hoping to receive anything back? Remind yourself of that. Can you figure out the time interval between the last time you freely gave and this present time.

For some people it would just be a day difference. Some too would have their interval as some days, weeks or even a few months. That could not be too dangerous. But I must tell you some others would have the interval between the last day they freely gave and the present time being years. Some others cannot even remember. Here lies the danger which determines they will test positive under the test for selfishness. So just sincerely test your own self in your own conscience. Don't deceive yourself; be true to yourself and let that still voice from your conscience place you where you sincerely belong; whether a freely giver, conditional giver, self-seeker or a selfish man.

Maybe you are too stingy and nothing of yours goes out of your corridors if it will not be of benefit to you. Thus, the only instance some people would try to give is when they will also benefit from it. That's selfish and conditional giving. Maybe you are the type who cares about only yourself, your wife/husband and children; nothing more, nothing less. How then do you expect God to bless you for your barns to overflow? You should manage what you have like that because it is always about you, your wife/husband and children.

Nevertheless, if indeed we desire to receive the overflowing blessings of God, then we must test negative upon being tested for selfishness. If we have even tested positive now, it is not too late. We just need to follow the isolation protocol where we think through our mistakes at the secret solitary place to have a communion between us and God. And I'm sure when our hearts and minds are corrected through the Holy Spirit's help, we would emerge out freshly nourished as people who now understand how to offer our possessions to meet the needs of others. Consequently, we will test negative to selfishness and be allowed to mingle with people operating in the supernatural blessings of God.

It is worth noting that to be blessed is to have obtained the heart of God, which is a heart of love towards all people you come across regardless of their kind. Hearts are blessed before material wealths are given out. Ask God to bless your heart before you request material blessings. We count from one before we get to two, then three and four and so on. You cannot bypass divine protocols and expect to reach higher levels in specific aspects of the grace of God. The grace of being blessed begins from the heart. Let's pray earnestly for that; then we would be good to go from there. Then when our hearts are channelled to be unselfish such that we become ready givers, we would become eligible to access the supernatural blessings in the hands of God. It is possible to get blessed so far as you are a child of God. Just work it out in the right process and God will manifest Himself in your corridors for your breakthrough.

The Accountability associated to Riches

There is the possibility of finding great wealth and resources at the disposal of some selfish people nowadays. Now someone would ask that if God wouldn't bless selfish people that much, how could such people be blessed as such. Thus, identifying some bountiful wealthy men who do not care even for the closest needy around them, might trigger one to wonder how possible it could be for God to touch their lives as such. It is possible though for one to find some seemingly selfish man with bountiful wealth, but one must not judge by sight of one incident alone. Maybe the fact you went to some wealthy man and your need couldn't be met does not completely conclude that that man is selfish and hence he does not deserve his blessing. Someone could be doing some good giving at some secret ends which you might have not recognised but God is aware. Therefore, God who is a witness to secret things can bless people like that. As a result, care must be taken about how we might want to jump to quick conclusions about whether some wealthy man is selfish or not.

Apart from that, remember Satan also can bless. So, it's not everyone you see with great possession that you can attribute the person's blessing to that of God. People with such satanic blessings are bound to exhibit ungodly characteristics among which selfishness could be part. Even with that, how best would one be able to identify people with satanic blessings. Only God who sees all things knows all things and for that matter He can tell. He is the final judge and that must be left to Him alone. It is a waste of time and energy to get occupied with determining which among the wealthy men you come across are genuine or not. That ample time could be used to work on something better to improve our relationships with God so that we receive blessings from Him. That would be better than wasting it on what we cannot do anything about. Now, whether someone's blessing is from God or not, what can we do about it and how importantly does it affect us? If someone passed through dubious means to gain what he has, that shouldn't be our worry. It is between the person and God. For God's word makes it clear concerning those who are in that group that,

> "As a partridge that broods but does not hatch, so is he who gets riches, but not by right; it will leave him in the midst of his days. And at his end he will be a fool." (Jeremiah 17:11)

So, if you are not ignorant of God's word concerning such people, you will not just worry yourself unnecessarily about those people till it creates problems for you, yourself. You can read more on them in Psalm 37: 1 - 11. The psalm of Asaph in Psalm 73 also shows the experience of the man of God who taught about these people to the point that he nearly dropped his faith except for the intervention of God. So, we should come to understand that one might harm himself by trying to think and talk more about such people and for that matter, it is not advisable. Don't try it, and if you are already trying, desist from it.

The best we Christians can do is to preach to all men, so if there is any among the wealthy who are not from God, they can be saved through the power of the gospel. Many would not preach them but sit in some corridors to gossip about them with others. That's a waste of time and that can even lead to judging wrongly which also has its designated punishment. Let's therefore desist from that dangerous characteristic if we are fond of doing that. Preach His word, then when His name is lifted, He will draw men unto Himself including the rich who have diverted from the right path.

Notwithstanding, there still exists the situation where divine blessings are found in selfish hands as it stands now. For that blessing, it's divine, so why must it fall in selfish hands. What could have happened? There are two reasons that might have caused that. One is the change of mind of the wealthy man who once had a positive heart towards the needy and gave freely and for that matter got blessed by God. A man is subject to change except he who has fixed his eyes and heart strongly on Jesus, the author and finisher of our faith. If anyone loses the principles of faith which he used to hold high, there is a high probability for such a victim to compromise his faith. It is possible for Satan to deceive anyone who does not strongly cling to the Lord Jesus after receiving his blessings.

Some, starting in the spirit, end up being too flesh minded to the point that they forget their first love that bound them to the precepts of God. So, you can find someone so kind and generous in the beginning but after gaining a lot and allowing himself to be influenced wrongly, his character changes. Such people's actions then become very opposite to their old character which was the foundation for their promotion. Many men disappoint God that way. Instead of honouring God who raised them from nowhere to where they presently are by satisfying the needs of the needy around them, they shun their spiritual obligation. They now become 'wiser' in their own eyes to follow what the world says rather than what God of the bible says.

Some such people buy the idea of poisonous worldly advisors who beguile them to believe in the fact that 'throwing away' most of what one owns will eventually leave him broke. They call giving 'throwing away' which they think will lead the generous man to become broke. Forgetting that this same person was more than broke from the point where God lifted him from. Many swear all kinds of oaths before God that they would help others once they are blessed. Others go to the extent that they would even want to use the name of God to swear that they would never remain selfish but would use their blessing to raise others, and for that matter, God should bless them. Most such people disappoint God. They just do the opposite.

Sometimes it is not that God does not see the future of what they would do. The faithfulness that one exhibits with regards to the little entrusted to him would determine how far God walks with him. Some of them could have been blessed more than the level they are now. All because blessing has got levels and different forms. One can be blessed in his work but not in his household. There is a level of blessing that a man can reach such that he becomes peaceful in all sectors of life. Thus, the person does not only have a booming business but also a successful and peaceful relationship with people all around him. Surely, there are people who live in the atmosphere of total internal peace even amidst the chaos this world presents. That is another form and level of blessing. Therefore, one must not gear his attention towards money and properties alone and consider that attaining such materialistic wealth only could be classified as a blessing. Without peace, all attainments are not enjoyable. Without peace from close and distant relationships, one can easily lose his possessions that class him as a wealthy person.

Therefore, failing to be faithful, these once-kind-but-now-selfish wealthy men lose their opportunities of greater and higher heights before the Lord. Had they continued with their charitable acts as they started, a greater door of greater blessings would have opened for them. Since they are ignorant of it, they believe it is all well with them. Do you remember the parable of the Lord Jesus about the master who before travelling entrusted talents to his servants? Try and look through it from Matthew 25:14-30. Those who proved faithful, he gave them higher positions but he who proved to be lazy and stingy with unjustified ideology lost everything he had and received a punishment.

So, it should be noted that to be blessed is also to be put in a position to be tested! In conclusion, I want to affirm that there is the possibility for God's divine blessing to be controlled by a selfish man. One of the causes is what has just been described above. And I hope the related effects of such a character has been expounded enough such that if anyone is found in such a character, he would better refrain from it. Let's look at the second reason by which divine blessing can fall into wrong hands.

The second reason to tackle is inherited blessing. When blessings are inherited, the probability for it to fall into wrong hands is higher than falling into right hands. This is because it is very difficult for some people to keep safe what they didn't toil for. Since it wasn't through their strength and sweat that made them come by what is handed over to them, some fail to discover the importance of using those blessings meaningfully. And for that matter, such people could become very selfish to consume those inherited blessings on their wrong personal cravings. More often than not, the mind-set and visions of the owner who toiled to attain the possessions is very different from the one who takes over from him. This can really cause a negative effect on the nearby people who were supposed to enjoy that divine wealth. Though the blessing came divinely to the one who had a correct relationship with God, yet since that person is dead and has been taken over by another who does not love God as the former did, the latter begin to misuse the wealth.

See what king Solomon said when he was thinking about this very thing.

> Then I hated all my labour in which I had toiled under the sun, because I must leave it to the man who will come after me. And **who knows whether he will be wise or a fool**? Yet he will rule over all my labour in which I have shown myself wise under the sun. This is also vanity. (Ecclesiastes 2:18,19)

Who knows what the sort of calibre of personality the heir could be made up of, whether he will be wise or a fool? As if Solomon knew that this would happen after he is gone while he was ministering in his wise sayings. What is so interesting about these words of Solomon is that his son Rehoboam, who was his heir, also dealt foolishly thereby losing a greater part of the possession he inherited from his father, Solomon. Instead of dealing with his people in wisdom as his father did, he resorted to the advice of his peers and therefore suffered a loss for it. Solomon taxed the people greatly during his reign, yet he knew how to confront them wisely in order to appease their heart from rebellion. So instead for Rehoboam to have learnt from his father's wisdom, let's consider below his answer to the people his father left for him to rule over at one point:

Then the king [thus Rehoboam] answered the people roughly, and rejected the advice which the elders had given him; and he spoke to them according to the advice of the young men, saying, 'My father made your yoke heavy, but I will add to your yoke; my father chastised you with whips, but I will chastise you with scourges! (1 Kings 12:13,14 emphasis added)

Look at the kind of heir who comes after king Solomon who had been bountifully blessed by God and who used his wisdom to protect his possessions. The words of Rehoboam determine how shallow his mind was to control the wealth handed over to him. Eventually, he lost the greater part of the kingship to another man who had no right to the throne. If divine blessing ends up being controlled by wrong hands, that's what results; people who don't have right to it take it away with less effort. All because the controller himself does not have the heart of God hence, God also removes His protection from the blessing. All divine blessings are established by the spiritual hedge of God and unless God takes that hedge away, no other can intrude to exploit it. Remember the blessings of Job couldn't have been touched by Satan until God gave him the access. Look at it because of its importance so far as the safety of divine blessings are concerned.

So, Satan answered the Lord and said "… Have you not made a hedge around him, around his household, and around all that he has on every side? You have blessed the work of his hands, and his possessions have increased in the land. But now, stretch your hand and touch all that he has, and he will surely curse You to Your face. And the Lord said to Satan, "Behold, all that he has is in your power; only do not lay a hand on his person." (Job 1:9-12)

As you can see from the text, Job was another example of someone experiencing the supernatural blessing of God. He had been blessed on every side, and Satan testified of that. The point of attention here which can be noted from the dialogue between Satan and God about Job is that there was a particular hedge around the divine blessings of Job that made the blessings untouchable. So, for Satan to be able to touch this blessing, he had to be permitted by God. Indeed, most of us who know the story of Job, are very aware of how it ended. The divine hedge around Job's blessings was taken away by the permission of God to allow Satan to get in. Satan could not have gone by any means when God had not permitted.

The blessings God bestows upon His beloved are fortified by His own hands. Except He removes His protection, no authority can take that blessing away. It is called His hedge of protection. It proves beyond doubt that God removed His hands from Rehoboam's wealth which were handed to him by his father, Solomon; as a result, he lost almost all of it. The scenario of Rehoboam's character in his possessions describes how divine blessings can also fall into wrong hands due to inheritance. The effects on it have also been duly treated and hence it serves as a lesson to anyone who has by chance taken over the blessings of other men due to absence whether because of death or travelling.

The lesson being taught all this while is that if someone has many resources and the person is still not extending his alms to meet other people's needs, then the person is not thinking right. That fellow is deceived to assume that his superfluous blessing is for superfluous flaunting of riches and extravagant living. That is the reason there is a day when everyone would account for what he was blessed with before God, the giver of all riches. As a matter of fact, apart from the resources that meet a person's personal needs, what should he be keeping the rest for? We must be aware that it is God who gives to all people, but He does so through other selected people. To these selected people, God gives them or hands over to them many resources relative to the other needy people or neighbours they would have to kindly reach through giving.

So, if one finds out that his resources are beyond his needs, he must be careful not to misuse the rest because it becomes his responsibility to now stand in the position of God to supply the rest to others who are also in need, thereby glorifying the name of God as the giver to all men. (… whoever serves, as one who serves by the strength that God supplies – in order that in everything God may be glorified through Jesus Christ. 1 Peter 4:11) Therefore, the act of refusing to give in some situations ends up restricting the glory of God in the lives of some people. This is because after every receiver had received from any giver and had expressed his appreciation, the receiver glorifies God in his heart for granting such an ability to the giver to render such a service of giving.

In this way, God obtains His glory as the source of every good work. Also, the glory due His name is not denied Him. For the particular reason of God receiving His glory in the lives of the needy ones, every capable giver must not refuse the honourable service of giving whenever such an opportunity comes his way. On this note, if one finds within his ability to give, he must not hesitate. Yes, in this world, just as one man said, "As we have awakened from sleep, someone's chop money is in the pocket of another neighbour of his." Thus, the tendency of someone's survival in a day depends on what he would receive from another person. So, one must do well not to play wicked on the needy person he meets along his path.

The other dangerous aspect of refusing to give either because you disregard the receiver, or you intentionally want to excuse giving is not that welcoming. Especially when God has commanded you to do that, or God placed you in such a position in order for you to offer such help to others. Let's look at that from the book of Esther.

And Mordecai told them to answer Esther: "Do not think in your heart that you will escape in the king's palace any more than all the other Jews. For if you remain completely silent at this time, relief and deliverance will arise for the Jews from another place, but you and your father's house will perish. Yet who knows whether you have come to the kingdom for such a time as this? (Esther 4:13,14)

Here is a common slave, Esther who has been shown the favour of God and has been raised to the position of a Queen. It was now her turn to offer her best to save her people who were under a serious threat of killing and utter annihilation. She had to now decide whether to forsake them because of fear or take on the risk of helping. She had doubts as to which action to take. Therefore, his uncle Mordecai sent a strong warning to her that cleared all her doubts and had her mind switched on to do everything possible to save her people who were about to perish.

Exactly so are many today raised to positions where they are obliged to help others to survive the heat of this present world. Like Esther many of them are doubting whether to help or deny helping. Unlike Esther who finally gave up her doubts and decided finally to help at all cost, many today have excused and denied the mission to offer their best for others to survive. That becomes too dangerous when the needy is a person in the will of God. Thus, if God desires that one must offer some help to make it possible for others dear to Him to survive and the person denies, the matter becomes a divine concern attracting divine jurisdictions which could be tantamount to divine punishments.

Just as Mordecai said, who knows you were raised to the position you are now for such a time as this and for such a reason of helping others. No one should think he will escape if he plays wicked and deaf ear to the call of giving that would help a child of God to survive. As I said earlier, so far as God lives, His sheep shall not want. So wherever possible, God would make a way for the needy to have his needs met but he who excused himself might end up getting into a great problem. Queen Esther could have disregarded her people and think that she is now a queen, so she's got it all. Yet no one knows what would have befallen her if she refused to help her people. We must not think we are good to go since we are now comfortable. Remember from where you were raised and help others too. Givers therefore should not excuse their giving to get more blessed, and to also escape from the punishment of God.

Significant notes

❖ Giving is disowning your possession for it to become the possession of another person

❖ If the world were full of only givers, no one would give; likewise, if the world were full of only receivers, no one would receive

❖ The receiver makes the giver, a giver; and the giver makes the receiver, a receiver.

❖ A person who owns a lot and has not given out is never equal to a person who owns and has given out.

❖ The honour given to givers after they have given is greater than the honour given to receivers after they have received.

❖ It is good to be a receiver but better to be a giver with regards to associated blessings.

❖ There are spiritual blessings in the alms of God ready to be deposited on any who proves worthy. Such blessings are that which makes a man rich without adding sorrows.

❖ The problems of a God-approved and blessed man are inversely proportional to the envy of his enemies. The more you envy divine people the less their problems become.

❖ Don't do wrong transactions with your envy such that you get credited with problems while the one you envy who is beloved of God gets debited with more blessings.

❖ The act of wrongly anticipating and judging on others' blessings whether they deserve to be blessed or not can get you into a serious problem with God.

❖ Let someone laugh because of your giving. As they laugh and bless God for what you have done in their lives, God's attention would come upon you.

- ❖ God multiplies the resources of sowers so that much would be sowed and for that matter, much would be produced for the consumption of all eaters

- ❖ Givers are entitled to a double portion of blessing beyond the blessing of those who are only receivers.

- ❖ Better will it be for one to be positioned at where he receives first-hand blessings than to be waiting on man who can change his mind at any time

- ❖ To be a valid candidate for supernatural blessings, you must be a proven giver

- ❖ Righteousness and giving cannot be separated. Not every giver is righteous although; but every righteous man is a giver

- ❖ Natural blessings wither and perish as the beauty of a flower. But supernatural blessings live beyond lifetime

- ❖ There is this one kind of blessing that goes beyond what nature and human effort can offer.

- ❖ Ready-made supernatural blessings are up there in the Hands of God waiting for us to reach some level of commitment.

- ❖ A giver gives a natural thing and receives in return a supernatural blessing

- ❖ God gives out His blessing only to meet human needs, and since a stingy person thinks about himself alone, he is bound to receive what will meet only his needs; hence, his minimal blessing

- ❖ Without peace from close and distant relationships, one can easily lose his possessions that class him as a wealthy person.

- ❖ Preach His word, then when His name is lifted, He will draw men unto Himself including the rich who have diverted from the right path

- ❖ If divine blessing ends up being controlled by wrong hands, the result is that people who don't have right to it take it away with less effort

❖ The blessings God bestows upon His beloved are fortified by His own hands. Except He removes His protection, no authority can take that blessing away.

❖ Givers should not excuse their giving to get more blessed and also to escape from the punishment of God associated with refusing the divine obligation to give.

Receive
Give

CHAPTER THREE

How to Give and How to Receive

The Proper Basis for Giving

There is a proper platform for giving that makes the results lasting and remarkable. The ministry of Giving and Receiving is a very important avenue which God uses to restore and rebuild broken lives, unite parties, and most importantly establish relationships between God and men, and also between men and other men. God gave His Son, men received Him and got saved; thus, eternal relationship between God and man established. Men give back to God through giving to other men or supporting His work. In all the acts of men's giving and receiving, important relationships are established that have lasting impacts on the parties who are involved whether the givers or the receivers. As a result of this remarkable impact aimed to be achieved, Giving and Receiving must be treated as holistic and be done in the right manner.

Giving must not be based on compulsion. Givers must come out from their own free will to offer what they can give from their possessions to their needy neighbours. If, at an instance, one sees himself that he can give, fine, then he can go on based on his ability. On the other hand, if the same person sees himself at some other point unable to give, that shouldn't generate a problem between him and anyone. No one must force anyone to give beyond that person's decision and ability. That's against the word of God. In fact, it should be expressly known that giving is not compulsory. Giving is necessary but not compulsory. The proper basis of giving therefore should be out of free will and not by compulsion. The apostle Paul emphatically addressed this in his epistle to the people of Corinth this way:

> Each man should give what he has decided in his heart to give, not reluctantly or under compulsion, for God loves a cheerful giver. (2 Corinthians 9:7, NIV)

Giving therefore is a decision from the giver's own intent and the product of the dialogue that goes on within him towards the target point of giving. No man can decide for any other man when it comes to a point such as this. One can encourage another to give though, but not force him compulsorily to give. So just as the Apostle rightly advised, giving shouldn't be reluctantly on the part of the giver nor should it be under compulsion from external people. If this happens, there is the high probability of the result of such a giving being fruitless. There will be no proper blessing coming out from such a reluctant giving or the type of giving that was done under compulsion.

It would be better for reluctant givers to have stopped giving because their reluctance would cause them to be grudging inwardly after their giving and that could attract something very opposite to the expected blessing. People have received disappointments other than blessings based on situations such as these. All because they didn't give freely out of their own heart and as a result felt regretful afterwards. This act could produce some bitterness in their heart which would also spoil their relationship with the people they gave to and go a long way to destroy their faith in God.

It must clearly be acknowledged that the fact that a person does not have enough to give at a certain point in time or in a certain situation does not mean he is wicked. Sincerely, it happens that sometimes the requests of some needy people are beyond those whom they target to receive from. As a matter of fact, there is no measuring rod for someone to determine that indeed this person is capable of giving this or that. That should come from the person himself because he has the control over his possessions. It is God who can discern into all hearts for the truth behind an action. The best compelling persuasion would be thoroughly teaching people the importance of giving; thereby bringing them to the point of awareness of the need to give. When people are educated right from the basics of giving with realistic examples, they would not need anyone to force them to give. People endowed with such knowledge give with understanding rather than reluctance. This crucial responsibility of education must therefore be taken up by any person who leads and has the opportunity of transferring knowledge.

Though every sacrifice costs; yet the one who is sacrificing agrees over what he is about to do. As a result, though there is the presence of the cost, the agreement and willingness of the person who is about to sacrifice overcome the cost so that there is the cheerfulness of the heart towards the target point of giving. Consequently, there is a witnessing relief of peace that occurs in the person's heart after sacrificing despite the cost incurred. This way of sacrificing does not produce any grudging and negative murmurings afterwards because the giver in this case made a complete decision by himself on what he decided to offer as a sacrifice. The agreement of the heart that produces willingness to finalise on a decision to buttress the act of given is the key!

When people decide for themselves to give, they give out of happiness. That's the cheerfulness the Holy Spirit communicated through Apostle Paul in the text above. People should give while laughing both externally and inwardly. Reluctant givers as well as those who are made to give under compulsion could put a fake smile on their faces whilst they feel bitter inwardly. That's not congruent! Your inner man should support what you do outwardly. It should not be that your mind and heart are against what your hand has stretched forth to do. Human beings are not robots. We are not programmed and configured to be controlled by external systems.

Therefore, to give out a gift which you are not alright about, would not please God. People would be pleased alright but God who sees how your heart is darkened concerning it and your unwillingness would not be happy with your gift. That would not help because the right blessing that could have come out from that giving wouldn't be witnessed. God does not desire that offer of sacrifice. God assesses the individual's heart before considering what the person has in his hand to offer as a sacrifice. You would better understand this when you read the story about the sacrifices of Cain and Abel. Your being must be pleasing before thinking of what you are presenting when it comes to offering to God. So, your heart cannot be darkened while you expect your offering in hand to be pleasing to God. One's offer of sacrifice would be validated before God only if his heart also is rightly appropriated with regards to the target point of the act of giving. (You would better comprehend this in my other book entitled, The Worthwhile Giving)

In spite of this and also to clear up any doubt, if one gets an ill feeling and decides not to give at one point and later on changes his mind and comes back to give, God will not be displeased with that. Thus, the person in this case was not willing to give but upon further internal considerations, decided later that he would now give. His later decision is now backed with his mind and heart which validates it as free-will giving. The underlying factor is the expression that goes within the giver at the point of giving and the afterward feeling. The basis on which the mind is being made up towards the point of giving is what is paramount.

So, if a person refused to make his mind to give at one instant but later made his mind based on his free will to give, this giving would be blessed and rewarded by God. So far as it was not under any compulsion and the present act is without reluctance, the giver's heart is filled with joy which will attract the required blessings of God proportionately. This is because there are instances such as these when God tests the obedience of men as Jesus mentioned in one of His parables. In Matthew 21:29-31, the son here who refused to run the errand for his father but later decided to go was termed the obedient son. Let what the Spirit of God is saying to the church be heard by our ears.

Raising the alarm of necessity of giving among people will be better than raising that of compulsion. When people get to know the absolute need for them to act on something, they come all inside out towards it; thus, they do it with all their will. Akin to salvation, God does not force salvation on men. In as much as salvation is the most necessary thing with regards to men's existence here on earth, God has left it absolutely to the will of men. God has commissioned the preaching of the gospel to raise the necessity of salvation to all men. Now, whoever hears the gospel, and is willing to admit that he is a sinner, accept that Jesus is the Son of God and receive Him into his heart, that person will be saved. If salvation, despite how necessary it is, is not on compulsion, then giving too is not. The best those who advocate giving can do is to continue to preach its necessity and leave the rest to the compliance of their audience based on their will. It is worth noting from these analyses above to establish that the correct and proper basis of giving is a person giving out his own will.

Wrong Ways of Claiming to Receive

Though we are dealing more with giving here, it's also important to consider the right and wrong ways receivers claim gifts from givers. Most assuredly, the proper way receivers could receive from givers is when the condition under which the giver gives is free from compulsion. Thus, when the giver comes out from his own will directly from the heart to offer what is within his capability to give. Else, if any receiver claims any gift from any giver by compulsion and for that matter against the giver's will, the reception is wrong. Whatever be the case the receiver might have met his need with such a giving but there is no peace after that giving and reception. Proper giving and proper reception establish a continuity and longevity of good relationship between the giver and receiver. Yet when gifts are claimed by compulsion and even if the givers are able to offer what is being requested, the cordial relationship between the giver and receiver breaks up from that point. We want to consider these incidents which happen between men and God and those between men and other men. Let's continue.

Men to God Requisition Relationship

Absurd Character of Receivers from God

We must be very keen on this kind of illogical attitude on the part of some receivers because that is the character of most children of God which is absurd. They have got a problem created between themselves and God based on this very character. Once their request tarries or is not answered, such people want to throw insults back to God. How dangerous that is! Yet some people in our generation do so with such an ignorant ease. Once they feel God hasn't or didn't give them their cravings, they manage to utter, silently in their hearts and sometimes with their mouths, lots of blasphemies against God. This character does not incline God to act in their favour, but it rather spoils their case.

It is God who is so merciful and the atoning blood of His son Jesus Christ which keeps advocating for some of us, else we would have been swallowed by the earth as it happened to Korah and his supporting allies. Even with the propitiation we receive from Christ, some people are bound to face the judgement of God because of their blasphemy against the Holy Spirit. Some have such an incorrigible attitude to the point that they are unable to be tamed by any measure of correction; yet that comes as a result of either total ignorance, or too knowing a character which amounts to arrogance. Children of God of such sort must better amend their ways and surrender humbly to God before God Himself humbles them.

You can't force God to give. In fact, who does that? And who is supposed to do that? No one! Though He is gracious, He is kind, He is generous, etc. He does His giving based on His own will. No one can control God. So, if God, in His own wisdom and will, has not decided to release a particular blessing on anyone, who is it that is worthy to question His intelligence. It's a shame many have gotten the lack of fear for God. We've got to honour God by recognising His supremacy and giving Him the reverence we ought to have for Him as His handiworks. Our required position is to please Him per what His word demands us to do. When we obtain His attention that way through our obedience, we can obtain what we don't even ask and indeed what we also ask through His name, He will give to us.

We cannot do for ourselves what we are seeking for. It is only God we look up to for an answer. So, if it is God who would answer you and do what you require, then patience, honour, and respect for Him is very necessary because He holds what you need. If it were the case that you could do your request for yourself without the help of God, then do it for yourself! Yet if we believe it is only God who can do what we need, then we better wait in reverence. Notwithstanding, some people who get weary obtain some unjustified anger to leave the presence of God in an act of going to find another way on their own to obtain what their hearts desire. And indeed, some are able to obtain their cravings but to the detriment of their own souls. Some end up bitterly in tears while they also lose their salvation. Yet, if we are the kind who want to secure our salvation in God and hence, we have no help anywhere other than to look unto God, then we must better wait patiently without blasphemy believing God's time is the best. The fact that having to wait for longer days, weeks, or even years for an answer is not easy is well know. It is well understood how weary one can be whilst waiting for an answer to prayers for a long time. Yet there are reasons that could result in the delay of answers to prayers that believers sometimes experience. Let's explore some of them.

Reasons Some Blessings Delay

God's divine timing is the reason we might see some blessings delayed. Sometimes it is the wish for the children of God to see what they have envisioned or been prophesied to be manifested as early as possible. Nevertheless, every prophecy has got its processing time. Unless it is fully matured, it will never manifest. It's akin to childbirth. The time between conception to the time of delivery is the processing period for the child to come out. No one can force a child out if its time is not yet up and expect the child to be normal. Unless someone has decided to abort it or due to other conditions, the child's life needs to be terminated to save the mother. Else, if any woman wants the manifestation of what she has conceived, then she must be prepared to take the nine-month journey patiently.

That gift of the womb needs to be mature enough to survive the conditions of this world immediately it is out. If not so, and the undeveloped foetus is forced out, the process of maturity would not have been completed and hence many abnormalities are bound to occur. Exactly so are the blessings God prepares for His people, whether gifts, deliverance or promotions. They all pass through the divine process of maturity till they are matured enough to be stable. Else, due to its immature state it will not last. Whatever also that is given by God is supposed to last. It could also be put in another way that before God releases a blessing, He prepares the receiving hands or vessel to be matured enough in order to be able to receive, contain and use it. Therefore, you might be crying all your tears out at the point of waiting; yet, if yourself or what you desire is not matured, you are bound to cry a little more. Yes, just a little more but not forever!

The Israelites cried for deliverance from slavery but until the time was right, it seemed as if God didn't hear them. So are prophecies! '**Though it tarries**, according to prophet Habakkuk, wait for it; because it will surely come to pass, **it will not tarry**'. Take note here that though it tarries with men; yet, with God, it will not tarry. God would never leave His words empty without accomplishing them because He cannot deny Himself; for He is His word. Yes, it is worthy to accept that indeed the vision is yet for an appointed time; but at the end it will speak, and it will not lie. (Habakkuk 2:3)

King David advises all who have waited for long that it is not easy but 'Wait on the LORD; be of good courage, and He shall strengthen your heart; wait, I say on the LORD!' (Psalm 27:14) He also added his own experience which buttresses his advice that 'I waited patiently for the LORD; and He inclined to me, and heard my cry, …' (Psalm 40:1) So waiters do not keep mute, they cry in prayers while patiently waiting for the appropriate time of the Lord's answer. They do not blaspheme or lose faith but they cry in hope of the salvation of God who alone can deliver them. Indeed, God will never forsake them as King David had also confirmed that, 'And those who know your name will put their trust in You; for You, LORD, have not forsaken those who seek you.' God shall surely show up in His divine appointed time and make all things beautiful.

In addition to believing that God's timing is the best, children of God must work out His commandments in obedience while we wait. Some people do not receive their request and others too have theirs delayed due to their disposition with God. Some are stingy and hence are not qualified to be blessed as it is explained in the previous chapter. Others too are comfortably living with sins that defiles the very hands they have lifted to receive from God. How can you dwell in sins and see them to be normal and yet you want a gift from someone who detests sin? You entertain the abominations of God, yet you desire Him to bless you, that isn't congruent. Check this out, going to a king for a request yet you hold in your hand what is an abomination to the king, what do you think will happen? Receivers must therefore check all these things before they complain beyond their designated level for it to turn out to be a blasphemy. The Lord therefore corrected such a class of receivers who are waiting for an answer from God yet are not in line with Him through Isaiah the prophet of God. Check it out:

> Behold, the LORD's hand is not shortened, that it cannot save; nor His ear heavy that it cannot hear. But your iniquities have separated you from your God; and your sins have hidden His face from you, so that He will not hear. For your hands are defiled with blood, and your fingers with iniquity; your lips have spoken lies, your tongue has muttered deceit.... (Isaiah 59:1-3)

This message is not meant for the people of Israel alone. It is now inscribed by the Holy Spirit for you and I. Just screen your life through the text above and discover why your prayer might have not been answered. It's just a matter of correcting ourselves. Identifying our faults, we just need to ask for forgiveness through remorseful repentance and forsake all the evil which is an abomination unto God. When we shall have done this, through the blood of Jesus Christ, our sins will be forgiven, and we would have a close relationship with God other than the time when we were separated due to our sins. All because the text above here shows us that it could be our transgressions that have made it look as if God's hand is shortened or His ear is heavy.

God cannot look unto sin because it is not His delight. So, deal with the sin attached to you by the power of the Holy Spirit and you will have the right to deal with God in a closer relationship than before. Sometimes one might need some help from others who are more spirit-filled to help him; if it happens so with your case, don't feel shy and ashamed. Seek help! It is rather shameful to be living with your sin secretly as a child of God. It gives Satan the ability to manipulate you the most. Revealing your secret sin to the right people, in itself, opens the door for the light of God to shine against the darkness of deception Satan employs against you. Satan therefore becomes less powerful against us when we reveal the affair that he is secretly having with us. Then from there, he can be driven out of our vessels by necessary correspondence with other men filled with the Spirit of God. Seek the right help and do away with the sin and God will automatically draw you nearer and your long-awaited answers will manifest out of the blue. Let's consider yet another point.

Another reason blessings could delay is because of discouragement to be persistent in prayer towards a request. The tendency of leaving the place of prayer the moment our blessings tarry, could deny us obtaining it. It is improper to accept a 'No' as an answer when a 'Yes' is on the way. Sometimes God can give you a sign of an upcoming positive response about an issue you are praying about; yet human beings would be presenting negative responses to you. This is where one ought to be persistent in pressing on through prayer to witness the manifestation of what God has said.

My Testimony

I remember when I travelled the first time to the UK to study and got myself into an immigration issue at the border to enter Scotland. Together with three other prospective students, we were detained for almost twelve hours at the very point of being deported. In the detaining room, I started praying. Though CCTV cameras were on us, I bowed my head and prayed. While some others had already lost hope, I felt very positive that the will of God for me was to move forward not backwards. One of us was deported that same day. This incident happened in January 2022. Out of the three of us who were allowed to enter the country and submit further appeals, two were deported after two months. I was the only one left who had my permit to stay and study after three months of difficult times. My long-awaited positive response came precisely at the end of March 2022 with all my documents to stay and study in Scotland. This is where I am writing this manuscript from, by the inspiration of God. I didn't just receive a positive response. I remember I received a letter in February to pack and get ready to go back like the others on a proposed day in March. Yet that was the answer I had been prompted by God's Spirit to receive so I discarded it. I had already devoted the full month of February to fasting and prayer. I had also connected a chain of prayer links to many honourable men and women who stood with me in prayer. To cut it short, God brought my desired answer on the last day of March 2022. A fervent prayer made would cause Heaven to look for the right connections to make a way even when all men say there is no way. I reckon that no matter how overwhelming your situation seems to be, don't give up, just tarry, worry less, pray more and believe that your answer will surely come. We serve a faithful God to whom all things are possible. Hallelujah!

There are instances in the Bible where the Lord Jesus addressed this notion of tarrying in prayer to receive. He talked about the parable of a widow who continuously presented her case to a lawyer without giving up, till she was vindicated by the lawyer. (Luke 18:1-8) That was to show us that unwavering persistent requests yield positive results. Another one He narrated was a certain man who went to request for bread from his friend at midnight because he had had a visitor; here, this man knocked at the door of the friend countless number of times till his friend couldn't help but to come and give him what he desired. (Luke 11:5-13) This also shows us that persistency during requesting yields a positive response if we don't get weary and quit. These parables, as the Bible states, Jesus told to let all His audience know that 'A man ought to pray and not to faint'. In the act of requesting through prayer, until we have obtained what we are praying about, we ought to persistently pray and not to give up. As far as our request is in the will of the Father, it is the desire of the Father to answer our request to glorify the name of Jesus through whom we make our request. It is also the desire of the Lord Jesus to see our prayers answered so the Father would be glorified. Therefore, men ought to tarry in His presence believing that He will ultimately respond to us.

The case of the Prophet Daniel (Daniel 10) is also a good example here. The story of Daniel's answer, in the hands of an angel, captured for twenty-one days shows us that we ought to persistently battle through prayer to receive what we have desired according to the will of God. Daniel's account portrays to us that every blessing battles its way down to the recipient. Therefore, till the person who is praying gets hold of what he is requesting, continuous prayer is very important. For we wrestle not against flesh and blood, so says the word of God. Let us pray, continue to pray and never stop praying until our eyes see our desire in our hands. God bless you.

Whilst dealing with prayer, let me mention what the Holy Spirit told me about how to increase the intensity of our prayers even when requesting from men. This is what He whispered to me: 'A helper's enemies increase at the very point he accepts to assist a needy person.' I asked how? He continued, 'The enemies of the needy person will make that helper a target because the helper's assistance will elevate the needy person to a level against the wish of his enemies.' So, one ought to pray not only to receive from a helper but also to pray against extra attacks the helper might encounter just by the decision of accepting to help. In the Bible, the Israelites made a covenant with the Gibeonites and by that the enemies of the Gibeonites became the enemies of Israelites. It thus throws up a caution to both helpers and the needy.

To a helper, this doesn't suggest that you should forsake the act of helping for the reason that you will be receiving extra attacks; no, just that you must always be in line with the consent of the Spirit of God in the act of helping. Never give consent on the basis of compassion only, but by seeking the counsel of the Holy Spirit. The Israelites in this act of making a covenant with the Gibeonites never asked whether that was in the agreement of the Spirit of God. They just reacted by sight and made their decision only to discover later that the Gibeonites had deceived them; upon realizing, it was too late because they had already established a covenant with them. At the point of communicating with men, one should simultaneously communicate with God; or postpone his final consent to men until he receives God's viewpoint. You can always postpone men but not God. Agreeing with men before coming to God could be fatal and regretful. Once God's positive consent is ascertained, have no fears about attacks that will come along the path helping the needy. The guaranteed protection of God upon a life-saviour who steps in the gap to help a needy will be thoroughly dealt with as we proceed.

One thing I cherished about my head pastor and father Rev. Yaw Fosu whom I stayed with is his regular sayings such as 'The Holy Spirit said to me, ...'. I learn a lot from ministers of God I come across but there is one thing I'm jealous of: when someone has direct connection to the Spirit of God through communication. I just love to hear that God spoke to a man and its genuine. All because whenever God speaks, there comes clarity about an issue of interest; all confusion is eradicated the moment God speaks. In as much as recognising that it's not everyone who can hear the audible voice of God, there are many ways God can confirm His consent about any issue one is deliberating on. God as dear

Father communicates to every child of His through many forms which are specific to His children. So, it pays to seek the consent of God who always answers anyone who sincerely seeks His face.

To the needy seeking to be helped by someone, the inference from the above inspiration means more prayer should be invested in the waiting period to receive from a helper. All because the helper might be willing alright to help but there could be obstacles that would want to stop him from being able to offer such a help. Once someone has given you a promise, it does not mean that the promise will be smoothly honoured. There could arise reasonable excuses to cause the helper to just dishonour the promise on the day of expectation. Even though some excuses are sincere and hence would cause the helper to postpone his help. Yet many of such of excuses are because of negative influences arising from physical or spiritual roots. Just as was stated above from the Spirit of God's inspiration, the enemies of the needy make any helper who tries to be of help to the needy a target immediately the helper agrees to help. So, continuous prayer made towards receiving request would be helpful especially when majority of the prayers are directed to support the helper. **For if the tool of help is captured, the helper will become helpless**. The needy must therefore continuously pray that God will do away with any obstacles that might arise in the path of their helpers.

So, it is good we have established that continuous prayer to God with regards to our request made to God or men is very paramount. This reason will lead us to consider yet another interesting reason below. Let's get going.

You know what the problem of some children of God are? They are fond of asking from God what will eventually kill them. So, no matter what it is, God should give it to them so that they die ignorantly. Far it be from God to give His children poisonous blessings! God would never grant what would eventually cause His child to break away from Him. He is intelligent. He sees far and beyond the end of all things. What we intend and plan to do are already in His view. Look at how the Lord Jesus hid this mystery when teaching on the act of requesting from God.

Ask, and it will be given to you, seek, and you will find; knock, and it will be opened to you. For everyone who asks receives and he who seeks finds, and to him who knocks it will be opened. Or what man is there among you who, if his son **asks for bread**, will **give him a stone**? Or if he **asks for a fish**, will he **give him a serpent**? If you then, being evil, know how to give good gifts to your children, how much more will your Father who is in heaven give **good things** to those who ask Him! (Matthew 7:7-11)

After giving us the assurance that we shall be given whatever we shall ask for, the Lord now questions our intelligence from there. Thus, whether we would give our children stone for bread and serpent for fish if we were in the position of being requested from by our children. Everybody would straight away answer no, because no sympathetic parent would do that. Now, the question here is, what about if your child asks not for the bread but for the stone and also for the serpent but not for the fish? Would any parent grant such a request arising from the desire of his child?

It is just like your child asking you to give him poison. Your son one morning asks you that his appetite is for the poison he has seen in the shells at the back of the corridors. And he adds that the poison is what he feels to take for breakfast. What do you think would happen that day? It would not be surprising that day to expect a long cry of no response with regards to the exact object of request. If anything would be given to the child by a loving parent, it would be something else to keep him away from crying all his tears out. Nevertheless, giving our ignorant children what they wrongly crave for which would ultimately cause us to lose them would never be done by any caring parent. How much more God?

It's high time the children of God checked the sort of request they are making before God. Thus, whether we are asking for bread or for stone and whether we are claiming to be given fish or to be given serpent. Bread and fish sustain the life of man; yet stone and serpent pose danger to the sustenance of the life of man. To be given bread and fish is to help you maintain your life and relationship with the giver who is God so that your fellowship with Him continues. To be given stone and serpent is to be given something that is a threat to your relationship with God such that your fellowship with God becomes at stake. God does not give stones and serpents. He gives **good things to those who ask Him**.

What do we infer from that? It means if one will only ask for a good thing from God, he will surely receive it. Therefore, this also is showing us another reason for some people having their request not granted before God. All because they might not have been asking for good things. They might have been seeking for stones and serpents which are a danger to their own spiritual health. And as a result, our heavenly Father being so caring and sympathetic would not provide them with such provisions to the detriment of their own souls. Again, far it be from God to give out poisonous blessings!

The bible text above compares the character of man, the sinful (wicked) and God, the righteous (sympathetic) in the aspect of giving. Thus, if men who are unmerciful know how to offer good gifts to their children, how much more God who is merciful. Would God give good gifts to His children; yes, He surely would. The opposite of this is also very valid. That if even men who are unsympathetic would not give bad things to their children, how much more God who is sympathetic. Would God give bad gifts to His children; no, He would never. Watch out! The text above (Matthew 7;7-11) should therefore be pondered over again by whoever thinks that it means 'whatever' comes from the mouth of anyone as a request at the point of prayer would be granted by God. The inference of that excerpt from the Lord Jesus was to reveal the pattern by which God, our heavenly, responds to our requests through prayers.

An example to discourage us from making such requests was given to us through the parable of the prodigal son by Jesus. (Luke 15:11-24) You can have a quick glance through that excerpt from the bible if you are not familiar. For us who are familiar, we all know what happened to this younger son who made such a wrong request and insisted on it till his father got weary. Though this son had what he craved for, he got lost from home, he broke relationship with his father, his guide, and eventually ended up suffering in the foreign land. This son particularly made the right decision and came back, and his merciful father also received him; so, he got lost but was later found.

Let me ask, 'How many of such sons are able to come back home as did the prodigal son?'. Some get lost forever such that their dead bodies are not even noticed by any relative. That's the mistake God doesn't want any child of His to make. The bible is written for our guide and therefore the mistakes in there are not supposed to be repeated by us, the readers (students). The first dangerous thing after receiving such requests is that you break relationship with God, and beyond that boundary you are at the mercy of Satan, who comes to steal, kill and destroy. When you have not even gone to him, he wishes to come to where you are to steal, kill and destroy you; how much more going into his territory. Though it is not impossible; yet there is very little chance of coming back. Only few make it back to god in such circumstances. Secure your life in God by refraining from requesting for stones and serpents.

At least we have dealt with four solid reasons for which our requests can be delayed: one, due to genuine God's divine timing, two, because of our own sins, three, failure to persist in prayer to draw our answer and four, as a result of making wrong requests. Before we go on to the relationship of men receiving from other men, let's deal with the need for being grateful to God.

A Ceaseless Cause to Show Gratitude to God

Most of the time, some children of God would want to wait for another great miracle in order to be fully grateful to God. Looking all around them yet being unable to perceive what they ought to see well, they fail to find something substantially worthy to stand on to show gratitude to God to the fullness. Hearing testimonies of what God has done in the lives of people around them; they yet don't get understanding into the manifold acts of God that's going on now and then. The wonders of

God are made manifest in all His creation and are evident to the living as evidence against those who fail to believe in God Most High.

There are some people who believe in God; yet not to the extent of accrediting full gratitude and honour to Him who has blessed them; all by dint of the fact they claim not to have seen what they hear about as the wonders of God for themselves. Their prayers of thanksgiving are therefore based on the fact that they have to begin prayers by thanking God; and hence, they do thank God because that is their method of praying. There is therefore no intensity of zeal or truthfulness in the words they speak out to God in the act of raising thanks to God with regards to what they have received from Him. God seated up on His throne hears mere mumblings from His children coming out of partial appreciation in terms of giving thanks to Him. That's when the word of the Lord through the Prophet Isaiah that was quoted by the Lord Jesus is made manifest, and it reads:

> These people draw near to Me with their mouth, and honour Me with their lips, but their heart is far from Me. (Matthew 15:8)

The hearts of many children of God, at the point of worship, get drawn far away either by the circumstances they are currently facing or other unanswered requests which they have previously made through prayer. As a result, their worship, whether singing or professing, becomes mere uttering of words without any meaningful supporting urge from their heart. Yet, it's worthy to note that **one must not wait for the next miracle to become fully grateful to God**. The next miracle is not, in any way, going to increase your gratitude if you are not grateful now for what He has already done. Investigate more into this statement for better clarification of the character of the Israelites towards God while they were in the wilderness.

No matter how wonderful the next miracle in the pipeline is going to be, it would not alter the constitution of an ungrateful hardened heart. Nevertheless, there is always a cause to show gratitude to God no matter the condition one might find himself. When it comes to thanking God, we have a ceaseless cause to do so no matter what is at stake. Whether we have attained our heart cravings or not; there is still a reasonable reason for us to become fully grateful at the point of worship. Our worship should always be overflowing with gratitude such that we become short of words in perplexity of how reverent God is to us, the awesomeness of His love towards us and the uncountable blessings He has ushered on us.

Past, Present and Future Causes to Thank God

Casting our minds back, there is a lot to reflect on that should inspire us to be grateful to God. As much as possible, there are some of us who have accelerated in life as we displace with time along the path of our lives. These displacements I mean here are the promotions that have occurred along our lives through getting positioned and repositioned for better places by God's favour. There are a lot of changes that have occurred when we carefully analyse long days or years ago. Though some of these changes could be very negative; yet there are significant positive changes that we could sincerely testify. Thus, the negative past conditions, positions or troubles that we do not find ourselves entangled in again and we are always filled with joy at the remembrance that they are gone forever.

Amidst troubles and somewhat unfavourable circumstances, God has sustained us and brought us out from one point in life to another. It is substantially enough to count such dispositions and turn-arounds that occur in the phases of life as God-influenced impacts in our lives. As a matter of fact, one must not easily forget the positive transitions that have transpired from whence he has been dispositioned to the present position. To ignore past testimonies while just considering current circumstances to draw conclusions would be an analysis full of errors.

What meaning do we make out of it when we say, 'God is good, all the time'? Someone would appreciate consenting with this saying when everything around is going on well as expected; but would want to know why he should agree with that when, looking at the past or even presently, certain instances are right oppositely negative than normal. Nonetheless, God is good whether in good or bad conditions. All the time, God is good. **It is instances in time that change, but the goodness of God doesn't.**

When things are good and normal as we desire, God is good. So is God good to us when we are also facing troubles of life. It is the time that has changed to a time of trouble, yet God is still good towards us to help us go through those trouble-imbedded times without being harmed beyond expectation. We should therefore not lose faith when we have passed through or are presently passing through hard times. The devil might want to cause us to easily believe that God has left us; but that's not the truth.

Trouble is part of life. Trouble is a necessary condition for building a strong character and hence it is God's will for it to form part of our encounters of life; and hence, He legitimates their appearance along our paths. Yet, when we reach those seasons, levels or times, God Himself is committed to be of aid in strength and comfort to us so that we are able to pass through them safely. Then when we are fully out, He glorifies us while we too would have obtained proper experience out of the trouble necessary to building a good character. One thing one must be aware of is that God trains His children; He doesn't just pamper them for them to become morally deteriorated. He wants His children well-groomed to become like who He is in character-wise.

The adverse conditions that come along our path to test our faith are all necessary to building a proper foundation as children of God. Through all those conditions that seem very unpleasant, still He is good. His goodness does not cease. In fact, if it isn't His goodness, no one could pass through some of these hardships that come along our ways. The adverse conditions would have swallowed us up if not by the goodness of God. The Psalmist does well in integrating all the salvation of God from troubles of life into one Psalm. Let's check it out.

If it had not been the Lord who was on our side, let Israel [**replace with your name**] now say. If it had not been the Lord who was on our side, when men rose up against us, then they would have swallowed us alive; when their wrath was kindled against us. Then the waters would have overwhelmed us, the stream would have gone over our soul; then the swollen waters would have gone over our soul. Blessed be the Lord who has not given us as prey to their teeth. Our soul has escaped as a bird from the snare of the fowlers; the snare is broken, and we have escaped. Our help is in the name of the Lord, Who made heaven and earth. (Psalm 124, emphasis added)

Sincerely analysing this psalm, one would possibly find himself to have passed through at least one of the different instances being suggested by the psalmist; yet received God's help. Surely our help is the name of the Lord who would faithfully come to our rescue when we are apprehended by times of trouble in this life. He has promised us not to leave us as orphans nor forsake us. He has done it before, presently doing it and shall forever save His dear children from being drowned by waters of trouble. He is the God of Moses; He shall surely make an escape way for our total deliverance.

Testified to by Apostle Paul, he stated in his epistle,

'No temptation has overtaken you except such as is common to man; but God is faithful, who will not allow you to be tempted beyond what you are able, but with the temptation will also make the way of escape, that you may be able to bear it.' (1Cor 10:13)

It stands to mean therefore that no matter what we have been through in the past till now, whether good or bad condition, God has been good to us. All because He provided the way of escape that made us bear what we passed through such that we were not overtaken by them. God is good at all times. He is good in all conditions and in all situations to keep those circumstances below the threshold of our ability to endure.

Still casting our attention to our past state of slavery to Satan as sinners who were wallowing in the pool of sin amidst this world of darkness; but now having been purchased by the blood of Jesus into royalty and freedom of the light of God, we can't help it, but to be extremely grateful. The cost of our freedom was beyond our capability. Without Christ therefore, we had no hope of escape from the chains of the devil. All because, the devil had legally captured us into his web based on our sins that resulted from our origin of birth or obedience to him at one point in time along the path of our lives. For that matter, he had captivated us; hence, controlling our bodies towards executing all sorts of filthiness of the world.

As much as he could, the devil employed all his schemes to deceive us each time through the lust of our flesh which sin had weakened. Yet, by the sacrifice of Jesus, all standards of transaction with regards to our salvation have been met; such that we can walk freely out of the darkness of deception of Satan into the light of the saving knowledge of the Messiah Jesus Christ to be led by His Spirit to glorify God. There is nothing tangible to reciprocate what the Lord has done for us with regards to saving our souls which were bound and doomed for destruction. We can't imagine the type of words or thankfulness worthy enough to give to Lamb of God who offered up Himself to take our punishment upon Himself and to die in our stead. All we can do is to be forever grateful and shout 'You are worthy, from everlasting to everlasting' to the Lord Jesus, the Messiah who died, and is risen and behold, He lives forever.

Much more, there are a lot of things to count on when our attention is driven to the present. When we are able to consider very well, we would come to a profound knowledge about how thankful we ought to be to God for our current being; thus, the point we are now. Indeed, some people might have more to count on than others with regards to possessions because of differences in attainments; yet no living person would have nothing to count on as a reason to become thankful unto God. Again, the adage, 'God is good, all the time' is prevalent here no matter the circumstance one might be facing in his current life.

Most of us enjoying the fruits of the mercies of God through great achievements which have made us joyous have obvious reasons not to keep our mouths shut; but to utter the praises of God who helped us. Yet for some others, it might be a season of darkness or night where weeping is enduring; yet God is still good during such tough times to help such victims to pass through all those divine hours of the night till daylight appears without leaving them destroyed. As a result, one must not allow some difficult circumstances he is passing through now to take out from his heart and mouth the gratitude due God. As long as we are alive, we have a reasonable cause to bless the name of the Living God. The gift of life itself is worthwhile enough to cause anyone living to be continuously grateful unto God. So, the psalmist proclaims:

Let everything that has breath praise the Lord. Praise the Lord!
(Psalm 150:6)

Being alive with breath through our lungs and nostrils gives us the responsibility to praise the Lord who owns the breath. Had many others had the opportunity to breathe again, they would have been very grateful unto God; but their time of breathing to live on the earth is past. Therefore, gaining the opportunity of retaining the breath of life should not be taken lightly. Many a time, circumstances could push people to the wall such that there are many who have uttered words as they wished they were dead. Yet, it must be reckoned to anyone in that state that the opposite of that very statement is strongly yearned for by the dead. If you wish you were dead; be notified that many more others who are dead wished they were alive again. Many who are dead now wished they could have the access to borrow your breath for some few years, months or even for days in order to make up with something important they couldn't finalise due to their unforeseen end of time. Why would they, being dead and gone, wish to be alive again if having the breath of life is not precious. The wise king Solomon puts it this way:

> But for him who is joined to all the living there is hope, for a living dog is better than a dead lion. (Ecclesiastes 9:4)

It stands to mean that it is a privilege to be joined to the living. We go to bed with the multitude but not all who sleep are able to rise the next day. To be selected among the lot who slept yesterday to be joined to all the living again today is a privilege to be valued. All because the living have been granted the access or ability to continue the process of life that embodies their story on earth. With the dead, the process of life on earth ends the point the breath of life is evacuated from their body. There is therefore an ongoing authentication process of granting access for joining the living every new day under the auspices of the Lord of lives. If one is denied the authorization by divine decision, he fails to be joined to the living. Yet, but for him who is joined to all the living, the implication is that the Lord has authenticated that individual to continue his process of life on earth. Would one not be grateful for being granted the access that many others were denied? It is worth being grateful unto God to be alive today. Certainly, that's a reasonable cause to bless God.

One should therefore not desire that he were dead knowing that it pleased the Lord to grant a person who is alive today the access to live. Sometimes circumstances could be so terrible that we can't imagine what the next phase of life would bring. Yearning to run away from the disgrace or pain that we perceive that would befall us, many who face difficult challenges wish they were dead before the next phase of life reaches them. Yet, the good news is that no matter how terrible the circumstances have turned, could you realise that it is not mighty enough to take your life away; that's the reason you are still alive. So, no matter what has transpired, the fact that your life is preserved means that there is something greater than that trouble. That greater thing is what is keeping you thriving in life in spite of the trouble that looks overwhelming.

King Solomon said, there is hope for the living. No one knows what will occur tomorrow. We have seen what we have seen today and heard what we have heard, but for what will happen tomorrow lies in the hands of God. He who will then lay his burdens on the Lord will surely survive the next day because it is God who makes provisions of life for all who trust in Him. Before the day dawns, the provisions for all the children of God are fast arranged to carry them throughout the day. The people of God shall not be put to shame; neither shall they be outlived by their troubles because God is their present help in time of need; and indeed, God appears at the right time, every time. God would not fail those who put their trust in Him. The waters, streams and swallowed waters would swallow the lot; yet those who sincerely trust in the saving power of the living God would be preserved, separated as the holy and chosen of God to glorify He who delivered them out of their troubles. Hallelujah!

Come to think of it, would you agree that as humans as we are, there is the tendency for us not to assign due value to conducive conditions when there is the constant flow of goodness. Men are characterised by the act of devaluing or looking down on what we always have in abundance. We tend not to attach a great sense of worth to things we easily lay our hands on because maybe we think they are so cheap. It is only when we are denied such things for some while, then after we had yearned for them for a moment, but they are now far from our reach, then we come to realise how necessary they were at the point when they were so close and abundant.

We do not value good health until we fall sick. We are less appreciative of good relationships unless they are broken. We don't attach the necessary value to natural resources unless we become short of them. Some people do not value the life they have been granted by God to live unless it reaches the point where God would take it away. For some others, the only time you would see them glorify God is when they have come out from something bad or some terrible situation. When everything is smooth, they fail to recognize the hand of God present with them facilitating those good conditions and hence take it for granted. So now, as a corrective measure, sometimes adversity or difficulty strikes our lives to cut the flow of some good conditions such that we are not able to access those conditions as in the normal trend. When this happens, men become appreciative of the sources of provision for those good conditions. We become more appreciative to God and value His provisions when we now yearn for them.

Therefore, problems of life serve as means of tuition to children of God driving our attention to how appreciative we should be to the provisions of God and how we should assign necessary value to continuous flow of good things. Never should we be familiar with God or His provisions; else, too much familiarity will steal away the honour we ought to ascribe to God who does all things for us. As we are awakened today, let's glorify God and be appreciative for our lives and everything He has provided around us; yes, we have a tangible cause to praise the name of the Lord for today.

Apart from that, it is testified in modern-day Christianity that the only moment some children of God would lift a sincere or effective prayer is when they have encountered trouble. When all is well, praying is a choice for many children of God. Yet, keeping our mouths shut and not communicating to God in order that divine ordinances would be decreed in the spiritual realm to yield our victory would give the enemy an upper hand over our lives. If we cease praying, then it means that we have opposed God's word. Failing to pray is therefore a sin because God has cautioned us not to cease praying. For sin is opposition or disobedience to God's word. So, for some people who are triggered to pray only at the sight of calamity, the approach of the calamity does them some good also. All because, they now become conscious of the necessity to pray which drives them to the presence of God and hence renews their relationship with God; thereby keeping them from the sin of failure to pray.

Nevertheless, whether we face calamity or not, prayer, as the Lord taught us, is a daily necessity. We can enter more into temptation or trouble without prayer. In either case, lifting a prayer and acknowledging the presence of God Most High in all circumstances would grant us the expected victory. Therefore, there is a reason to lift a prayer today whether laughing or wailing. Commencing the prayer is the honour and praise we should give to God for granting us the ability to survive what we have been through. Surely, He would also make provision for us to survive what we presently face. We have a cause then to praise the Lord right now!

For our future, there is yet a more significant basis for us to be grateful to God for our lives ahead as children of God. Counting on His unfailing promises in the word of God for our lives as we live on with our families here on earth, we ought to be grateful. Whatever good promises God has said shall come to pass in this life shall surely come to pass. The word of the Lord says, not even a jot of the scripture shall fail being accomplished. Just as God was faithful to Abraham, Isaac and Jacob, so does He keep His covenant with those who hold Him in reverence by trusting in His word. The believer of the word of God is therefore much assured that his life ahead is catered for in the Hands of God.

Do you know what makes those who have insurance over their properties and lives here on earth so comfortable? I mean those who register with insurance companies and go into ties with them concerning their properties and even their lives. You can see such people so comfortable about those properties they have insured. Their basis of comfortability being that no matter what happens in the near or far future about those properties or lives they have insured, they have had them catered for. Should anything bad happen to them, either they are going to get brand new ones, or they or their families are going to be compensated. The same applies to believers of the word of God.

The promises in the word of God are our insurance agreement with the divine cabinet of God. As far as we remain His children, He is faithful to play His role as our Father because of the covenant He makes with us. We are therefore assured through the word of God about our future even before we reach there along our lives. The lives of the children of God are well catered for through the agreement between their faith in God and the faithfulness of God in keeping His word. If men who run insurance companies do it so well for their clients such that they do not fail them, God's system of insurance, His Word, is far more reliable. The God of Abraham, of Isaac, of Jacob and of Israel never fails nor disappoints. God shall see to the fulfilment of His promises to His children on the earth.

For this reason particularly, we cannot keep mute; but to be grateful unto God who holds our future.

Beyond the reliability of God's word for our lives here on the earth lies the hope of dwelling with God peacefully in eternity. When all is said and done; when Christ had accomplished His desire on this seen world at the end of all things, there lies the hope for all who believed in Jesus, the only begotten Son of God to dwell eternally with God in His rest. Our hope therefore does not fall within the span of this world alone. The greater part of the hope of a true child of God goes beyond the limit of life on earth.

No matter what is obtained and achieved here on earth, a person is bound to be entangled with problems and troubles that would deny him the fulfilment of true peace. Whether we like it or not, as long as we remain in this corrupted world, we are bound to be disturbed here and there. Even if one tries as much as possible to keep himself out of trouble, there is the possibility of being affected by the problems caused by other people. Everything happening around us in this era declares that the peace of the world is unstable.

We are just witnessing a cycle of a trouble-embedded world. One wakes up every day only to be notified of frightening news that renders all plans that had been made the day before to be at stake. Not only the pauper is terrified but even the wealthy panics at heart by how surprising things are happening. Meanwhile, true children of God are also at the centre of persecution in every setting of the systems of this world. Therefore, together with the general hardships of the world, the true child of God, today, suffers from a lot of oppressions, oppositions and restrictions.

There is no happiness for the children of God who are not of this world; it is just the joy of the Lord that sprouts out from within them, and it's seen expressed to strengthen them in their missions. Apart from the joy of the Lord, which is their strength, there is no actual taste of happiness for the children of God in what is done in this age of the world. The world we live in today presents a lot of things that are abominable to the Holy Spirit that resides in a child of God.

As a result, the true children of God witnessing scenes of acts and systems which are rampant everywhere roundabout them, which are also against the desire of God, become extremely distressed in his spirit. I say 'true' children of God because if one finds himself to fit happily into the disorderly and God-disregarded pursuits of this world, then there is a problem in that person's relationship with God. So, the Lord Jesus warned that woe unto him whom all men of this world love. No true child of God feels delightful in the surrounding atmosphere of defilement and rebellion in this present world. This brings more meaning to what the Spirit of God spoke through the Apostle Peter about Lot dwelling in Sodom and Gomorrah. Thus, the bible says:

> ... and delivered righteous Lot, who was distressed by the filthy conduct of the wicked (for that righteous man, dwelling among them, tormented his righteous soul from day to day by seeing and hearing their lawless deeds) (2 Pet 2:7,8)

What is seen, heard and smelled today across our streets and in the media is distressing to the Holy Spirit-filled child of God. To certain extents, the systems of this world try to limit the full expression of the desire of people of God. Enacted laws and bills have been filled with granting liberty to many abominable acts in God's viewpoint while simultaneously presenting a lot of boundaries to the child of God not to exceed. The taste of sin to the highest extent has been granted as normal by our approved norms and there is the quest for the interesting lot to explore even more above what is done that is detestable in God's sight. What a world! A world where 'anything' is permissible, but the will of God is strongly opposed! Gaining a stance of operation by what is termed 'rights and freedom', sin is prevalent and presented at the doorstep without shame. Shamefacedness is out of the book; virtue has no place to dwell; moral integrity has been ripped out of this generation. Yet, there is no cause for alarm in the consideration of the proletariats who have assumed authority and are exercising their time-bound power.

Sin has a positive pole that strongly attracts the negative pole of the wrath of God; the more sin abounds, the nearer the wrath of God receives an invite. Only if the people of Sodom knew how nearer the wrath of God had approached them due to the high altitude their sin had attained, they would have thought twice. Nevertheless, when men sell their conscience to the devil, they hardly see what is really right. There is therefore no true happiness for a child of God dwelling in this present world. There are a lot of sorrows and pains running through the hearts of true people of God. All because the world now is turning into an uninhabitable place for serene moral living due to the high acceleration of immorality without boundaries.

Our hope as children of God is then not driven towards obtaining ultimate peace here on earth, because that cannot be achieved. All by dint of the fact that the systems of this world are not governed under the auspices of the Prince of Peace. The future of this earth is already determined; we are just witnessing the unfolding of prophesies God has already given through the mysteries of His word. The hope of a child of God for dwelling on the earth the rest of the days ahead is therefore built in the word of God to obtain provisions for the fulfilment of assignments and missions.

Yet, the greater hope which is well assured by God for all who believe in the Messianic mission of the Lord Jesus is for them to obtain eternal living with God beyond this world. As the word of God confirms, all our tears that we shed due to the oppressions, distresses and restrictions the world entangled us with would be wiped off. We would then be given citizenship into the new Jerusalem, a nation without sin, sorrow and trouble ruled and governed under the auspices of the Prince of Peace; hence, peace abounding everywhere. The happiness of this assurance that this present world is not our end keeps the children of God moving on in their commitment to God.

vIn conclusion, whether in the past, present or future and whether we have encountered or now encountering either good conditions or tough circumstances, there are significant as well as ceaseless causes to show gratitude to God. Let's now consider from here the negative ways in which men receive from other men.

Men to Men Requisition Relationship

Wrong Approach for Requesting from Men

Some set their eyes on things they see that some people have and try to base their requests on that. Fine, maybe those wealthy men may be in possession of those items but who knows what plans they have on those possessions or whether they have already given them out for something else. Some receivers also forget that they might not be the only people being served by a particular giver at a particular time. Thus, some givers have some other commitments that their receivers must understand and therefore desist from letting their request be on the basis of what they see that the givers possess at a particular time. To request as if you are entitled to all that you have seen that a giver possesses is not appropriate. It is a very wrong way to request something that way; yes, that's indeed an improper basis for request.

A person's capability to give must be between God and the person alone, period! So, if a man in need approaches another person he expects to receive from, and that person cannot help the needy as at that point in time, that does not position that potential giver among selfish and wicked people. No man can judge that way, only God knows rightly and can judge rightly. We must therefore stop that character because it can lead us into judging wrongly and that could place us into the wrath of God. This advice goes mostly to receivers and those who would want to persuade and urge others to give.

Some receivers, on the other hand, are not content with what they receive from their corresponding givers with the reason that they think the givers could have given more than what they gave them. With some unjustified murmurings as 'Look at your possessions and accomplishments', 'Look at the job you do', 'Look at where you stay' 'and look what you are giving me', etc. they fail to appreciate what they receive from those givers claiming that the givers could have done more than what they did due to their status. Giving is not influenced by status but love and compassion.

The tendency for a giver to give much or less should not be a function to what he possesses. That only relates to the evaluations that go on within the mind and heart of the giver towards the target point of giving. Being touched by the need to give at some point, someone can be having a little, and yet give much based on the need intended to be met. Someone would also give a little though he has much possession. It all depends on how the giver views the need at stake and the inward calculations of how helpful he thinks he can make up resources available from his possessions to meet the need; all of which should be authorised by the Holy Spirit residing in the giver. It is therefore unfair for the direct receiver or an eyewitness to conclude that a giver's giving was not up to expectation, judging only by sight. This is a very key point here because people base on the incident that happened in the bible to conclude wrongly. Thus when the Lord Jesus witnessed some people who came to give to God and among them was a widow whom the Lord commended to have given more than the other rich men. Look at this instance and see how wrong only-sight judgement could be! This is what happened:

> Now Jesus sat opposite the treasury and saw how the people put money into the treasury. And many who were rich put in much. Then one poor widow came and threw in two mites, which make a quadrans. So, He called His disciples to Himself and said to them, "Assuredly, I say to you that this poor widow has put in more than all those who have given to the treasury; for they all put in out of their abundance, but she out of her poverty put in all that she had, her whole livelihood. (Mark 12:41-44)

Let's consider this very cautiously. The rich came and gave much, while the widow only two mites. At the end, the Lord says something that corrects the judgement of all eyewitnesses who might have concluded wrongly from their own points of view. The little the woman gave became more than the much the rich gave. It proves that it doesn't matter the much or little that someone gives at a point; but then, what matters is how that giving counts in God's judgement.

Those around, depending on what they saw, could have judged from their own points of view and concluded that the rich gave more than the widow; yet they got corrected when the Lord spoke. Until we get the idea of God about a particular giving, it's not enough to use physical calculations to draw a conclusion on it. The disciples were there, and they might have gotten their points of view about the giving they all witnessed. Now, Jesus was worthy to give the final verdict. The reason is because He saw beyond all what the disciples saw. The Lord knowing all things knew the capabilities of all those who came to give to the treasury; so, He was right in His judgement. That's what makes you a wrong person as an eyewitness to judge whether a particular giver did give up to expectation or not. All because your knowledge is limited with regards to finding out the content of the coffers of a giver at a particular point in time.

Yet, for the Lord Jesus, He just knew everything about everyone who came around. What we see with our physical eyes is always not enough. There is more behind what is presented to the physical realm of visualisation. Sometimes, we don't know very much about the secrets about some people's possessions; yet we would want to hurriedly judge on their capabilities of giving. Making this error, some receivers would want to defame their corresponding givers. Since either they did not receive what they sought for from their corresponding givers or they were not content with what they received, they tend to misinterpret things and misbehave towards the givers.

A lot of people make this mistake and due to that they destroy the relationship between themselves and their corresponding wealthy men who could have helped them in the other way round. Since they didn't get what they requested specifically from their corresponding givers, they just conclude those wealthy men are wicked. Yet the basis of their conclusion is weightless. Some go on to the extent of spoiling the names of such wealthy men with all sorts of insults. When this happens, if even the wealthy person was about to change his mind on the denial of your request, that is not going to happen. Also, if the wealthy person had any other plans for you, all those plans are also going to be cancelled. It is a very negative way of claiming gifts from others this way which victims fond of doing that must desist from.

Allowing givers to give from their own will is the best so that there will be an established peace and good relationship between the giver and receiver. Compulsorily claiming gifts is not proper with regards to proper receiving. That erroneous character on the part of some receivers must be cleared enough so that people would have the right over their own conscience to conclude for themselves when they are at the point of giving.

One other negative approach to desire to receive from men on the part of some receivers that leads to the character described above is pinpointing on a particular man for their help. Yes, that's how some receivers do; no matter what, they somehow have the strong conviction that it is a particular giver from whom they would receive their help. Hence, they sort of put their trust in receiving all their needs from that person. This results in a big problem when that man turns them down. Since they had put all their trust in receiving from that end and they did not get their heart's desire, these receivers tend to be so much disappointed that they begin to have ill-feeling for such givers. Yet, since giving, as we learnt earlier, should not be on the platform of compulsion, it remains unjustified to hold it against such givers.

After all, no one has gone into a signed rigid agreement to give any of his possession to anyone at a particular time. Such receivers therefore need to be aware that they are not on contract terms with those givers that bind the givers to compulsorily give to them. In order not to be disappointed this way, one must not cast all his expectations on a particular giver. That's wrong expectancy. All because this giver is but a man who can change his mind at any time even if he has given a promise. Conversely, the person can die before reaching the point of attending to the need of request though he had concluded to willingly support the receiver who needed help. Never should you forget that a man is a mortal whose end point of termination of life is undefined by himself and other men.

It is also biblically incorrect and dangerous to trust in man, hoping to receive your help in a specific man. Victims of that character receive a blow other than their desire; God's word comes into play on them; no wonder such receivers get stricken with unresolvable issues leading to heart breaks as well as disappointments. All because God has already cursed the attitude of men trusting in other men. It is God who touches peoples' hearts to give; and He does so in diverse ways. God sometimes brings help from places where receivers least expect. He who trusts to receive from a particular man would always be disappointed. Yet, those who trust to receive their help from God always get their hearts fulfilled because God knows where to create the next way of escape from hardships. God has always got how to reach the needs of His children by whatever means or persons He desires to choose.

When the people of Israel got stuck behind the red sea, not knowing where to pass and being terrified also by the fast approach of their enemies, Pharoah and his troops, they never knew where God was going to make the way for their escape. Yet God Himself knew how and where He had planned to surprise both the Israelites and their enemies at that very moment. **Only God knew that there was a way through the Red Sea** at that point in time. He had already drawn the path through the sea without the notice of the people of Israel. The escape way is with God only.

That which the Israelites nor their enemies never expected to occur was what God had pre-designed for it to occur to prove Himself as all-possible God. Yes, it seemed outright impossible for the Israelites and every eyewitness how the Israelites could get to the other side of the sea. If when they got there, there had been a pre-booked ship arranged to hurriedly convey them across to the other side, that would have been fair and reasonable for the normal man. Yet, here was the case that they got there only to meet an empty space, no transportation to aid them cross to the other side of the sea. How were they going to do that? That was the present need of the Israelites; thus, to gain a possible way of escape from their enemies. What to do had become so baffling for the whole congregation as well as their leader, Prophet Moses. Until Prophet Moses contacted divine direction, human calculations and contemplations had concluded that they were at the point of doom and hopelessness. Yet, God who is a present help in time of need was right there with them; He only had to be contacted so He could show them the way through the sea that is hidden from them.

You see the problem that arises at some point in time as God leads His children? God sees the escape way; but His children do not see. That makes Him God who knows everything, the Alpha and the Omega who declares the end from the beginning. If care is not taken at such points along the path of our walk with God, we might be tempted, by sight, to disbelieve in the capabilities of God and become faithless. All because we have got limited knowledge about what God has in store for us in the future which could be the next ten minutes ahead of time. What God was about to do in the next few hours in the lives of the Israelites was completely out of their knowledge; yet, for Him, He knew it!

The only proper thing to do at such points in time is what Prophet Moses did. He sought a divine view from God about what to do about the present situation. When God came in with His view, it was then that the Prophet received some peace of comfort at heart and hence had to pass on that comfort to the others who were more terrified than he was. Peace of the heart amid the heat of troubles could be obtained only by contacting God who knows where to create the next escape way.

It therefore stands to mean that receivers who find themselves in critical needs must prioritise contacting God above all other avenues about how their needs would be met. God must be contacted first before casting our minds on men or other sources. All because it is God who foreknows where and how He's bringing the escape way for that need. He is the one who touches the hearts of men to help other men. So, if a needy person forsakes putting God first, there results a breach of protocol of hoping to receive. The individual would then be hoping in man rather than in God who will touch the heart of that man to provide.

Apart from that when a person hopes in receiving from a specific man, it limits the solution of escape to only one end, which is not the same with God who can choose any other point of contact He desires to use as a medium of deliverance.

When God is contacted first, where He usually brings the help from is 'abnormal'; that's supernatural that is beyond the reasoning of men and beyond the natural order of how problems are solved. The channels of God-provided solutions to needs are least expected by the needy whose hope falls all on God. The provision from expecting from men is ordinary but the provision from expectation from God is divine. Divine provisions prove the power and authority of God over nature such that the normal process of natural occurrence could be altered for the will of God to be done. All to show that God is Lord over all creation and to demonstrate to all men and spirits that He rules over all the seen and the unseen as the God Most High.

Put in another way, one must expect to be blessed by God through His chosen channels He desires to use. That is when God becomes the centre of focus with regards to hoping to receive the solutions to our needs. Don't expect a man to bless you; else, the man now becomes the centre of focus with regards to hoping to receive your solutions. I have come to realise that human based blessings or giving turn around to become a burden for the recipient. In addition, those blessings also do not last. It is something that is tested and proven in many settings which could be testified by many people. Yet the blessings attained from claiming the promises of God through His word become permanently established for the individual whose life afterwards becomes peaceful. God blesses and gives without reproach.

There is that atmosphere of increasingly inexpressible joy beyond the giving that was influenced by God. Check out the response after receiving a gift and get to know whether it was God-influenced or human-influenced. Manipulating gifts out of the coffers of people can turn out to be a menace in the lives of both the giver and the receiver. It is better therefore to seek to be blessed originally from original sources and funds which come from treasuries of heaven.

Don't pinpoint some specific wealthy men and trust them to receive their gifts; you will end up creating a grudge in your relationship with them. Better trust in God and He will bring the right person at the right time to serve you in a way you never imagined. The Psalmist sang, 'I lift up my eyes to the hills. From whence comes my help. My help comes from the Lord who made heaven and earth.' (Psalm 121:1,2) It is better to side with this Psalmist to believe that our help would drop from God who created everything and even created that giver who holds what we need. In fact, the possession and possessor all belong to God. Why do you worry yourself trying to convince a steward over a property while you have access to request it from the real owner? At the command of God, any gift, no matter where it is kept or whoever holds control over it, must be released to where God directs it. All because God holds the right of ownership over all things. He is Lord of all lords and King of all kings. God needs our hearts to be directed more on Him than on men; else, we end up making men our God. Nevertheless, if we trust that whatever offer that comes our way is God-provided and that He can do that through any other person, we then show appreciation to the givers and give glory to God who brought them to our rescue.

Summary points to note

❖ Giving is necessary but not compulsory.

❖ Giving is a decision from the giver's own intent and the product of the dialogue that goes on within him towards the target point of giving

❖ Denying to give is better than giving reluctantly against one's will with inward grudges.

❖ When giving, your inner man should support what you do outwardly. It should not be that your mind and heart are against what your hand has stretched forth to do.

❖ A giving that pleases God is one supported by heart and mind.

❖ Properly receiving is when the condition under which the giver gives is free from compulsion

❖ Proper giving and proper reception establish a continuity and longevity of good relationship between the giver and receiver.

❖ Every prophecy has got its processing time

❖ Before God releases a blessing, He prepares the hands or vessel to receive the blessing to be matured enough, in order that the vessel would be able to receive, contain and use it.

❖ To entertain the abominations of God, and yet desire Him to bless you isn't compatible

❖ It is rather shameful to be living with your sin as a child of God than sharing it for help

❖ Far it be from God to give His children poisonous blessings

❖ God does not give stones and serpents. He gives good things to those who ask Him

❖ Stone and serpent blessings eventually influence one to terminate his relationship with God.

❖ The wonders of God are made manifest in all His creation and is evident to the living as evidence against those who fail to believe in God Most High

❖ One must not wait for the next miracle to become fully grateful to God. No wonder is wonderful to a callous heart.

❖ When it comes to thanking God, we have a ceaseless cause to do so no matter what is at stake

❖ Our worship should always be overflowing with gratitude such that we become short of words

❖ To ignore past testimonies while just considering current circumstances to draw conclusions would be an analysis full of errors

❖ God is good whether in good or bad conditions. All the time, God is good. It is instances in time that change, but the goodness of God doesn't.

❖ In fact, it is the goodness of God that cushions us to survive bad conditions and seasons and come out safely.

❖ Trouble is a necessary condition for building a strong character and hence it is God's will for it to fall part of our encounters of life; as a result, He legitimates their appearance along our paths.

❖ The adverse conditions that come along our path to test our faith are all necessary to building a proper foundation as a child of God.

❖ There is nothing tangible to reciprocate what the Lord has done for us with regards to saving our souls which were bound and doomed for destruction.

❖ As long as we are alive, we have a reasonable cause to bless the name of the Living God.

❖ If you wish you were dead; be notified that many more others who are dead wish they were alive again

❖ To be selected among the lot who slept yesterday to be joined to all the living again today is a privilege not to be less valued

❖ To be alive means that the Lord has authenticated you to continue your process of life on earth. Would one not be grateful for being granted the access that many others were denied?

❖ We have seen what we have seen today and heard what we have heard, but for what will happen tomorrow lies in the hands of God

❖ Before the day dawns, the provisions for all the children of God are fast arranged to carry them throughout the day

❖ As humans as we are, there is the tendency for us not to assign due value to good conditions when there is the constant flow of goodness

❖ Problems of life serve as means of tuition to children of God driving our attention to how appreciative we should be to the provisions of

God and how we should assign necessary value to continuous flow of good things.

❖ Too much familiarity will steal away the honour we ought to ascribe to God who does all things for us

❖ The lives of the children of God are well catered for through the agreement between their faith in God and the faithfulness of God keeping His word. If men who run insurance companies do not fail their clients, God's system of insurance, His Word, is far more reliable.

❖ A person's capability to give must be between God and the person alone, period!

❖ Giving is not influenced by status but love and compassion. The tendency for a giver to give much or less should not be a function to what he possesses.

❖ It doesn't matter the much or little that someone gives at a point; but then, what matters is how that giving counts in God's judgement

❖ What we see with our physical eyes is always not enough. There is more behind what is presented to vision of the physical realm.

❖ Only God knew that there was a way through the Red Sea, neither the people of Israel nor Pharaoh did. The escape way is with God only.

❖ If a needy person forsakes putting God first, there results a breach of protocol of hoping to receive

❖ Divine provisions prove the power and authority of God over nature such that normal processes of natural occurrence could be altered for the will of God to be done for His trusting child.

❖ Human based blessings or giving can turn around to become a burden for the recipient

❖ In fact, the possession and possessor all belong to God

❖ At the desire and command of God, any gift, no matter where it is kept or whoever holds control over it, must be released to where God directs it.

CHAPTER FOUR

Overcoming Barriers to Giving

There are certain factors that could hinder the act of giving. As much as the importance of giving has been highlighted, these hindrances that occur at certain times to disturb the smooth process of giving and receiving ought to be also treated. Let's look at a few of them here in this chapter.

Ungratefulness

One very discouraging factor against giving that could affect the positive action of givers is ungratefulness. Failing to recognize the significance of what someone has done for you is ungratefulness. In this case, what will make it worse is not only failing to recognize what the giver has done for you; but going a wrong step further to do what is reproachful to the giver. Ungratefulness can turn the hearts of givers upside down to the point that all the compassion they had towards a particular receiver could be redrawn. Unfortunately, some receivers tend to assume this character of repaying the evil of ungratefulness for the good they receive from their corresponding givers. As a result, many potential givers have either quit or have now become 'careful' in their act of meeting the needs of the next needy person they meet.

This character particularly caused God to decide to terminate all the lives of the Israelites whom He had just saved from Egypt. Except for the intercession of the Prophet Moses, all the Israelites were bound to face the wrath of God at that very point of their journey due to ungratefulness. After they had been delivered by the miraculous salvation of God, their return reaction was an abomination before the very eyes of God. They made an image and referred to it as their saviour. 'How is this possible?', God thought. No image came to rescue them when they were suffering in slavery in Egypt. Blocked by the Red Sea and left to be consumed by the fierce anger of the troop of Egyptians, no image showed up for their deliverance. Yet, they were now proclaiming that whatever progress they had gone through was by the grace of an image. So ungrateful were they!

God became so furious by this action of theirs and decided to remove all such ungrateful entities from His sight that very day. The thin line of salvation that delivered them was through the intercession of the prophet of God, Moses. Even when they were forgiven, since ungratefulness was in their genes, they couldn't refrain from it while journeying in the wilderness. Eventually, those in that generation, except two, perished along the line because they failed to acknowledge God's hand of salvation in their lives. Their ungratefulness made them lose faith in what God can do in the future. All because, recognizing what He has done before should produce a concrete reason to believe that He is able to do what is ahead.

Yet, their minds could not remember; neither could their hearts prompt them to what God has done and therefore is able to do because of ungratefulness. As a result, such an unappreciative generation couldn't reach the promised land, the very reason that they had set off from Egypt. For mighty signs and wonders, their eyes witnessed enough; yet they were denied the opportunity to reach their destination, a land flowing with milk and honey. That's what ungratefulness can do, it can deny a receiver from reaching the destined end which is planned and intended by the giver. Men ought to be careful not to be ungrateful, especially we who receive from God; thus, all men ought to be careful because God provides for us all.

Cease from the thought that God created us and so it is compulsory for Him to provide for us; and for that matter being grateful to His provision doesn't matter. Yes, that's how some people imagine it to be. They believe God has created them, so it remains His responsibility to provide for them and therefore they do not need to beg or be too grateful for His provision. They make it look like it's God who has given Himself His problem by creating men; so, He is duly responsible for catering for them. They would want to hold God responsible! Therefore, such people do not appreciate the eminence of the supply of nature by God.

Nevertheless, one must not forget that even a child must be grateful for what his father offers him though it is the responsibility of the father to cater for the child. The child must not beg for provision from the father but should request. And upon receiving the requested item, the child must show a sense of appreciation to the father in order for the father to know how grateful the child is. And that's the very episode that causes a father to love some of his children more than others. All because, in this imperfect world, it's very possible that some children will appreciate the father's provision, but others will not. Provisions provided must be appreciated by recipients. Respect and appreciation after receiving from givers must come automatically and willingly from receivers. That is not compulsion but common sense. That is good manners worthy of a morally trained child.

Some others go to the extent of connecting it to salvation that if it is God who created us then He holds the responsibility to save us. Therefore, they do not attach any sense of gratefulness to salvation in order to respond positively to it. Your reason for claiming that God must save you Himself if He created you is good enough though;

but ask yourself some proper questions that would let you come up with some proper reasoning. How come we are living in God's created world but obedient to Satan? How come our forefathers did not recognize this Almighty and Creator such that they replaced Him with other objects as an insult to His integrity?

Our forefathers, just as us, meandered from the right route of obedience so as to be under the rule of the majesty of the King of Heaven. Like fathers, like sons, we faltered out of the right path to listen to Satan's voice rather than hearkening unto the calling of God. Therefore, we needed His mercy to bring us back on track so that His divine will for creating us would be fruitful. So, we have already rejected Him though He created us, and for that matter we must be substantially grateful for His provided Way to lead us back to Him. The Way is The Lord Jesus Christ.

The provision of salvation to all by the Lord Jesus does not lie on the basis of what any man can boast of. Salvation is being favoured through the grace and mercy of God through Jesus Christ. This favour is not a product of the fact that any man is deserving. All have sinned and come short of the glory of God, thus says the word of God. When God looked on earth to even find one man who was right, He found no one. (Psalm 54:1). As a result, no man was worthy to intercede for any other of his kind. All because the unrighteous cannot intercede for the unrighteous; so is a sinner not qualified enough to stand as an advocate for another sinner.

Therefore, the righteous Jesus had to come and die for the unrighteous men as the book of Romans says. A man therefore obtains salvation not as a result of the fact that he deserves it; no, it is because God has shown him mercy through the Lord Jesus Christ. A saint you see now was once a fallen sinner who has been helped by the hand of grace to rise to his feet. This, as a result, must keep everyone humbled enough to be forever grateful unto the Lord Jesus and God, His Father.

The act of ungratefulness can go a long way to discourage givers to the extent that some would even quit giving. Yes, people nowadays have stopped their act of charity due to this very act. They find no reasonable thought in helping someone who would at the end of the day throw insults of ungratefulness back at them. They had better keep their possessions than 'waste' them on ungrateful people. People today, I mean some receivers, are very ungrateful.

Many men in need are like chameleons; they have got the ability to change their characters as soon as they change environment. They are only humble and respectful at the point of need. Nevertheless, let them sail through their difficulty and get some proper grounds and you will get to know that they are people who can express themselves in the wrong way. That's a bad characteristic. It is deceit and hypocrisy for one to act as if he is good only to get help and afterwards show off a bad attitude of ungratefulness. The effect of such behaviour has now got a negative notion imprinted in the minds and hearts of some kind givers who feel they must better quit giving. Many others have already stopped giving to some people because what they currently witnessed from those people who were once in need has discouraged them out-rightly.

Forgetting previous help from givers such that receivers base on current conditions to conclude on a reaction is also a sense of ungratefulness. When some receivers do not get what they desire in their subsequenvt requests from a giver who has been of help to them before, they tend to act ungratefully. Some react as if they have never received anything from the givers before. A giver could be of help at one time while at another time he could sincerely not be of help. When this happens the receiver who did not get his request from this giver at an unfavourable condition should not be enraged. All because proper remembrance would spell out that the giver has really been helpful at other times past.

How happy and satisfied the receivers were when they received the former help in the past should be remembered so that they become tolerant in the current unfavourable time. Yet, some receivers would not think of anything like this. So far as their corresponding giver expresses inability to be of help to their current request, they react so badly. They just depend on the present denial of their request or the insufficient help from the giver and conclude to react ungratefully towards the giver.

The act of ungratefulness from such receivers does not only affect them alone for not receiving again from their corresponding givers; it also goes against other different people in need who might need the offer from such givers. That actually is not good news for the next needy person in the pipeline who might need some help from such givers who have been treated with disdain by those whom they gave to. When some givers witness such ungratefulness in their corresponding receivers, they tend to believe that any other needy person they see again might be like the others they have had correspondence with before. Some come to have the thought that every other person is a liar or deceiver who might want to exploit them by describing themselves as being in need. As a result, when such givers come across some needy who might not necessarily be ungrateful as those earlier, these givers do not have any confidence to help them. Ungratefulness really discourages giving.

Many potential givers have now refrained from freely giving because they have got trust issues with those whom they would want to help. Since the former needy whom the giver helped has been so unfaithful and ungrateful, it becomes very difficult for the giver to trust the current needy he comes across. The reason being that such givers would imagine that all people in need are not trustworthy. When some of these receivers are in need, their humble demeanour and multitude of begging words might let one believe that they are angels. The devil in them manifests as soon as they mount the throne of high-handedness by the support they received from the givers. Some of these people would even want to control their corresponding givers by whom they rose to their current levels.

As a result of what some givers witness along their act of giving, they tend to be reserved and hesitant in the next point of need that requires their help. People have lost trust in others such that even the next faithful person whom they encounter is mistaken as unfaithful. 'After all, that's how they all begin; help them and see what they would return to you,' 'A human being has no remembrance,' 'Never will I offer help to anyone again', etc. are the words that come from givers who have witnessed ungratefulness from some receivers. They never trust anyone anymore.

To the Betrayed Giver having trust issues

It is good though not to trust man because God alone owns our trust. Let all men be liars, and God be truthful. Yet in matters such as this, the level of distrust that can restrict one from executing a divine assignment could be dangerous. So, we've got to know whom to trust when we face such instances. The only person that can be trusted at these points is the Holy Spirit. A giver can go ahead to give when the Holy Spirit has granted him the go ahead. All because, men are disappointing! Hope to receive something worthy from man and your heart will be broken. Yet, God never disappoints. So, if you give on the basis of having your trust in God, even if the receiver disappoints you with ungratefulness, the Holy Spirit will strengthen you with the hope that your reward of doing good awaits you in the future on earth and in heaven. On earth, God will bless you here, and in heaven, He will surprise you; all because you gave based on trusting Him.

With that said and done, it takes the power of the Holy Spirit, our comforter to heal those wounds created by the ungrateful acts of some receivers on some givers. So that such givers would be refreshed in their thoughts and decisions about being kind again to the same receivers or to other men in need who would come across their path. Considering that all other men in need are deceivers and liars is not a right conclusion to be made by any giver no matter what he has suffered from. The Holy Spirit should be allowed to lead in situations such as this to direct our paths towards the right kind of people and lives we must touch with what we have in our possession.

Don't let the wrong reaction of someone dissuade you from your mission in the sight of God. You can lose man; but don't lose God. God would always urge you to do what would please Him. Though some ungratefulness is painful and heart-breaking, kind givers ought to look to the cross so that their hearts would be strengthened. Look at how men are ungrateful to God, yet He still came to die in our stead. Our insults, denials and abominations did not dissuade Him from completing the mission of our salvation.

A mission of God does not need to be abandoned. If God begins it, He does not quit at the middle of the journey. He is the alpha of every divine mission and the Omega of it also. So, if it's God who touched your heart to offer some help to another person, then don't get discouraged to the point of quitting. All because every good act of service a man does is unto God, not unto men. God will reward us according to our deeds and the impacts we had on our neighbours which were according to His will. So far as it is God's will for you to help others, let nothing dissuade you from doing it, not even the action of the direct beneficiary.

The reason is because Satan has got a lot of ways that he employs to deny us from getting to the point of receiving the glory of God. That's the finishing point of God's mission. It is a glorious point. It is the point the Lord Jesus reached that there were great shouts of trumpets and honour from the dignitaries in heaven to declare that He alone is Worthy. Innumerable angels, the twenty-four elders and the four living creatures all rose to the Honour of the Overcomer who overcame death and hades because He did not fall to deception and resistance Satan brought along His path. Yes, the Lord Jesus is worthy to receive honour, praise, thanksgiving, power and might because He is the Unbreakable Overcomer.

Why do you want to stop the honourable mission that God has placed on your heart with regards to saving someone in need by giving out your possessions? Maybe it might be because of some formal experience of ungratefulness you have witnessed from some people you were generous to. It might be that those who have been raised to higher levels due to your kindness do not recognize you as their helpers anymore. It could also be that you have received assaults of insult despite all the goodness you did to someone else. For that matter, your experiences have now blackened your conscience such that you can't even have the openness to freely offer help to other people. That's not a strange experience, child of God.

People are bound to be ungrateful sometimes. Yet, there must be a reason that pushes a child of God to continue doing charitable works even amidst unexpected responses such as ungratefulness. You see, worldly men only dwell on past experiences to act in the present. Nevertheless, children of God do not do so. We are not moved by what we saw, are seeing or will see. We are moved by the Spirit of God. Let us therefore not act as people of the world, because we are in the world but not of the world. If you are not so careful in matters as this, your flesh will dictate to you how to react; but the flesh profits nothing.

To be led by the flesh is death, thus away from the mission of God; but to be led by the Spirit is life, thus at the centre of the will and mission of God. Other worldly givers can quit their giving based on their own reasons but not we who are led by the Spirit of God and hence are children of God. If God started the mission which He has laid on your heart, He is the only One worthy to stop it, and not you yourself or anyone else. Don't quit it because there is a glorious point ahead of you where angels of heaven would arise to your honour because you could overcome the destruction Satan brought along the path of the mission God placed on your heart. God bless you that you will not abandon God's mission He has placed in you.

Fear

Fear is a weapon that paralyses the capable to become incapable through its grips of imaginary pictures of a terrible future. Many potential helpers cannot be up and doing with the burden on their hearts to impact the lives of other people in need because of fear. Either internally or externally, they are pierced with a strong jerk on their conscience such that they are just broken at heart to act positively towards the target point of giving. They shiver and panic at heart in either way to the point that their spirit wished they did the act of charity; yet their body becomes so weakened with fear. That becomes a barrier strong enough to keep them away from reaching the needy just at their doorstep. They are people who are nearer to the point of need of receivers yet become stacked behind the barrier of fear hence are unable to approach the needy with an impacting help by giving their possession.

Fear is a stronger unseen authority that exerts more powerful damages on men than some visible weapons. Many men die without implementing their visions and missions because of fear. Dr. Myrles Munroe said, 'The richest place one can find on earth is the cemetery,'. Yes, that is certainly true. This is because many people die with their rich visions and plans which they couldn't unveil from within them. Their inability to bring into fruition what was burning so hot within them can be attributed to a lot of hindrances; yet a lot of those people who have died with their visions were victims of the fear syndrome.

Internally, many potential givers would like to calculate how offering a fraction of their possessions would afterwards affect their personal conditions. They would have to deal with the internal threatening 'What-ifs' at the point they come into contact with the needy. Some of these are 'What if I give this out and I also fall into an unforeseen incidence of need', 'What if my own wife and children come afterwards with an urgent need', 'What if I go bankrupt because of giving this out', etc. Fears galore! The power of fear begins to take over the individual's whole being such that he becomes enveloped with the panic not to attempt to open his arms.

Some others get the thought that instead of giving out a possession that would threaten their businesses, they would better use that which they could have given to establish other business or extend their business territories. Fear becomes a dragging rope pulling them away from being of help to the needy. Lives need to be impacted. Those perishing needs to be rescued. There are people who are about to exit from the land of the living who need just a bit of help in order not to die. Yet, fear, fear, fear!!! Fear has gripped and restricted many potential helpers who could have given their possession out to be of help in such situations from responding positively.

Lives are being lost and people are thinking of protecting their properties. People are securing their business from not collapsing while human lives are collapsing. Which do we weigh worthy, the material wealth or lives created by God? Denying offering some help within one's ability to save a life due to fears of losing one's property would mean that the person involved is valuing the property more than the life at stake to be saved. Personal and internal fears have kept some capable givers locked behind doors. Sometimes it is not the lot that would come from a particular person that is needed. Yet if only those people could break through this barrier of fear and recognize the necessity of showing compassion to the needy out there, they could have known the little God seeks them to do in some instances. A quota from every person could do something that giving nothing cannot do. A penny out from your account could do something substantial. A cloth from you could be helpful. A word from you could cause some great change in someone's life. Yet, reasoning about fear of personal threats after giving, a capable giver might want to exempt himself from the life-saving team God is raising.

There are also other external fears that could bind someone to be inactive towards giving out what he possesses to save a life. Just around the target of giving, many get stricken with fear based on assumptions of probable surrounding threats they might encounter in the process of trying to be of help to the needy. Some can overcome the internal barriers of fear and hence would want to go ahead to help the needy except for external fears. This fear particularly develops through what is seen and heard around the capable giver relating to the needy to be helped.

The negative words some capable giver hears from another person about the needy can deter him from giving. People are very good at tarnishing the image of others that way. How they would speak about a certain needy to someone who is touched to help that needy would just discourage the giver. Some husbands/wives would not allow their spouses to give; so, they would just discourage them by giving negative reports about the needy which poses a threat to giving at that time. Other people who are anti-giving are found exhibiting the character of always not happy about the decision of others to give; hence will do their best to provide threatening reasons to discourage the ready givers.

Some other capable givers would stop giving because they think other witnesses would get to know that they are rich. That alone poses some fear to them that can restrain their compassion from coming into action. Such people are of the view that being too generous at some places means flaunting your riches which can attract even robbers to attack you. Other such people would not want their neighbours to know how rich they are. With some others too, fearing that many other needy people who will see them giving at a particular point would all come thronging at their doorstep for help, they would better stop and remain safe. Besides, other capable givers reject giving because they are of the belief that some needy people would base on what has been given them to spiritually work against their wealth. Fears, fears, fears! Whole lots of external fears keep some potential givers blocked behind the barrier of incapability though they had whatever it takes to save those needy whom they encountered and whose lives are at stake.

While these potential givers are delayed in their action to give, due to fear, death continues to work its course on the victims. As they continue to contemplate on whether they should forsake those internal and external fears and help the needy, death does not delay in its activity on the needy. As a result, a good number of the needy lose their lives or gifts or potentials in the process their available potential helpers are kept behind the barrier of fear. Such potential helpers, gripped with fear, would rather watch their corresponding needy men lose their lives or potentials than attempting to help because of fear. Unless some other brave helper who does not care about internal or external threats comes to the aid of the needy, those who are close but restrained by fear would watch the needy to die. How sad! That's the reality in the recent world which should not be the case and because of which this manuscript is written by the Holy Spirit to get the hearts and minds of people to be channelled towards the appropriate way to respond to the needy we come across.

To the Potential Giver gripped by Fear

How possibly could these fears be dealt with so that these potential givers could be freed to go on with saving lives with their possession. One thing any child of God must be aware of is that God has got anyone whom He has sent, covered and catered for. The Spirit of God will not prompt you to take a step and leave you or your family unprotected. It's very possible for any giver to think through these fears because the devil will just shoot it at you. Yet, it depends on the individual to allow that shot a place to reign in his heart and mind. The devil will engage your mind to think about many things that can be used as an excuse to stop giving. Sometimes it's just virtual reasoning which is never bound to come into reality, but the devil will let it look like that thought will manifest the next minute.

Nevertheless, they are just a scheme to frighten the capable giver off from doing something worthy. Even if those fears were real, which mostly are not so, one must realise the company of the Spirit of God with him towards doing an act that's pleasing unto God. Recognizing the presence of God with you alone must raise your faith enough to believe that all shall be right. Clear conscience and leadership of the Holy Spirit are necessary tools to be adopted here. The rest of it beyond the giver's strength would be taken care of by God. God knows how He would protect His child against internal or external threats.

More to that, if it becomes necessary that one should lose something dear in order to save something dearer to God, and the person is able to cooperate, he becomes a delight unto God. Thus, should what the giver fears come into reality, that also shouldn't be taken as strange. All because there are instances in real life where people have suffered a lot to free others from suffering. This is the place where opportunity cost comes into play. It could be that taking a time to see to the well-being of someone would cost you to lose an important business meeting. Sometimes too, responding positively to the call to save a needy person would mean losing something greater that would cost you much with regards to your emotions, finances, relations, etc. At this point is where one must weigh the worth of the two things at stake; thus, to save the needy or save what he had planned for the day/week/year. A choice needs to be made there and then. Only brave and committed people can touch the heart of God by choosing what God wants them to do over their own preference at instances such as this. When they have passed through the ordeals for the needy to be saved or relieved, the liberty which the needy gains at the end wipes off the sorrows they passed through in the past.

There is always a fulfilment of purpose after a successful giving and that takes care of all suffering the giver might have gone through in the process of giving. In fact, it should be known that the act of giving, in itself, does not happen without the giver having to lose something valuable of his. So, when it comes to critical points like this, it depends on the individual to decide to lose something of his to save some other person in need or to save his possession. So many people who come to this point tend to value their possession over the lives at stake. Blessed are those who overcome the odds they would have to go through just to save someone in need. Fears are bound to come; yet the committed giver will overlook and overcome it and afterwards laugh at it by the power and strength of the Holy Spirit

Discrimination

Discrimination is when someone treats another based on prejudice; thus, a partiality that prevents objective consideration of an issue or situation. The explanation of the term gives us the clear point why discrimination could be a barrier for someone to stop giving out his possession for the well-being of another. Within discrimination is an element that prevents objective consideration which in turn leads to partiality in an act of service. Objective here means emphasising things as perceived without distortion by emotion or personal bias. Now, what this means is that the consideration and emphasis of people who are discriminatory becomes distorted by their emotions and personal biases. As a result, the need of taking an action towards a particular situation would be very obvious to them; yet they become driven back by their emotions and personal bias if the targeted needy is not of their delight.

Much is needed to be said when it comes to this subject but less touches would be made here because it seems this problem has become chronic for most people of this present age. It has really developed to become a genetic problem with some people such that generations impart the trait into forthcoming generations to become emotionally biassed to some kinds, types and groups of people. It therefore becomes almost impossible for such people to develop any sense of compassion towards certain needy people because of how they see those needy people. Only the Spirit of God can heal such a chronic disease and uproot such a deeply rooted trait. With God, all things are possible.

Discriminatory people have got a sense of selection in their approach of association and offering of service. Should it be a needy person they know, they would have done their best to ensure his survival from the difficulties at stake. Should the needy be someone they have relation to either by blood or birth, they would have done what is required of them and even beyond that to save him. They would do their best possible for someone belonging to their selective category of choice whether of colour, blood, birth, ethnicity, association, etc. Yet, if the person at the point of need does not belong to any of their selective liking, they would ignore being of help because they cannot get touched with any sense of belonging that would enable the connection of their hearts to the needy through compassion.

As a result of that distortion of consideration caused by personal bias, discriminatory people fail to extend their resources to save the about-to-perish needy who fall within a group they dislike. It isn't that discriminatory people do not give; they do give but not to 'some' people. Nonetheless, giving based on such a platform is devoid of the divine love of God that is shared abroad in our hearts to impact the world in a broad scope beyond our likes and dislikes that result from our personal biases. Giving should be based on the leading of the Holy Spirit influenced by the love of God through the heart of the giver to reach the needy, which love is divine and devoid of the discrimination that could arise from the personal biases of the giver.

If the world demonstrates such an act of discrimination in their association and service, it's quite understandable. Yet, it becomes divinely undefined for such an act to be witnessed under the roof of God's household, where the food that is eaten every day is love, which is the word of God, served on table of grace, standing upon the carpet of the sacrifice of the cross, laid on the foundation of the Rock - Jesus Christ. All because, according to the Spirit of God through the Apostle Paul, certain things are not to be named among children of God, as is fitting for saints (Ephesians 5:1-3). The act of discrimination is worthy to be named among such things because it serves as a barrier for the holy communion among the children of God which impedes the unity of the body of Christ. All because giving and receiving is actively among the acts that facilitates the adhesive force of combining people from different roots into becoming one people of God.

When children of God are joined together as one, our differences die out, even as there is the revelation of the light of God in our lives; even as we begin to speak one language which is love. The nature of the Son of God begins to take over our formal differently originated lives such that we begin to develop individually into the image of God which was lost right from Eden. Giving, a means of caring, is one act that facilitates such a process of adhesive combination and reformation of new people, of new descent, whose citizenship has no relation with any country on this earth. Yet, discrimination stands as a strong barrier to giving and communicating the true love of God.

First Root of Discrimination - History

The root of discrimination could be traced from different sources. We would want to help ourselves here with only two of them. The foremost is history. One of the foundations of discrimination is the act of making references to written, told or experienced historical interactions between individuals or groups of people. Many rely on histories of the dark ages to choose how to relate to humanity in the present and the future. Wars, rivalries and strife that have occurred between individuals, groups, countries, etc. in the past tend to have a negative influence on those involved and their descendants such that some of them become discriminatory towards other sects of people. The hatred that such rivalries implant in the hearts of some of the victims tend to influence how they also raise their children. They thenceforth would want to train their offspring in such a way that their descendants would also detest going near certain groups of people; let alone to relate to them.

As a result, there are many who are living in the present day that did not get in-person experience with the rivalry between their parents and other groups; yet, what their parents told them have caused them to also develop a strong sense of hatred against certain groups of people. They must obey their ancestors because they are their parents and for that matter their directors so as to ensure keeping the traditions of that family, group or nation. Train a child the way he should go, when he grows, he will not depart from it, so it goes. They train their children while implanting that sense of discrimination in them such that when they are also old, they do not depart from it. As they grow, that seed of hatred that produces the sense of discrimination also grows within them; when they are fully grown, the seed of hatred would have also fully grown into a plant bearing its intended fruits which is evidenced in the outward bias reaction and absurd relations towards some kind of people. They become bitter against those people whom their parents and formal generations were bitter against. How possible ever would such people be touched to help or give to any other person in those groups they have been nurtured to never get associated with. It is almost impossible with men, but not impossible when God comes in.

To the Historically discriminatory Giver

History, history, history! What sort of history must children of God reflect on? We don't have any other history than what Christ Jesus did for us on the cross. Earthly history only gives us the whispers of how incidences of the past occurred in order that the forthcoming generation will be informed about their great grand generations. Yet the effect and impact of these earthly histories obtained from books and stories could be better understood through considering it through God's viewpoint. If not, the literal or personal inference a person could obtain from a narrated or studied history could have immense effect on him either to have a bitter heart or live the rest of his life burdened with anxiety. For instance, a child who was made to believe his father was very wicked would never grow to love him. It happens the same way with how hatred is planted in people when history is not properly handled.

The bible is not a history book. The bible is the word of God. Though it is made up of some histories of the lives of people; yet it is the embodiment of the word of God which is alive and powerful. It is a living book. Other history books refer to only the deceased making imprints of the overshadowing instances of the dark past. Nevertheless, the totality of the bible reveals the Christ who is and who was and who is to come - Jesus Christ the same yesterday, today and forever. Most key characters of history books are dead; but the key Character of the bible is alive, He is Jesus.

The life of Christ on earth and His sacrifice on the cross remains the only history worthy for us to reflect on as dear children of God. That alone can bring life into our relationships because pondering on Him who is alive is livelier than the doom pondering on the history of the dead brings to us. That alone can help us to live exemplary lives as He lived as a lover of the world which is full of sinners who are not on good terms with God. Jesus Christ loved us and came to die to save us. He didn't depend on the fact that we loved Him back or we were on good terms with God before He came to die for us. All men, because of our sins, hated God; yet He delivered His only begotten Son, His very image, into agony of torture in order to reconcile men unto Himself. If God was to look at our history to react, Christ would not have come. Men had a very bad history with our relationship to God. Yet, God responded to our hatred towards Him with love. What wonderful feedback! Only the Wonderful Mighty Father can do that. The bible makes it so clear this way:

> For scarcely for a righteous man will one die; ...But God demonstrates His own love toward us, in that **while we were still sinners**, Christ died for us. (Romans 5:7, 8)

To find someone to die even for a righteous man will be very difficult as the bible puts it; but the wonderful thing is Jesus Christ went beyond that. To an unimaginable extent, He came to die for the unrighteous. Looking at the bolded phrase in the text above, '**while we were still sinners**', the great unsearchable love of God becomes so evident to the point that the mind of man cannot fathom the in-depth foundation of it thereof. Jesus did not wait for us to repent before coming down to die for us. Men were still in the process of railing insults and blasphemy against God; yet Christ decided to come down. Sinning and never having any intention to repent in the near or far future, men kept drawing away from God; yet Christ found it necessary to still serve as a bridge to bring back the falling-away men to God, their creator and love.

Christ did not depend on our history with regards to our relationship with God to decide on whether to offer Himself up or to stop. Discrimination could be dealt with if men could wipe off the negative past experiences and the dark-age encounters that they or their parents have had with other people and try to look at people the way God sees them to be. Viewing others through the lens of God could help deal with the hindrance that discrimination mounts up in-between the giver and the needy irrespective of the kind, type or group both belong to. Approaching the needy through the love of God will do away with any negative historical imprints in the heart as a result of formal occurrences.

What about the fear of the fear that those people would repeat the negative behaviours as they or the predecessors did in the past? That's the reason the approach of Giving is influenced by the Spirit of God. God gives you the go ahead with the promptings of His Spirit; hence, He would as well help with any difficulty you might encounter. Children of God are Spirit-led to do good. The Spirit of the Lord knows the end of the task that one is just beginning. In other words, He is aware of the outcome of whatever act anyone begins. That's the reason we must depend on Him and His fellowship day in and day out to make decisions, whether to consent or not to consent, to taking an action that calls for our concern. Evang. Marthus A. Zimboiant, an end time Witness and Prophet, once said, 'Christianity is physical by spiritual'. So, advancing in the physical alone without spiritual correspondence in an act done in the Christian journey would be an error. Rejecting the leading of the Holy Spirit and predicting what the future outcomes would be, with the basis from past events, would not be proper.

Maybe one might do that with the view that he doesn't want the past to repeat itself. Yet, being urged by the Spirit of God, if one denies acting positively, the person would be the one rather repeating the hatred of the past. Thus, the person's act would be rekindling the past thoughts and pains that should have been lost long ago. Reminding oneself of the past pains would eventually pull the past into the present and that would be delaying progress. May the Spirit of the Lord help you and I to deal with all past pains and traumas that would want to impede our pace of progress in our divinely assigned tasks. Forward we go with the Holy Spirit as our leader, no turning back to past influences and impacts.

When Christ saved us, He cleared off our own personal history of sins as well as the history we have had with other people so that our present and future relationships with God as well as other people will not be based on those histories. He did so in order that we would have rich godly relationships with Him and other people after being saved. The mind of God concerning the new creation beings reborn by believing in Christ is that they would be led by the Spirit of God right from the transformation point. The newly created believer's future, with regards to his justification, has no reference to his past. No one stands worthy to pinpoint on our past sins to judge us presently or in the future; all because of the purchasing power of the blood of Jesus. Just the same way, it is not welcoming for anyone to be influenced by histories between himself and other people to react unwholesomely with regards to a divine mission in the present time, as long as that person is in Christ and is therefore a new creature. A child of God therefore need not to remind himself with negative earthly histories that would eventually pollute his heart from doing the right thing that God is pleased of.

To be a child of God is to be given birth afresh with no memory of the impact of what Satan did or could do in the past state; but to just reflect on the work the blood of Jesus has done in your life. Anyone who therefore reacts based on the chaos and negatives that occurred to him through the devices of Satan in the past would be easily influenced again by Satan to rekindle the bitterness which should have been dead long ago. Born again means born with a new mindset which does not reflect on past occurrences in order to react in the present or future incidences. Yet, since the flesh part of man needs always to be subjected by professing and practising the word of God in order to reveal the desire of spirit, it is very necessary for anyone to be renewing his mind periodically; so as to be divinely and fully transformed into the likelihood of the image of the Son of God. It is because of which the Apostle Paul said:

> And be not conformed to this world; but be ye transformed
> by the renewing of your mind, that ye may prove what is that
> good, and acceptable, and perfect, will of God. (Romans 12:2)

The flesh would always remind you of fleshy, earthly or worldly things that do not profit the soul; yet, to prove that one is at the centre of the will of God, he must renew his mind every now and then. Not just as it used to be in the past; but what the Spirit of God desires it to be now. Not remembering and being reminded of the bad old days; but to travail through the present and future challenges that come our way through being led by the Spirit of God. No earthly tradition is older than God; hence, the tradition worthy of keeping is to act in accordance with the desire of God. Therefore, if anyone wants to keep tradition, then let that person keep God.

Certainly, just as people do not want to throw away tradition; more than likewise, God must not be thrown away. Yet what would be invaluably proficient is for men to replace all other traditions with God, His precepts, love and character. He is the oldest and it is He Who can properly narrate long previous happenings and concepts, adding the proper reasons behind them. If some people discriminate because of tradition, then there is a better characteristic to trace backwards which ends up on God; for He is the Alpha who began all things.

You know, one thing about history and the past that everyone would admit being helpful is that the past, and for that matter history, gives us experience especially if we are directly connected to those incidents. The experience obtained becomes knowledge for the individual as a pre-information for tackling present and future situations which are in like manner as the ones that happened in the past. Yet, whether directly connected by in-person experience of the past or being told as a story, sometimes the basis for those happenings become hidden to the natural man. I mean the root or origin of some misunderstandings that resulted into conflicts or contentions among people in the past cannot be fully told by the historians. Sometimes not even the direct people who were involved can tell what really ignited those conflicts. Only God can tell; yes, only Him alone!

If men could turn to God to enquire about the reason certain things that are termed tradition and history came about or happened, we would get enlightened and appreciate the original truths behind them more than what we know ourselves or have just been told. Satan remains the origin of chaos. He designs the plan on a deceitful sheet spread on the wicked table of his heart and afterwards seeks his way out to execute it through any means he gets. Going to Eve in the garden of Eden to cause such havoc that resulted in the loss of the position and relationship Adam and Eve had with God, he knew what he was up to. His cunning questions to Eve demonstrate his pre-planned agenda against them. Yet, the descendants of Adam would only get to hear what occurred in reality but not the intention of Satan who was behind the scenes.

Sometimes if we forget to immediately turn to God in times of our trials, we will eventually fail our tests. That's what happened to the first Adam; he failed to turn to God as and when he was under serious attack to compromise his obedience to the voice of God. The Second Adam – Jesus – overcame the devil when he was tempted even more times than the formal. How did He do it that is worthy of emulation? He turned to the word of God every time the devil came. All three times He kept answering back 'It is written.' I believe if the devil had come hundred times, Jesus would have gotten hundred scripture quotes to cast him away. This shows us that those messing ups that we have heard our predecessors encountered or we ourselves were involved in, could have been overcome if they or we turned to the word of God. So sadly, those misfortunes have already occurred, and we label them history because it belongs to the past now. Nevertheless, have we never thought of the authority that was working behind the scenes as it happened in the lives of Adam and Eve?

We might never know what the influencing power behind those bad old misfortunes was, whether in the time of our predecessors or in our own lives. In essence, it is evident that those past issues have caused many to generate hardened hearts not willing to even forgive their spouses, fathers, relatives, etc. while they are still ignorant of what was the influencing force behind those actions of the past. It's worth noting that no negative thing happens without the devil giving a helping hand. This includes most misfortunes whether divinely allowed or even arising from personal mistakes. He shows up quickly when he gets the wind of something negative about to happen so he can facilitate it. So, you can imagine those ones he plans himself, how devastating he envisions for them to happen. What's the point here then? Though the grudge one holds against people, whether close or far, from the past due to history could be from personal intentions resulting in negative actions and reactions; yet the influencing force behind those happenings is the devil who pre-planned to achieve some bitterness in the present time and future.

To create a chaotic world and atmosphere around individuals so that he can continue implementing his devices, the devil influences commotion and contention among people. The manipulations of the devil are then taken up by those who do not seek the consent of God and are not in relationship with Him to formulate principles they put up together to call traditions. As a result, traditions that do not relate to the will of God Most High were all built up principles resulting from the influencing power of Satan behind the happenings and experiences which natural men got out of past events. Those natural men did not seek the consent of God to get to know the origin of those happenings. If they were in relationship with God such that they could enquire into the mind of God about a particular event, they would have known the influencing power behind each of them. Traditions that do not include God therefore are not complete because they reject to factor in what was behind the scenes before compiling and enacting them into being. They must be revisited whilst seeking the light of knowledge of God to view all influencing forces behind each activity.

Notwithstanding, renewing our minds as children of God will bring us to a point where we will acknowledge what Christ did for us on the cross and for that matter know how better to respond to other needy people not based on prejudice. Dwelling on negative history does more harm than good to the victim because it renders the person to live on in life with bitterness of heart. Some people have their memory filled with stuff that do not help them to be open-hearted to execute proper missions for God. God bless you for discarding negative history from the bank of your mind. Let's renew our minds by the help of the Spirit of God through the word of God, on the platform of the sacrifice of Christ Jesus, in order to discard discrimination that stands as a barrier in our path of giving.

Second Root of Discrimination - Contempt

The second source of discrimination we want to consider is looking down on others. This is also a strong foundation upon which discrimination could be built. It is very easy for one to show a discriminatory attitude towards another he looks down on. To look down on someone means to regard the person with contempt. This attitude results from the internal calculations that go on within an individual towards the person that's being looked down on. For whatever reasons and conclusions derived from those internal calculations, people who look down on others tend to gain a negative picture about the state of being of those whom they target. As a result, the way they will deal with a 'normal' person will differ from dealing with such people whom they look down on and hence that forms a foundation upon which discrimination could be mounted.

There is a particular sense that's attached to the way we look at things. The way a nursing mother will touch her own baby's faeces would look to an eyewitness as if the faeces is nothing that stinks. Nevertheless, since the baby is hers, the mother's sense of treating the faeces would be outright different from when this same mother gets to the scene of other faeces from other people or other babies which are not hers. It happens the same with everyone. Negative excreta that we bring out from our own systems are given some 'respect' by ourselves. How we would squeeze our faces to signify a sense of unwelcoming towards other people's excreta is very different when it is our own. When there is an attachment of sense of belonging, there is this natural accommodation within the individual such that there is a peculiar reception given to what is even bad. Sincere citizens would agree very easily to this.

With this picture now, what makes people look down on others could be better understood. Everybody loves and cherishes his own no matter what. We can count on many of such instances where physically challenged individuals are loved dearly by their families. No matter how handicapped the victims may be, they are still cherished by their families; all because that's where they belong. So, the problem of looking down on others that could result in discrimination can be resolved if we could find a solution to the problem of the omission of the sense of belongingness.

To the Despising Discriminatory Giver

When people around us are viewed as people belonging to the family of God, of which we are also part, we would better attach a sense of regard to how we see them. Our actions are the products of what goes on within us. So far as we don't have a place within our reasoning to position people whom we come across, we can never show an outward hospitality without contempt to them. People cannot be accommodated within our confines so far as they are not accepted by our hearts and minds to belong to a place worthwhile. As a result, discrimination would continue to reign and that would also cause us to hesitate to give out any possession of ours as a support when the need be. Yet, when we discover that people that we come across are part of God, and since we also find ourselves to be part of God, then the sense of belongingness comes into play. Immediately a sense of belongingness is established, all contempt and disrespect die out; as a result, every barrier such as discrimination has no place along the path of showing goodness to such people.

All this discovery of a sense of belongingness is facilitated by the Spirit of God; for we cannot know the mind of God, except with His Spirit. To know the originality of the person whom you have just met, one must rely on the Spirit of God. It is better to see people the way God sees them than gaining your own conception about them which might be based on what you have just seen or heard about them. You could see some people to be very good and hear good things about them but later discover that what you believed about them was the outright opposite. The same way, some other people could be mistaken to be bad, wicked or even enemies by our sight but only to discover later that they were angels God brought across our path.

Sight could always be deceptive when that's all we are depending on to conclude. That's the reason the Holy Spirit stands to be the best discerner because He will always give the true picture about an individual. Sometimes instead of asking other people how they see some person to add up to what we also see to draw a conclusion, let's just resort to the Holy Spirit. Human judgement could always be lacking completeness; yet the Holy Spirit gives the right judgement. Human judgement is always influenced by fleshly interest which is against the spirit; yet the Holy Spirit would always reveal to us what is the divine view about who a person really is. When people whom we come across are viewed through this lens, we will not make the mistakes of wrongly judging people.

Look up on people other than to look down on them. To look up here means to see what God has got for those people. Instead of seeing people as not worthy, better think about what God, if He decides to, could do with their lives. In that attempt, we would get to know the purpose of their lives around us per divine appointment for such time we get into contact with them. God can take any vessel He desires to do something worthy to glorify Himself. Some of these purposes cannot be known just by sight and conversations. Whenever men resorted to God in the bible, they got correct answers that they needed to get per their instances particularly for their era. Those who also forsook God's council and acted based on their own intuitions and flesh judgements discovered how they must bear the consequences of their wrong judgements. (Read about the Israelites and the Gibeonites in the book of Joshua, the ninth chapter to better understand this).

No man can be truly careful without the control of the Holy Spirit. Carefulness devoid of the Holy Spirit's direction and consent will end up resulting in casualties beyond what carelessness could cause. With the drive of the Spirit of God, we would always be on the safe path. We wouldn't drive off the right people with the act of looking down on them. Also, when the need arises that we give to ensure the survival of such people we would not be blocked by any discrimination barrier based on contempt. May God help us in our decisions so that we would be driven by the Holy Spirit to arrive at a correct conclusion that tallies with divine view.

With this dealt with, let's get to the other aspects concerning givers and receivers.

Notable Points

- ❖ Human based blessings or giving turn around to become a burden for the recipient
- ❖ In fact, the possession and possessor all belong to God
- ❖ At the command of God, any gift, no matter where it is kept or whoever holds control over it, must be released to where God directs it
- ❖ Provisions provided must be appreciated by recipients.
- ❖ Respect and appreciation after receiving from givers must come automatically and willingly from receivers. That is not compulsion but common sense
- ❖ The unrighteous cannot intercede for the unrighteous; so is a sinner not qualified enough to stand as an advocate for another sinner
- ❖ A saint you see now was once a fallen sinner who has been helped by the hand of grace to rise on his feet. This must keep everyone humbled enough to be forever grateful unto the Lord

- ❖ The act of ungratefulness discourages giving; by it, some givers have quit giving
- ❖ It is a deceit and hypocrisy for one to act as if he is good only to get help and afterwards show off a bad attitude of ungratefulness
- ❖ Let all men be liars, and God be truthful. A giver can go ahead to give when the Holy Spirit has granted him the go ahead.
- ❖ Fear is a stronger unseen authority that exerts more powerful damages on men than some visible weapons.
- ❖ Fear has gripped and restricted many potential helpers who could have given their possession out to be of help in critical situations from responding positively.
- ❖ Denying offering some help within one's ability to save a life due to fears of losing one's property would mean the person involved values the property more than the life at stake to be saved
- ❖ The negative words some capable giver hears from another person about the needy can deter him/her from giving
- ❖ God has got those whom He has sent covered. He assures them of His protection at every time.
- ❖ Recognizing the presence of God with you alone must raise your faith enough to believe that all shall be right
- ❖ God knows how He would protect His child against internal or external threats
- ❖ Sometimes, responding positively to the call to save a needy person would mean losing something greater that would cost you a lot.
- ❖ Only brave and committed people can touch the heart of God by choosing what God wants them to do over their own preferences
- ❖ There is always a fulfilment of purpose after a successful giving and that takes care of all suffering the giver might have gone through in the process of giving

❖ Fears are bound to come; yet the committed giver will overlook and overcome it and afterwards hoot at it

❖ The consideration and emphasis of people who are discriminatory becomes distorted by their emotions and personal biases

❖ Discrimination has developed to become a genetic problem now such that generations impart the trait into forthcoming generations to become emotionally bias to some kinds, types and groups of people

❖ Discriminatory people have got a sense of selection in their approach of association and offering of service

❖ Giving based on discrimination is devoid of the divine love of God that is shared abroad in our hearts to impact the world in a broad scope beyond our likes and dislikes that result from our personal biases

❖ It becomes divinely undefined for discrimination to be witnessed under the roof of God's household where the food that is eaten every day is love which is the word of God served on table of grace standing upon the carpet of the sacrifice of the cross laid on the foundation of the Rock - Jesus Christ

❖ Giving, a means of caring, is one act that facilitates the process of adhesive combination and reformation of new people of new descent whose citizenship have no relation with any country on this earth but of God

❖ The bible is not a history book. The bible is the word of God. Though it is made up of some histories of lives of people; yet, it is the embodiment of the word of God which is alive and powerful

❖ We don't have any other history than what Christ Jesus did for us on the cross. The life of Christ on earth and His sacrifice on the cross remains the only history worthy for us to reflect on as dear children of God

❖ Pondering on Christ who is alive is lively than the doom pondering on the history of the dead brings to us

❖ Christ did not depend on our history with regards to our relationship with God to decide on whether to offer Himself up or to stop

❖ Discrimination could be dealt with if men could wipe off the negative past experiences and the dark-age encounters and try to look at people the way God sees them to be

❖ Viewing others through the lens of God could help deal with the hindrance that discrimination mounts up in-between the giver and the needy irrespective of the kind, type or group both belong to

❖ Approaching the needy through the love of God deals away with any negative historical imprints in the heart as a result of formal occurrences

❖ The Spirit of the Lord knows the end of the task that one is just beginning. It pays to rely on Him to make decisions whether to consent or not to consent to taking an action that calls for our concern.

❖ Rejecting the leading of the Holy Spirit and predicting what the future outcomes would be with basis from past events would not be proper.

❖ Reminding oneself of the past pains would eventually pull the past into the present and that would be delaying progress.

❖ To be a child of God is to be given birth afresh with no memory of the impact of what Satan did or could do in the past state; but to just reflect on the work the blood of Jesus has done in your life

- No earthly tradition is older than God; hence, the tradition worthy of keeping is to act in accordance with the desire of God; therefore, if anyone wants to keep tradition, then let that person keep God

- God is the oldest and it is He Who can properly narrate long previous happenings and concepts, adding the proper reasons behind them

- The root or origin of some misunderstandings that resulted into conflict or contentions among people in the past cannot be fully told by the historians

- If men could turn to God to enquire of the reason certain things that are termed tradition and history came about or happened, we would get enlightened and appreciate the original truths behind them more than what we know ourselves or have just been told

- It's worth noting that no negative thing happens without the devil giving a helping hand

- It could be that the grudge one holds against people, whether close or rear, in the past due to history could be from personal intentions resulting to negative actions and reactions; yet the influencing force behind those happenings is the devil who pre-planned to achieve some bitterness in the present time and future

- Traditions that do not relate to the will God Most High or are out of the desire of His will were all built up principles resulting from influencing power of Satan behind the happenings and experiences natural men got out of past events

- When there is an attachment of sense of belonging, there is this natural accommodation within the individual such that there is a peculiar reception given to what is even bad

- People cannot be accommodated within our confines so far as they are not accepted by our hearts and minds to belong to a place worthwhile

❖ Immediately a sense of belongingness is established, all contempt and disrespect die out; as a result, barrier of discrimination has no place along the path of showing goodness to people

❖ To know the originality of the person whom you have just met, one must rely on the Spirit of God

❖ Human judgement is always influenced by fleshly interest which is against the spirit; yet, the Holy Spirit would always reveal to us what is the divine view about whom a person really is

❖ Look up on people other than to look down on them

❖ Carefulness devoid of the Holy Spirit's direction and consent will end up resulting in casualties beyond what carelessness could cause

❖ With the drive of the Spirit of God, we would always be on the safe path. We wouldn't drive off right people with the act of looking down on them.

CHAPTER FIVE

The Necessary Queries on Giving Answered

It is very important to know because of all the reasons dealt with in the previous chapters, the three Ws: who, what and why, that are associated with giving. Therefore, this chapter addresses the questions, 'Who must give', 'What at all can one give?' and 'Why is it necessary for one to give?'. It is better to begin with Who so that we better understand when it comes to appropriating responsibility. Is it the wealthy alone that are supposed to bear that responsibility of giving or has the pauper got something to do? Should the poor man who is left with very little resources to survive on also give out his little or, due to his impoverished state, is he exempted from the act of giving? We've got to know this so that we shall be well informed since as we have already agreed, giving is very dear to the heart of God. If anyone gets to know that he is exempted, then he can forsake giving and would not have any problem with God with regards to the associated penalty for those who refuse to give. Yet if one identifies that there is an obligation laid on him to give, then he can obey fairly. So, let's begin.

Who Must Give?

With the conclusions arrived in the above chapters about givers, it is worth addressing the question: 'Who must give?' Knowing that at certain points in time, a person can sincerely, due to his inability, refuse to give because he does not possess what the corresponding needy person is requiring, how do we take it from there. Should one assume the position that every day and every time he doesn't have what it takes to help someone? Yes, it is true that at certain points in time people are actually broke and cannot give specific things. But would someone want to acknowledge that he is always broke on all sides at all times? Maybe it is one aspect of the request that he was not in the position to help at a particular time, that's understandable. Now, what about other times when requests on other aspects are presented to him? Would one say that, as for him, all other aspects are the same at all times so he cannot help any needy person?

That's not true. That's a lie. Lies come from Satan because he is the author and finisher of all lies. It could be the sense of selfishness born out of the deception of Satan that's producing lies from anyone who would want to affirm that. Thus, those who would want to say, 'As for me and my household, we only consume, we cannot give anything out.' As for them and their household, they would not serve God through what they can offer, but they only consume. That would position those people in the set of 'Only Eaters' as described previously (You can refer back to the subtitle: 'The Sower and the Eater'). That is not a better place to be although that's where people of such a category exist; meanwhile they are the very people who are seeking to be bountifully blessed by God.

The moment the subject of giving is raised; a lot of people tend to assume that it does not concern them as they do not have enough. They would want to exempt themselves with some excuses such as, 'Look, I have nothing, I myself lack this and that, I do not fall in the position to give, etc." Meanwhile, they have forgotten what the Lord has proclaimed that,

For to everyone who has, more will be given, and he will have abundance; but **from him who does not have, even what he has** will be taken away. (Matt 25:29)

I want us to take notice of the phrase in bold type: **from him who does not have, even what he has**. He does not have; yet, what he has will be taken away. If he does not have, then what is it that he has that will be taken from him. Now if something of his possession would be taken from him, then it really means that he had something. Applying this school of thought here, it suggests that those who always say they do not have, really have; but they would want to selfishly consume what they have alone. They say they do not have when it comes to giving; yet, for their personal expenses they have more than available resources to meet them. To give to others, they do not have, but what will satisfy their own wants, apart from their needs, they have. Meaning that the only instance in which such people would give is when they are giving to themselves, which amounts to selfishness.

If one is unable to let go of the little in his possession, it will become difficult for him to give out large amounts when he has abundance. Training oneself to give in large proportions is to start with giving in the small proportions he now possesses. So that the Lord will consider your faithfulness in the little you possess to bless you further. For everyone who has, more will be given, and he will have abundance. Amen.

Apart from that, one must be aware that there are always some other people who are in a worse condition. So, if one wants to excuse the act of giving with the reason that he is poor, he must not forget that there are some others who are poorer. Everyone can do something. The poor can relieve those who are poorer than themselves by the little they can offer; so exactly can the afflicted comfort those who are more afflicted than they are by whatever desirable form of giving. A child of God therefore has no reasonable stand to exempt himself from this desirable act of charity.

For in this lies the demonstration of the love of God towards one another when we help each other, when we develop the act of reaching out to the nearby needy neighbour; and when the wellbeing of our colleagues is among our greatest concerns. We cannot overlook the act of offering a helping hand in the form of giving to the needy and still claim that we are exhibiting the character of God here on earth. All because the God whom we say we are representing is a full-time giver. He gives gifts all the time, continuously! He gave in the past, just now he is giving, and He continues to give every time.

It means, therefore, that the appropriate answer for the question, 'Who must Give?' is **EVERYONE**. No individual is exempted! Every person is required to give so that some who are in need of the fraction of your possession to survive can survive through that. When we all understand this concept and practise it, then everyone will become a saviour to everyone through the provisions God lays at our disposal. Then life wouldn't be more difficult in some sections of the world, some parts of the country and some sectors of the society. Individuals in families would be joined together in unity of the supply chain of giving. Families would be reaching out to help and team up with other families to form a joint society who helps one another. Each society would also contribute immensely to help build the country in such a way that the cry of the needy would be responded to. And then countries would also reach out to the help of other countries thereby helping one another to generate a world in which the needy is not forsaken.

What can One Give?

Among men, there are many ways through which one can support his neighbour through giving. This suggests that we have many forms and types of giving which are all very invaluable to the lives of men. The manner in which a person can offer help to his neighbour who is in need might be completely different from the way in which another person would also give in another instance. The principal aim of giving is not centred on the form or way one gives; but it is mainly focussed on the needy having their needs met and afterwards getting their peace of mind in their lives. So that the needy who were worried can now shout joyfully because they have been relieved from the hardship which had swallowed all their happiness. When those chains of necessity are broken and the burden of difficulties are now laid off from the heads of the needy, then one can say the target point of giving has been reached.

All because, we give to solve problems, to mend broken relationships, and to also keep one's life and potentials alive from dying because of hardships. One can give his time, knowledge, money, or any other possession to support his neighbour depending on a particular kind of need that must be met. Therefore, the principal aim of giving is centred on the needy being set free from that which once entangled them and made them feeble to the point of drowning them.

The Wrong Gift and Wrong Reception

The gift being offered must be the possession of the giver because one cannot give out what does not belong to him. You cannot give what you do not have. The service of giving must therefore be biblically legal. This first principle is very essential for a giver to be aware of before he sets out to even have that concern to give. Else, the tendency to offer what is not in your possession as a gift becomes a wrong way of trying to help. **That is a wrong gift!** There is the possibility of that happening where people would intentionally take a property which they do not own themselves and offer it out.

Though the receivers would receive it in happiness; yet there would be no peace at the end of it all. As a result, if a receiver also gets to notice that the gift being offered to him is not coming from the original or legal owner of that gift, it would be better to reject and not to accept. This is also not an easy thing to identify. Trying to get full information about the gift in the hand of a giver being presented to you as a receiver is not that easy. Sometimes too, it is not polite to be asking any giver where he got the gift to offer from. It would be a personal investigation that could bring out such notices.

Most often, the haste of reception because of the pending needs that the gift is coming to meet can deny receivers that second thought of seeking to know whether the givers are rightful owners of their gifts or not. Nevertheless, if it really comes to the notice of any receiver that the gift being presented to him does not rightfully belong to the giver, then it must be rejected. Else, if such a receiver overlooks the fact that the gift does not legally belong to the giver, and continues to receive it, it is not right. That's a **wrong reception**! All because that could even cause one to be prosecuted by law if it is later found out that the gift, for instance, is a stolen item. Be ready to receive as a needy person because you need the gifts; yet be careful in receiving the gifts. Not every gift is worthy of reception; yes, that's certainly a reasonable caution. Either side must beware of not doing the wrong action.

In spite of that, one must not give out his gift to support someone to sin no matter the urgency of that need. Giving your possession as a sponsor for evil is not only a wrong giving but also a dangerous offer. No matter how urgent the needy person expresses his need to be, if the giver finds out that the gift is going to be used to support an evil act either directly against the receiver himself or indirectly against others, the giver must refrain from that giving. That could cause one to end up in a bad position in the legalities of men as well as in the sight of God. Knowing that a particular needy wants the gift to satisfy a wrong need, be careful of your response. This is not to deter you from freely offering what you have but to sincerely let you be aware about all what giving entails. Even God does not give poisonous gifts as explained in the previous chapter. So, **don't be so good to do bad**.

It is sad these days that people support evil missions more than good ones. The structures established in the world that destroy people, that render people useless and leave people addicted to negative conditions are those that mostly receive immense help from wealthy men. Whatever such institutions want to mount up, they do so with ease and almost no restriction because they have the support of the state laws as well sponsorship of the noble and wealthy men. Such structures do not lack financially because financially sound men are shareholders in their businesses. Other wealthy men even give freely to such negative institutions so that these institutions can flourish in their services that have a negative impact on the youth and people in the society.

I would not mention any but they are rampantly interspersed in the communities, countries, everywhere around the world. They have solid foundations because they are backed by the government and leaders; yet their service is of no proper impact on the citizens. In fact, that's a wrong support. To support a service that would go a long way to destroy your future generation is out of proper reasoning and consideration. If we really care about our children and their children, we wouldn't devote our support to those structures. You wouldn't invest in the institutions that destroy your fellow neighbours if you have love in your heart towards the wellbeing of the people of your community and country. If you really envision and desire that very sound and proactive personalities do rise and take your place when you are no more, to build onto what you have already built, you will never promote such evil producing structures.

The products of these structures are addicts as drunkards (who have lost their dignity of being due to addiction), sexual immoral people (who have no control of their feelings), wicked killers (who have lost sense of humanity), etc. These are the products of such numerous structures and institutions accepted and supported in this era of the world. I believe by now their names are rhetorical. Yet to offer such a gift of support for them to produce such unproductive products of personalities is a wrong gift.

It is a wrong gift to help someone to sin, as a child of God, because you become a partaker in the very evil act which he uses your gift for. We must therefore be circumspect about the kind of help we are about to offer and the kind of need that gift is going to meet. This proposition is no reason to be employed by anyone as a basis to stop giving. Thus, the decision for one to stop giving for the fear that the needy might be using the gift for a wrong thing is not a good conclusion if done in a haste. It is not everyone that would use your gift to sin. Again that's why children of God must be led by the Holy Spirit. He is our help when it comes to situations like this. Let Him lead you to reach out to the kind of person He would want you to help. All because giving itself is not by any man's will but God's. Therefore, He knows the particular person He would like you to reach with your possession. It is when we lead ourselves that we fall into such errors.

Someone would want to give just to please another man. Sometimes we give to those whom we might want to receive some favours back from them in the other way round. In other times when our interest and fleshly desires drive us to some inappropriate points, we might want to offer our gifts to satisfy our own pursuits. Sometimes people even offer their bodies to satisfy the burning lust passions of some other people which is not according to the will of God. That's really a wrong gift. Others too offer their properties in the act of satisfying the desires of some people without the approval of the Holy Spirit. It is some of this wrong giving that the wrong receiver now uses the gift to do an evil thing. In consequence, that can lead one to be prosecuted by law though he gave kindly to the receiver.

It must also be said that some people also get to know the very evil act because of which their receiver is asking for their possession, yet they go on to deliver their gift. If that evil act is accomplished with your gift and even if men do not get notified to prosecute you, you the giver as well as the receiver all would stand faulty in the judgement of God. Run away from the fierce judgement of God by refraining from giving a wrong gift. Better look for some talented but handicapped individuals and help them rather than supporting someone to sin. Those talented people are all around who need some help from benevolent benefactors to help them develop their hidden potentials. There are numerous such people out there. It takes the leading of the Holy Spirit and a compassionate eye to find them and support them. It is much more worthy to help such people to become productive than to waste your resources on someone to sin.

Also, not to leave it unbalanced, a receiver must also refrain from a gift that would compel him to sin. Sometimes people would want to entice other people to sin by way of giving them gifts. A gift that would result in pushing or pulling one to sin is not worthy of acceptance. Else, if the receiver knows for sure that receiving a gift would compel him to sin, and he continues to receive it, it is not right. That's a wrong reception. That can lead the receiver to be prosecuted by law of men and the most dangerous part, he/she would also stand faulty in the judgement of God. To avoid the severe judgement of God which must not be taken lightly, every receiver must refrain from wrong reception.

Why Must One Give?

Now, we might want to ponder on the reason for one to give knowing from the previous topic of this chapter that everyone has the responsibility to give. Someone would want to know the reason he too should be counted among givers; thus, why such a responsibility. We have indeed known a lot concerning giving from the beginning chapters. This chapter deals vividly with the main reasons a person who is living must offer something from his possession for the benefit of others around him. As a result, it's going to give more sense of meaning to anyone who joins the sect of givers from now on. As it has already been pictured to us, every giving must have a proper basis. A baseless giving is an empty one and hence nothing much would come out from it. Therefore, the reasons going to be dealt with here would buttress the foundation upon which any giver makes his decisions towards the target point of giving. Now, let's consider from here the reasons one after the other.

Freely Given, Freely Give

The first reason we want to consider is the fact that one must give because everyone received what he now possesses. Ponder on that for a few minutes about your own life and what possessions are at your disposal. Number them one after the other and try to trace their origin; thus, try and get to know where those possessions came from into your lives. After doing this sincerely, we would realise that almost everything within and around us was obtained from some other place. Either directly or indirectly we would come to know that almost all we now possess came as a result of a chain route of giving. Yes, you did receive what you now have. The few possessions we can count on as self-generated would all have been obtained on the foundation of what was received externally. Thus, you could get what you have your own self due to what you received from some other people. Our self-acquired products were as a result of processing the raw materials we received from other external beings. Let's look at a few.

Breath of Life was Given

The basic element of life that serves as a foundation for all other things in the life of an individual is the breath of life. Everyone was given the breath of life freely by God. To be granted the visa into the system of living on the earth, one must have been provided with the breath of life. That is the basic and functional unit of life needed by a person in order to enable him to be called a living being. Our reasoning power, strength in our muscles, abilities of our organs, etc. all depend on this basic functional unit of life. It is the breath of life that sustains a man to go on with all other activities in life. Without it therefore, all the boast of a man in this life becomes nothing. A very exuberant and well recognized man just vanishes off the scene when this foundation of life is taken away from him. A dead man is just like a deflated balloon; it cannot bounce any further. The breath of life is therefore considered the most important element of life among all others. And no man on earth can boldly say he provided for himself this breath of life. The creator who created man facilitated this basic need of existence so as to set man into the atmosphere of living.

Akin to other manufacturers of machines, after they had finished their products, they would have to provide something worthy to ignite the motion or start the activity of those products. For instance, without filling the petrol tank of a petrol-based car, no amount of effort can ignite the starting mechanism of the car though every other part of the car would have properly been fixed. The individual parts are important though for the car to become complete in structure and fascinating for view; yet, per how it was manufactured to operate, without the petrol, it will be of no proper use. Else, it might then be left only for tourism so that people would just come and catch a glimpse of it and go away. But if it would move on the highways as it was intended by the manufacturer, then it must be provided with petrol by the manufacturer or owner.

A human being is no different from that. Our creator did not deal wickedly with us. After fearfully and wonderfully creating us, He also deposited into us the fuel of life so that we would not remain immobile and become insensitive. The breath of life is the fuel for our lives. Every man was given this before he could enter this realm of the earth. Those without the breath of life are sent to the mortuary to prepare them for burial. Nevertheless, whoever is moving up and down and having, at least, one of the five senses functioning properly possesses this breath of life which is not self-provided. The breath of life we, living beings, possess does not have any connection with the effort of any personality. It was divinely delivered by the creator Himself. God gave this freely to any human being He created. Hence the Psalmist reveals this that

> The Lord is the strength of my life (Psalm 27:1c).
> Apostle Paul also makes us aware through the Holy Spirit that

> For in Him we live and move and have our being as also some of your own poets have said, 'For we are also His offspring'. (Acts 17:28)

Acknowledging God as the strength of our lives is worthy because His provision of breath into our nostrils is the very foundation for every other attainment in our lives. For that matter, He is the source of our lives. We came into being right from Him hence other people referring to us as the offspring of God. All because God produced us and sustained us with the breath of life. The genesis of life makes it evident when God breathed into man; 'And the Lord God formed man of the dust of the ground and breathed into his nostrils the breath of life; and man became a living being (Genesis 2:7). A man is left with no other choice to submit and accept that without God he is not. God is the giver of life; and the taker of life also.

We learnt from the previous chapter how God took away the life of a certain rich man who did not acknowledge God. So, God can take lives and allow lives to be taken because it is He who gave all lives. By His will, lives are freely given to men; it is unto His will that all lives are taken; and without His consent, no life can be taken. Therefore, we are alive and hold our breaths intact because God desires that we should be in the possession of our lives. God has not desired taking our lives, that's the reason we are still alive. The day He desires or allows, our lives would be taken from us because He gave it to us. There are no two ways about that!

Now, knowing that our lives are sustained by the breath of life which we freely received from God, we come to understand that the very attainments we have built in this life all stand on this fundamental element of life. This would, first of all, help us to give honour and reverence to God more than we used to because without God, we also would not be. Without God, man isn't! No God, no man! A man exists because of the existence of God who began the beginning of man. God was before the start of all things and so is He beyond the end of all things. This acknowledgement of His supremacy over all things is worthy for every living man. Together with this, the reason for a living man to also give some portion of the material thing of his possession so that his other colleague would survive becomes more enlightened. The need for giving becomes alive when a man realises that the very breath that keeps him ongoing everyday was freely given to him. As we were freely given, so must we also freely give to others. It is therefore needful for everyone to give as far as we live on the breath of life which was freely given us.

Just Custodians, not Full Owners

Apart from the breath of life, whatever a person attains along the path of his life are all things which are given. Right from possessions that are inherited to those that are fought for, individuals and groups receive directly or indirectly those things from external ends. Talents or skills are given divinely by God. Intellects are developed as a result of one attaining knowledge directly from formal and informal teachers or indirectly from resources. One would say, a person pays for some of his education. That's right; but from where comes that money for the payment. Tracing the sources and origins of our financial support for successful attainments, we would come to know that we did receive it at some point in time. Others who cannot pay for their education themselves are supported by some benefactors whether closely related or distantly far; and such is a very clear link demonstrating that those beneficiaries were direct recipients of the sources of their attainments.

Conversely, others have to work and pay for their education themselves or to finance their visions to come into manifestation. That is where if care is not taken, one might attribute his accomplishments to himself because he might strongly and wrongfully believe that all his attainments were through his own toils. But the strength from which one attains the ability to work in order to get money cannot be attributed to any personal quality. One can eat the necessary balanced diet as prescribed; yet the mechanism of digestion that takes place within the body to cause the release of energy is not under the control of any man.

It forever remains unjustified to attribute quality health to obtaining quality hospital care, optimum exercise and eating proper food. All because those that have beyond abundance of these conditions continue to fall as prey to the strike of adverse conditions that is beyond the ability of humanity. Royals, rich men and honourable dignitaries lost their lives to the pandemic covid-19; though they had all the necessary measures put in place. It is not only covid-19 that brutally kills wealthy men who are able to afford expensive treatments but just that it has been popularised by its unexpected impact to the whole world recently.

The strength of the indwelling life that keeps us fit to work does not depend on proper conditions we manage to surround ourselves with; but it is God who provides it. After a day's toils, we can become very stressed out to the point of feebleness; yet, the next morning, by the time we realise, we are awake with full strength as if we have been refilled with the strength we lost. This is a divine act and not attributable to men's effort. Our strength we dwell on to work to produce whatever achievement is therefore ascribable to God alone.

What shall we say then, to whom does all what is in our possession belong to? What reference does everything we hold on to as our belonging worthy to be attributable to. All because we've got our names printed boldly on our properties declaring that we are the sole owners of them all. That's how the world knows what possession belongs to whom in order to isolate the classic affluent from the poor puir. Yet in the sight of God, **we are all just custodians, but not full owners of the little or much we might have in our possession**. That's the sad truth; very sad for the one who has all his trust and reliability on what he owns, but quite manageable for the one who has come to know that he has a temporary stay here on earth and hence a stranger and a passer-by.

Yes, in reality, everyone is just a custodian of what he thinks belongs to him but not the outright owner. **The overall owner of everything seen and unseen is The Lord of lords, Jesus Christ**. (For by Him all things were created that are in heaven and that are on earth, visible and invisible, whether thrones or dominions or principalities or powers. All things were created through Him and for Him. Colossians 1:16) The Lord Jesus just entrusts properties and possessions to people who are termed lords in earthly point of view. On the earth, these lords are mortals and hence temporarily enthroned in their office of lordship over what is assigned to them by the Lord of lords who sits enthroned in heaven. This is the truth that made King Solomon worried when he finally found it out that he was not going to lord over his attainments forever. This was his words out of anguish of spirit when he meditated into this truth by the multitude of the wisdom God gave him:

> Then I hated all my labour in which I had toiled under the Sun, because I must leave it to the man who will come after me. And who knows whether he will be wise or a fool? Yet he will rule over all my labour in which I toiled and in which I have shown myself wise under the sun. This also is vanity. (Ecclesiastes 2:18, 19)

You see, the king had initially thought, as many of us do, that he was going to rule over his toils for ever. He might have first imagined that he would be enjoying all the riches he has kept in store, if not forever, for a very long time to the fullness of his own desire. Yet with a second view through the insight of his wisdom, he came to the knowledge of the sad truth that he is just a custodian of whatever that is at his disposal, temporarily. In addition, his appointed time of exit at which point he would have to leave all these possessions and post behind was kept hidden from him. Meaning he could go at any time whether prepared or not; as such, he might have to leave them behind at a point he has not had enough enjoyment of them.

The reality of life in this regard began to resound in his mind probably because he had been granted authority to know thanks to the multitude of the divine wisdom that was given him. Due to this wisdom, he was granted divine authentication to access this knowledge that becomes latent to many men yet that's the true end of them all. It began to hit him harder when he was getting older and as he could reflect on all his attainments through the strength of his youth. Then he started hating his labour because all the products of his toils will not go with him when he dies. He will just have to leave it for someone else whom he doesn't know whether the person will be as wise as himself or not.

The most distressing part of that reasoning is how this unknown heir will be treating and handling those possessions. How that person would take care of the royal family and how he will use the available properties gave King Solomon a headache such that he hated all what he had toiled to do under the sun, and hence termed it as vanity. Vanity in the sense that it is not worth clinging your heart to possessions you think you own now. All because, at the end of the day, you are going to hand it over soon to another man you can't guarantee would have the heart, conscience, love, wisdom, etc. as you have. Yes, more often than not, men depart from the earthly realm sooner than they had thought; and eventually, another man would have to take over their possessions.

If you read the account of Rehoboam, the son of Solomon who took over from him, you get to understand why Solomon was deeply worried. As discussed in the previous chapter, Rehoboam ruined his father's heritage with just a poor decision. Sometimes, the sad thing is that some of the heirs who take over properties act as if they are the ones who obtained them from scratch; thereby not recognizing again the deceased who toiled all his life for them. Some people's properties are in operation in the present day, but their names are covered. No one living knows and will ever know that such people toiled for such properties because they have no mouths to defend themselves once they are dead and gone.

Vanity upon vanity is when a man believes that the totality of his wellbeing and future depends on what he possesses. It is an arrow of lie and deception shot against those who do not have Jesus Christ as the Lord and Saviour of their lives. It is a strong weaponry employed against wealthy and successful men who believe they have had it all and will never lack again and hence do not need to worry because whatever they need is available for them. The possessions of such people are the source of hope for their future which is very false.

The wellbeing of man in the future does not depend on what he possesses in the present time. Some of them sometimes believe they are going to be driven far and far by what they have in store; only to come to a point where they have to rather leave all those possessions behind and exit the earth. Calamity comes banging their door without prior notification. Some of those calamities serve as media of exit for such people to leave the earth while they had no plans of leaving that soon; and importantly while they did not know who was going to take over all the products of their toils. Yet, they have no say once death stretches forth his cold hands towards them.

Sometimes if it were possible for some men to bribe death with some of their possessions, they would have been happy to do that and live on to attain more possessions. Someone would even give all that he has in exchange for life; because with his intellect, he can gain all those possessions back again. Sadly, money is not a transacting medium on the market of life and death. Neither do possessions count when it comes to pacifying the angel of death. The land of Egypt would have given a lot to prevent all the first born of her strength from being driven away just in a day. Egypt had the multitude of wealth that many nations did not have in the time God rescued His sheep by the hand of Prophet Moses; yet her wealth did not save her firstborns.

When God has issued the sentence of your departure from the earth, don't bother yourself about thinking to be saved by your possessions. No health care is sufficiently sophisticated enough to stop death when the appointed time of God is up. It is God himself who can extend the lifespan of a person whom He is pleased with, as in the account of King Hezekiah. Nevertheless, one's own possessions cannot save him; and at that very point of exit, another man would have already been elected to be enthroned to rule over the possessions the deceased is leaving behind. God will just appoint another person to take over because the person dying was just a custodian of what he had but not a full owner. In fact, the world or the universe at large is something else than we might think it to be! Only God, the maker, can give us a better view of it.

Therefore, being just a custodian but not a full owner must give one a proper reason not to hoard that which he has while other people suffer in need. Realising that our possessions are temporarily handed over to us by God, one must avail himself to be led by the Spirit of God to supply some of his possessions to satisfy the needs of the needy neighbour. All because whether you keep it or lose it, you will finally lose it. The accountability that awaits a custodian makes it proper for a man to know how to reasonably use what is entrusted to him.

Properly appropriating properties entrusted to us would help us to render a proper accountability before the Lord of lords. The fact that it is the Lord that entrusted it to us means that He has intentions of what He would want us to use those possessions for. That's what every possessor must search for so that he does not misuse what is now in his possession. It is also a big problem for others to realise the reality that they were enthroned to their present state of ruling by selection of grace through unmerited favour; and hence would need to humbly submit and operate under the auspices of the majesty of the King of kings who gave them that opportunity. The Apostle Paul advises us through the Holy Spirit this way:

> For who makes you differ from another? And what do you have that you did not receive? Now if you did indeed receive it, why do you boast as if you had not received it? (1 Corinthians 4:7)

Some people in authority and possession now have forgotten that their post was just handed over to them from another who left; and for that matter, they would also hand them over in time to come. Therefore, they boast as if they did not receive it; and would want to misuse their power because of their office of authority. Conversely, some of such people would not want to use the right possession for the right purpose intended by whoever that handed over that post to them. This is the source of the menace we witness in both spiritual and physical offices that have been given to people by God. Being given a spiritual gift means there is a particular assignment at stake that God, the giver, requires the receiver to use that gift to accomplish. Ignorance has caused many to misuse the opportunities God gave them through gifting them with spiritual gifts and authorities. Instead of seeking to be led by the Spirit of God to be properly led as to how to use the gift, some people would rather want to misuse it.

Some boast, as the Apostle said, as if they self-manufactured their gifts and can use them anyway and anyhow no matter the negative impact it brings to other people. Looking down on other people, such people think their gifts make them superhumans over those whom they relate to. Nonetheless, nothing makes the man gifted different from any other, the Apostle confirms. All because the gift was handed over to the person; and maybe his new post is what might deceive him to have become different; yet there comes a time he too will hand it over. The only important thing about being gifted is what one would use his gift for in the appointed time interval that the gift rests upon him, which would determine whether the person would eventually be commended or condemned. Commendation and condemnation await gift holders and their fate between the two mainly depend on how they use their gifts in their appointed time interval of being in post.

The psalmist declares the undeniable fate that awaits all men, adding whom we must properly fix our eyes and our hope. Here it goes:

> Indeed, You made my days as handbreadths, and my age is as nothing before You; certainly every man at his best state is but vapour. Surely every man walks about like a shadow surely, they busy themselves in vain. He heaps up riches and does not know who will gather them. And now, Lord, what do I wait for? My hope is in You. (Psalm 39:5-7)

Certainly, every man at his best is but vapour. For the best part of man does not last; men operate in their temporal era or season. Sooner than their expectation they are wiped from the face of the earth by an approaching calamity or divine necessity. That is why it is important to leave a proper legacy by our present actions; for we cannot continue to do what we do best every day for all days. The positive impact of the actions that keeps living on, after the individual is no more, is what is important. Better is it therefore for the man who is in his highest strength today to seek the direction of God to focus on touching the heart of God by directing his efforts mainly on the will of God. Vain will it be to heap riches which are based on selfish aims without the direction of God on how to administer the resources to be of impact that would last more than your earthly life.

Calamity does not give prior notice before it comes. Before one is aware, the calamity he never expected pays him the surprise visit, which distorts all set plans and aspirations of the individual. If at that point the individual had not properly ordered the administration of his gathered resources, then the unknown available hands begin to gather what they did not toil for. Since every man is bound to meet this at one point in his lifetime, it is better for all living men to put their hope in God. It is He who can facilitate our triumphant victory over calamities which come with effects to alter the divine timings of an individual. Yet, if even the calamity falls within the divine timings of God and hence it is God-approved to befall the individual who has his hope in God, the person is still safe. All because his hope of survival was fixed on the Lord not on his possessions or qualifications; and for that matter, he was directed by God on how to administer his resources to please God and to positively impact the lives of other people.

The tendency to heap riches without letting go of some fraction of them to be of benefit to other people is a very deceptive sense which easily entraps many people. This is normally as a result of the self-esteem and the ego attached to who possesses which number of what riches in this era of ours. To some people, to reduce part of the resources to focus on something else apart from self, would mean to reduce their self-esteem or ego. This brainwashing is upheld by many to the point that they keep on adding up while forsaking the opportunity God brings to their doorsteps to become partakers of the divine mission of assistance to the needy which is under the move of God.

It remains better to become a partaker of God's mission through any means of participation that is within the confines of one's available resources. All people who forsake this great opportunity regret at the point when they see that they wouldn't have authority over their possessions again. To those who honour such a wonderful opportunity of extending what they have gathered to impact other lives, they are filled with a sense of worth when they are the point of exit from this earth. The Apostle Paul therefore gives a caution as he was influenced by humility concerning the level God has brought him so far:

For I am the least of the apostles, who am not worthy to be called an apostle, ... But by the grace of God I am what I am...
(1 Corinthians 15:9,10a)

To realise that we are who we are, by the grace of God, is very paramount as far as knowing how to act at a particular level in life is concerned. When one comes to the point of realising that his level of attainments and possessions are all by the grace of God, that sets a platform for the individual to be influenced by the Spirit of God to do the will of God with what falls within the person's authority. Yet not all people are able to realise this to come to that point of humility. The moment the possession of a person now controls him such that his associations and system of life begin to change due to what is now in his possession, the verge of drifting out of control is drawn. A critical analysis of one's conduct of life then ought to be accessed at such a point to ensure that the person is not taken off by the control of his possessions out of God's will. It is an undeniable fact that there must be changes that are bound to occur in one's life when the level of possession rises in life in the aspect of social life and other relationships. Yet, one's connection with God is a vital connection which cannot be compromised even in this state.

It is the maintenance of God's connection that will let someone continually remain humble no matter what level of attainment the person reaches. This will also influence the person's relationship with other human beings. A person in authority of possessions, yet humble, still sees other people the way God sees them and would react to them in that same sense. It is better to realise therefore that we are who we are not by ourselves but by the grace of God. Subsequently, this would help us overcome any high-handedness and draw us to the point of helping others in need with the possessions we have obtained by the grace of God.

Reflecting Increase in one's Divine Accounts

If the results of our deeds and acts of services all ended here on earth, most of the lives of people of God would have been termed tragic. The reason for this proposition is because one can tell from clear analysis that the end of lives of most people of God is not welcoming. In the sense that some men would die in pain and some in incidents and accidents that normal description from a human point of view would term it undesirable end. Yet, some of these men who die in somewhat terrible and undesirable incidents are all people whom God appreciates their services while they were on earth. Conversely, they are a delight to heaven such that God receives them in glory while the earth is giving them a doomed farewell. There are many instances in the Bible which support this proposition to the point that if the conditions of termination of life determined the success of a person, it might look like many instrumental people of God failed.

We can mention some of them such as Prophet Moses, Prophet Isaiah, the husband of the widow Prophet Elijah fed from who had died leaving debt behind, the poor Lazarus whom the Lord spoke about in His parable, etc. before the birth of Christ. After the death of Christ, an uncountable number of them in the Bible as the martyr of the disciples, the killing of the persecuted church, and many more. There are a lot of great men and women of God this earth has witnessed who departed in a very sorrowful episode. How would one consider this if the yardstick of judgement is limited to the earth alone. What meaning would one attach to serving the Lord if it all ended here on this temporary habitable planet.

Thanks be to God that the pronouncement of successful living is not limited to the conditions of termination from the earth. All Saints who died sorrowfully have received by the Lord into glory and in reverence awaiting their day of reward. That means the picture of their termination from the earth is not necessarily their real end of story; they are just switched from one realm of shame and suffering into another of glory and joy. Therefore, steps taken while living on earth should be done while conditioning the mind beyond the earth.

The seen is ruled by the unseen. The impacts made in the seen reflect in the unseen for a feedback judgement to be manifested in the seen. Yet, most of the rewarding feedback of the impacts of the seen are kept in the unseen. The determinant for success therefore comes from the review of the impacts of a man in the seen that are recorded in the unseen. The vessels whom we have heard about or seen pass away in terrible instances had already made their earthly impacts which are recorded in the unseen. Their impacts become tangible once they have left the earth. Their records which are not visible on earth are shown to them once they have terminated the earth realm. So, tragic would be the earth's judgement of their termination; yet, glorious would be their reception because of their records kept in their divine accounts. One very important thing to notice is that no one is staying on the earth forever. So better would it be for one to make impacts that will speak for him after his departure. This reality makes it a necessary reason for everyone not to deny the opportunity of giving. All because giving is one of the major ways of recording imprints of impacts on earth in divine records. Consider therefore the advice of the Apostle Paul to the Philippians:

> Not that I seek the gift, but I seek the fruit that abounds to your account. (Philippians 4:17)

Urging the Philippians not to forsake giving to support the work of God, the Apostle drew their attention to the records that are taken from the impacts of good acts. The fruits of our good acts would be rewarded to us. The good acts done today are therefore not thrown away; never, they have got a reflection in our divine accounts. Whatever giving one avails himself to give would never be missed from the sight of angels assigned to keep such records. Earthly structures put in place to reward good acts are prototypes to sections of the greater one in the unseen yet to be manifested in due time.

In the Bible, Mordecai was remembered by his good deed because it had been recorded in the chronicles concerning him. In due time, the fruit of his good work abounded to his account and through that he was saved and glorified. Exactly so could one's good works save him in the evil days. Mordecai's records of his good acts were right there to intercede for him at the right time by God's will to save, uplift and glorify him. A better reward and glorification await those who would make good impacts in God's name towards God's will through the act of giving.

The giver must therefore look beyond the earth when giving. All because you cannot enjoy certain fruits of your labour of giving on this cursed earth. For the purpose of increasing the records of impacts in one's divine accounts, it is therefore very necessary to give. One could sow into the lives of some people in need and reap his harvest beyond the limit of the earth. Giving while being expectant of what to receive back here on earth would not always be fulfilling. Rewards are kept in the unseen proportionally to records of impacts of the deeds of men on earth. We should therefore never lose heart if even our expecting feedback from our good works are not fulfilling here on earth. Men could be ungrateful and unrewarding because men are men. Some men are disappointing while others merely forget as simple and easy as that. Yet, God, our Lord who never sleeps nor slumber will never lose focus of any good act we do. He sees them all and would reward us accordingly in due time.

The records would surely speak when all is said and done. Therefore, Apostle Paul was very convinced by the Holy Spirit to also motivate the Corinthians that 'Therefore, my beloved brethren, be steadfast, immovable, always abounding in the work of the Lord, knowing that your labour is not in vain in the Lord.' (1 Corinthians 15:58) Apostle Paul himself was striving on with the mission of God when all that he was waiting for was the crown of victory. Hence his heart was fixed on a reward beyond the confines of this earth. As he strengthened the arms of the people of Corinth to abound in good works, so do I urge and pray that your hands of doing good would be strengthened. All because every good labour done in the name and will of God will not be in vain. Some people's hands have already got weary; yet by the help of the Holy Spirit it is more than possible to get revived to keep on doing what would touch the heart of God to reflect in your divine accounts.

Think about this: How is the state of your divine account? I mean the accounts with God that bear records of your good works here on earth. How well would your records speak for you once you are out of the realm of living? The impacts can only be done here and not hereafter. People who have gone already wished they could be given the opportunity to come back to make more impact. Probably because they would have now realised the importance of making good impacts when alive on earth. What about us who are still alive? The opportunity is now! Increase your divine accounts of records by making positive impacts through giving.

Former Experience

There is yet another reason that must urge every one of us to embark on giving. Remember the last time you encountered some serious difficulty that was almost unbearable and made you feel totally helpless. I mean the one which almost broke your heart. I believe I've reminded you of yours. It could have been issues relating to relationships, finances, health, accidents, or any unforeseen incident that made life almost darkened for you. I understand hardships come in diverse ways, and as such its difficulty or the ability to bear is relative with regards to individual differences. I want you to just ponder over yours. What you went through within that period before things came back to the normal state. I don't know how long that period of difficulty lasted. In case you are not aware, there are some people who are existing in such and worse conditions as you went through for a very long time without the hope of coming out.

I must tell you, yours was an unforeseen contingency; yet, for some others, it is a usual lifetime experience. The hard times you have been through before must trigger you to get to the aid of some others who are also in the same or other similar hardships. This is because while you were in those hard times, you can recall that you were wishing that some helper could come to your aid. Why not do the same to others once you are now out. For no one knows when the waves of hardships would again be directed to him along his life in the time to come. Besides, never forget that "Blessed are the merciful, for they shall obtain mercy." (Matthew 5:7) He who then will show mercy to someone in need now will surely be shown mercy when he also is in need according to the word of God.

169

<u>Notable Points</u>

❖ The only instance some people would give is when they are giving to themselves, which amounts to selfishness. That's not of God.

❖ If one is unable to let go the little in his possession, it will become difficult for him to give out the large when he has abundance

❖ Training oneself to give in large proportions is to start with giving in the small proportions he now possesses

❖ The poor can relieve those who are poorer than themselves by the little they can offer; so exactly can the afflicted comfort those who are more afflicted than they are by whatever desirable form of giving

❖ A child of God therefore has no reasonable stand to exempt himself from this desirable act of charity

❖ The appropriate answer for the question, 'Who must Give?' is EVERYONE. No individual is exempted!

❖ The principal aim of giving is not centred on the form or manner in which one gives; but it is mainly focussed on the needy having their needs met and afterwards getting their peace of mind in their lives

❖ The gift being offered must be the possession of the giver because one cannot give out what does not belong to him

❖ The service of giving must be biblically legal

❖ The tendency to offer what is not in your possession as a gift becomes a wrong way of trying to help. That is a wrong gift

❖ If a receiver, after knowing, overlooks the fact that the gift does not legally belong to the giver, and continues to receive it, it is not right. That's a wrong reception!

❖ Not every gift is worthy of reception; yes, that's certainly a reasonable caution

❖ Giving your possession as a sponsor for evil is not only a wrong giving but also a dangerous offer

❖ Don't be so good to do bad

❖ To support a service that would go a long way to destroy your future generation is out of proper reasoning and consideration.

❖ If you really envision and desire that very sound and proactive personalities do rise and take your place when you are no more, to build onto what you have already built, you will never promote evil producing structures which destroys the youth by their services they offer.

❖ To offer support to evil producing institutions for them to produce such unproductive products of personalities is a wrong gift

❖ It is a wrong gift to help someone to sin, as a child of God, because you become a partaker in the very evil act which he uses your gift for

❖ Run away from the fierce judgement of God by refraining from giving a wrong gift that supports sin

❖ There are numerous talented but handicapped persons out there. It takes the leading of the Holy Spirit and a compassionate eye to find them and support them

❖ A gift that would result in pushing or pulling one to sin is not worthy to receive.

❖ If the receiver knows for sure that receiving a gift would compel him to sin, and he continues to receive it, it is not right. That's a wrong reception.

❖ Either directly or indirectly, all we now possess came as a result of a chain route of giving.

❖ Our self-acquired products were as a result of processing the raw materials we received from other external beings

❖ Everyone was given the breath of life freely by God

❖ To be granted the visa into this system of living on the earth, one must have been provided with the breath of life

❖ A dead man is just like a deflated balloon; it cannot bounce any further

171

❖ The breath of life is the fuel for our lives

❖ The breath of life we, living beings, possess does not have any connection with the effort of any personality

❖ Acknowledging God as the strength of our lives is worthy because His provision of breath into our nostrils is the very foundation for every other attainment in our lives

❖ Without God, man isn't! No God, no man! Yet without man, God is.

❖ A man exists because of the existence of God who began the beginning of man.

❖ The need for giving becomes alive when a man realises that the very breath that keeps him ongoing everyday was freely given to him

❖ The strength of the indwelling life that keeps us fit to work does not depend on proper conditions we manage to surround ourselves with; but it is God who provides it

❖ In the sight of God, we are all just custodians, but not full owners of the little or much we might have in our possession

❖ The overall owner of everything seen and unseen is The Lord of lords, Jesus Christ.

❖ More often than not, men depart from the earthly realm sooner than they had thought

❖ Vanity upon vanity is when a man believes that the totality of his wellbeing and future depends on what he possesses.

❖ The wellbeing of man in the future does not depend on what he possesses in the present time

❖ Money is not a transacting medium on the market of life and death; neither do possessions count when it comes to pacifying the angel of death

❖ When God had issued the sentence of your departure from the earth, don't bother yourself about thinking to be saved by your possessions

❖ Properly appropriating properties entrusted to us would help us to render a proper accountability before the Lord of lords

❖ Being given a spiritual gift means there is a particular assignment at stake that God, the giver, requires the receiver to use that gift to accomplish

❖ Commendation and condemnation await gift holders and their fate between the two mainly depend on how they use their gifts in their appointed time interval of being in post.

❖ We cannot continue to do what we do best every day for all days

❖ The positive impact of the actions that keeps living on after the individual is no more is what is important.

❖ Better is it therefore for the man who is in his highest strength today to seek the direction of God to focus on touching the heart of God by directing his efforts mainly on the will of God.

❖ Calamity does not give prior notice before they come

❖ It remains better to become a partaker of God's mission through any means of participation that is within the confines of one's available resources

❖ One's connection with God is a vital connection which cannot be compromised in every state of life

❖ It is the maintenance of God's connection that will let one still remain humble no matter what level the person reaches

❖ A person in authority of possessions yet humble still sees other people the way God sees them and would react to them in that same sense

❖ It is better to realise that we are who we are not by ourselves but by the grace of God

❖ If the results of our deeds and acts of services all ended here on earth, most of the lives of people of God would have been termed tragic.

❖ Thanks be to God that the pronouncement of successful living is not limited to the conditions of termination from the earth.

❖ Steps taken while living on earth should be done while conditioning the mind beyond the earth.

❖ The impacts made in the seen reflect in the unseen for a feedback judgement to be manifested in the seen

❖ The determinant for success therefore comes from the review of the impacts of a man in the seen that are recorded in the unseen

❖ Giving is one of the major ways of recording imprints of impacts on earth in divine records

❖ Whatever giving one avails himself to give would never be missed from the sight of angels assigned to keep such records

❖ One's good works done could save him in the evil days

❖ For the purpose of increasing the records of impacts in one's divine accounts, it is therefore very necessary to give.

❖ Rewards are kept in the unseen proportionally to records of impacts of the deeds of men on earth

❖ The records would surely speak when all is said and done

❖ How well would your records speak for you once you are out of the realm of living?

❖ The impacts can only be done here and not hereafter. The opportunity is now!

❖ The hard times you have been through before must trigger you to get to the aid of some others who are also in the same or other similar hardships.

CHAPTER SIX

<u>A Life-saving Giver</u>

Having treated giving above and knowing the need to give and the conditions associated with giving and receiving, we would want to now know who a life-saving giver is. It is good to delve into the title of this manuscript after the highlights we have received so far from the previous chapters. As short as possible, a life-saving giver is someone whose act of giving aims at or eventually results in saving a life. Such a person is someone who offers his best as much as possible in order to ensure the survival of the neighbouring needy. Intuitively, he is characteristically fond of having a longing desire to intercept the process of death on someone's life or talent because of need.

Thus, the action of a life-saving giver resists the total completion of the authority of death on an individual, thereby restoring life into the victim whose life or talent was nearly approaching death. Their support extends the span of the exact lives as well as the talents, skills and potentials of individuals who face the fear of losing their rich innate capabilities due to circumstances beyond their control. Life-saving givers are channels through whom God reveals hope to the hopeless. A life-saving giver either plans in advance to save the targeted about-to-die needy or spontaneously gives at an unforeseen circumstance in order to save a life or lives.

We want to help ourselves with one impacting parable of the Lord Jesus entitled 'The Good Samaritan' to help us unravel the identity of a life-saving giver. Take time with me to look through this below. This is going to assist us dig out every essential element about our subject.

> *And behold, a certain lawyer stood up and tested Him, saying, "Teacher, what shall I do **to inherit eternal life**? He said to him, "What is written in the law? What is your reading of it? So, he answered and said, "You shall love the LORD your God with all your heart, with all your soul, with all your strength, and with all your mind, and your neighbour as yourself." And He said to him, "You have answered rightly; do this and you will live. But he, wanting to justify himself, said to Jesus, "And **who is my neighbour?**"*

> *Then Jesus answered and said, "A certain man went down from Jerusalem to Jericho, and fell among thieves, who stripped him of his clothing, wounded him, and departed, leaving him half dead. Now by chance a certain **priest** came down that road. And when he saw him, he passed by on the **other side**. Likewise, a **Levite**, when he arrived at the place, came and looked, and passed by on the **other side**. But a certain **Samaritan**, as he journeyed, came and saw him, he had compassion. So, he went to him and bandaged his wounds, pouring on oil and wine; and he set him on his own animal, brought him to an inn, and took care of him. On the next day, when he departed, he took out two denarii, gave them to the innkeeper, and said to him, 'Take care of him; and whatever more you spend when I come again, I will pay you. So, which of these three do you think was a neighbour to him who fell among the thieves?*

> *And he said, "**He who showed mercy on him**." Then Jesus said to him, "**Go and do likewise**"*

Critical attention is needed here in order to extract all the nuggets hidden in this very parable to uncover the divine obligation the Lord implied for all people. By dint of that fact let us take time and consider it section after section to reveal the character of a life-saving giver.

LESSONS FROM THE GOOD SAMARITAN

Characteristics of a Life-saving Giver

From the excerpt above, we can draw some qualities that come together to constitute the lifestyle of a life-saving giver. Referencing from the passage therefore, someone can be classified as a life-saving giver when that person:

Is Eternal Life Conscious

*Teacher, what shall I do **to inherit eternal life**?*

A life-saving giver's mind is set on eternal life. What triggered the parable of the good Samaritan was a question on eternal life. At the end, the command of Jesus, "Go and do likewise" meant that the questioner ought to go and do likewise as was presented in the parable in order to inherit eternal life. Whoever would then want to inherit eternal life would not exempt himself from the lessons this very parable teaches.

Now, for a person to be able to offer his belonging to save lives, then that person must have consciously concluded on some principles of this life. No one does anything without a reason. Those who give for the purpose of saving lives also have got enough basis for their action. This act of wholeheartedly giving out to the benefit of others must come from a reasoned intention in the minds of those donors. To be able to let go of what is of this world means that your heart and hope are not based on them. Therefore, life-saving givers set their minds not on things of this world which shall pass away. They do not consider holding their positions and possessions forever. For that matter, when the need arises for them to offer their position or possession by reason to save others, it doesn't become difficult for them. They do not love the things of this world.

He who loves the things of this world cannot offer them partly or wholly when the need arises. Such people would better die and leave worldly things behind than to lose them and live. This is because they value the things of this world more than their souls. Their position and possession are their treasures that make life meaningful for them. The bible says where your treasure is, there also would be your heart. As a result, those who prepare their treasures here on earth have their hearts strongly concentrated on the things they have amassed with their strength. All that their minds and hearts are based on is how to maintain their riches, positions, and attainments and how possible they can increase them. They see to it that their businesses are booming, their positions are retained, and everything that brings them income is kept in good shape. They consider all these at the expense of their souls. Ignorantly, they see the attainment of lots of earthly riches alone to be a successful and meaningful life. Yet, remember what happened to the rich fool in the bible? Let's look at it and know well the character and fate of those opposite to life-saving givers.

> Then He [Jesus] spoke a parable to them, saying: 'The ground of a certain rich man yielded plentifully. And he taught within himself, saying, 'What shall I do, since I have no rooms to store my crops?' So, he said, 'I will do this: I will pull down my barns and build greater, and there I will store all my crops and my goods. And I will say to my Soul, you have many goods laid up for many years; take ease; eat, drink, and be merry'. But God said to him, **'Fool!** This night your soul will be required of you; then whose will those things be which you have provided? So is he who lays up treasure for himself and is not rich toward God.' (Luke 12:16-21, emphasis added)

You see how God shouted the 'fool'. Unfortunately, that's how God sees those who cherish acquisition of possessions more than what will truly benefit their souls. All because they lay up treasure for themselves that label them rich, but they do not have rich relationships with God. Therefore, the Lord Jesus had already told the disciples that 'Take heed and beware of covetousness, for one's life does not consist in the abundance of the things he possesses.' (Luke 12:15). Covetousness restricts the urge to give. And that alone can lead a person to lose his soul. That's what exactly happened to this rich man. Yet, since those who are not life-saving givers are not eternal life centred, they also lose consciousness on this fact.

Therefore, people in such a category think their success depends on the abundance of their possessions, and hence it becomes difficult for them to give. They deny themselves the honour of saving the lives of those who come along their paths from what they possess. Are you conversant with the story of the rich man and Lazarus in the bible? The rich man could have done something to save Lazarus when he saw the state of Lazarus; yet he looked indifferent. All because he was not a life-saving giver. His concentration was not on how he can inherit eternal life but to enjoy alone the fruits of his labour. For some people, since they obtained what they have through their sweat and toil, they must consume and enjoy it alone. Yet that mind-set is likely to lead one to be self-centred rather than to be also concentrated on what to do to inherit eternal life.

Life-saving givers are different. They are eternal life conscious. Their readiness to offer what is in their possession for someone in need shows where their hearts are concentrated. Yes, they do not fully dedicate their minds and hearts to the wellbeing of their physical wealth, but they also have attention on their spiritual relationship with God. And that helps them to give. Apostle Paul puts it in this way that, 'The love of God constrains us.' As a result, life-saving givers become constrained by the love of God to give and they cannot ignore that burden laid on them because they revere the spiritual relationship they have with God.

Spiritual relationship with God is nothing to those who only chase after worldly riches and fame. The difference is therefore evident from the story of Lazarus and the rich man that, when all is said and done, worldly-riches-chasers find themselves wanting because they had no relationship with the eternal Lord. Everything shall pass away but God lives forever with those who are connected to Him. It is better therefore for anyone who has obtained a lot of riches to also look at how to secure a good relationship with God through believing in Jesus Christ, the beloved son of God. From then would that individual be directed how to properly administer his resources God had allowed him to obtain to save others and unto the glory of God.

Eternal life conscious people also always search the scriptures. It is evident therefore that after asking what to do to inherit eternal life, Jesus also asked the man, *"What is written in the law? What is your reading of it?"* All because you cannot reject the word of God and seek for eternal life. Inside the Word is life. He who therefore seeks for eternal life yet is devoid of the word of God is akin to someone seeking to pluck an orange fruit from a mango tree. It is impossible! One must be well versed in the word of God in order to know how to order himself to be in line with the will of God so that he can obtain eternal life. In fact, 'What is your reading of the word?' How often do men today turn to read the bible?

Children of God nowadays are too busy to the point that we almost forget the word of God that is our director and manual to eternal life. We are occupied with too many other things that some of us don't remember the last time they had a communion with the Lord through reading the word ourselves alone. We book appointments, schedule meetings and plan our work in such a way that there is no time left within the day to talk to God through His word. In fact, that's deadly so far as seeking eternal life is concerned.

You can find a Christian today who knows nothing in the word of God yet that person attends church every week. Totally empty-headed persons with regards to the knowledge of the bible are all over in our churches. The worst point is that some of such people occupy honourable positions in the churches. They have no desire for the word; neither does it occur to them to take the bible often to read. They open the bible only when they are in church and close it forever till the next meeting. In fact, some do not even have bibles or have lost them due to loss of concentration on it for long periods. Yes, it's only in Christianity that one can find such lack of commitment towards worship. You cannot find it anywhere in the other sects of worship. Yet, it is us who believe we have got the right path to eternal life, which is true. It's a shame! We have got to know the right way—Jesus—yet we don't study Him who is the Word of God. Note, what is presented here is not to insult but bring to light how poor God considers the attitude of His sheep who profess to be seeking life in Him. We've got to be more serious than we are now!

Some people can stay without reading the bible for weeks and even months while they feel alright. In fact, as a Christian, it is abnormal for you to remain without the word and feel alright. All is not right when you don't search on a daily basis what God has for you through His word. This is because God's word is new every day and it comes specifically differently to particular people in every generation; yet the same as yesterday, today and forever. How God will speak through His word to someone who lived decades ago would be different from us who are in the contemporary world today. God's word always shows the readers how to live in the unique setting and season in which they are; thereby fulfilling all prophecies spoken by the prophets of the word. Hence every child of God must characteristically be used to going to the word day by day for the refreshment of the Holy Spirit's inspiration. We must not find ourselves too much used to the bible such that we think that since we read it the last time, we are ok for the next days.

The act of seeing the bible to be a normal book will deny us the richness it possesses. There is life in the word of God. The characteristic of the word is evidently stated: 'For the word of God is living and powerful, and sharper than any two-edged sword, piercing even to the division of soul and spirit, and of joints and marrow, and is a discerner of the thoughts and intents of the heart.' (Hebrews 4:12) That's what the Word says about the Word. The word of God is tested and proven over the years that not even a jot from it will pass away without being fulfilled. Prophecies in the word of God have been fulfilled, are being fulfilled and shall be fulfilled because the word of God cannot fail. All because God cannot fail; God is His word, and He cannot deny Himself. Searching the scriptures therefore is searching into the wisdom and intents of God for the past, present, and future concerning man.

It is very critical here because if we would get to know a particular season in which we are per the prophecies of the word, then we need to constantly be searching and comparing. All because there are certain things ongoing now which are the exact things God has said would be happening; yet how would we recognize that that's what God said if we are not conversant with the prophecies. They are just encrypted codes within the knowledge of God which the Holy Spirit decrypts to anyone who is ready to know. During the time of Jesus on earth, whatever he did reflected to the disciples what had been written about Him in the scriptures by the old prophets. When He drove the traders and money changers from the temple, the bible says that's when His disciple remembered what had been written about Him that 'Zeal for Your house has eaten Me up.'

So, everything that was happening about Him had a connected prophetic word that had already been inscribed by the old prophets. The little Jesus being sent to Egypt to escape from being killed by Herod, and returning from Egypt, He being sent to dwell in the city of Nazareth, and many others all had prophetic connotations that had already been written by the prophets of old. The prophecy of God keeps on unfolding. Which part of the prophecies would we connect to what we are seeing now? We would know it better if we were constant students of the word. Yes, every action happening now has a reflection from what has already been written. Let's go back to the word and start comparing diligently what is happening now to the prophecies.

The bible would become more real and alive when we do this. Through that anyone who gets to know the intentions of God is not far from obtaining eternal life of God. All because knowledge is power. Even knowledge of this world gives some people power over others. The knowledge of the word of God has the transforming power on the reader to empower him to obtain the gift of eternal life from God. So, the Lord Jesus confirmed this in the lifestyle of the Jews who sought life through searching through the scriptures this way:

> You search the scriptures, for in them you think you have eternal life; and these are they which testify of Me John 5:39

Eternal life is therefore connected to searching the scriptures. The life in the scriptures the Jews were searching for was Christ yet they were ignorant of it. For that matter, the Lord had to correct their zeal and direct them properly on Him. For that which they searched for was right in front of them, yet they failed to recognize Him. Hence, He later confirmed that, 'I am the way, the truth and the life' to testify to them that the very life they were searching for in the scriptures is Him. That was to the Jews and how their desire for obtaining eternal life is seen in their act of searching the scriptures. What about you and I? How often do we search the scriptures? I desire with all my heart to obtain eternal life; I don't know about you. I'm not sure anyone will waste his time and resources in the house of God just for earthly recognition but not seeking for the life beyond this life. If it is so then that we all desire to have eternal life, then we have a lot more to do. We've got a lot of corrections to do in our daily organised routines.

Rescheduling must be done, so as doing new timetables. So that we can factor in the ample time of fellowship with God through searching the word of God. This must be done by fixing times of reading the word before, within, and after church services and work schedules. You must get a personal encounter of God with His word out of church hours. That's the moment the Holy Spirit can help you comprehend well what was preached during church. This was what the character of Christians of the church of Berea and hence the bible testified of them against the Thessalonians:

Then the brethren immediately sent Paul and Silas away by night to Berea. When they arrived, they went into the synagogue of the Jews. These were more fair-minded than those in Thessalonica, in that they received the word with all readiness, and searched the Scriptures daily to find out whether these things were so. (Acts 17:10,11)

Christians today are unfair minded just as the Thessalonians but not more fair-minded as those of Berea. The Bereans were ready to receive the word and not that alone but also went further to search whether what they had received from the Apostles were so. How can such people as these be deceived by false teachers and prophets? And how would they not discover the whole measure of the life hidden in the Scriptures. There is a reason behind the Lord referring to us as sheep; and we must look carefully into that to discover it. The sheep being a ruminant has four stomachs. It chews the cud. That's after plucking leaves and swallowing them into one stomach, later on it pushes those leaves from that stomach back into its mouth for proper mastication at its own peaceful time. The properly chewed leaves are then swallowed back into another stomach where digestion and assimilation occurs on the absorbable broken down leaves. What kind of sheep are Christians today, think about it?

Christians today would never look at what they learnt at church for a second time. Hardly would you find one looking back at the notes he himself wrote back at church. No, they don't have time; but they have got time for other things. Many think the time they can give to God is the only one to three hours period of the onetime-in-a-week they are at church. But that's not enough to enrich our souls with the power to obtain eternal life. Much of what is taught at church is not properly understood and some even not complete. All because the ministers must factor in all religious activities in order to work within the time arranged for the service.

Woe to any modern-day minister to go beyond the time scheduled for a meeting. The return response from the angry congregation will be shocking to that minister. Some congregation will not even come to church the next meeting in order to send a signal to the minister not to repeat that mistake of 'wasting' time. The teacher of the word therefore must rush to complete the bible teaching, so must the preacher; else, they get a problem between themselves and their congregation. More so, the preachers today do not want to offend their congregation in any way because it has gotten to a time in the world that some Christians must be pampered like little babes, otherwise they stop churching. How pitiful! There is something really missing. That ancient desire of hunger and thirst for the Lord's presence need to be sought for and rekindled. As a result of this rapidity in today's teaching and preaching of the word, many biblical texts are not better expounded for better understanding while some others are not even read at all for the sake of time.

It therefore remains the responsibility of the Christian to continue studying what was taught and preached at church so that the Holy Spirit will complement any misunderstandings and incompletions. Nevertheless, where will the Holy Spirit find Christians today to do that? Whenever the Holy Spirit draws them to sit at the word, they stand up because they have to catch up with other things they must not miss. The Spirit of God draws their minds on the word, their minds are almost immediately drawn away by phone notification or another prompting seeking their attention. It has become a striving matter between the Spirit of God whose mission is to lead the Christian into all truth and the busy present-day child of God. The word of God preached having it last in the minds of these Christians is just that day they received it. Some even forget it just as they leave the church premises. So, what could help them would be going back to the word at least one of the weekdays to ponder over the scriptures again and again. Nevertheless, they do not! Christians in this situation walk throughout the week with no word of God in their minds and hearts.

The result is therefore evident that the devil succeeds when he comes against such people. When deceivers also come along their line, these ignorant Christians fall as prey to them. All because they have no weapon to fight the devil and his agents. **The word of God is the**

overcoming weapon against the deception of Satan. The Lord Jesus used it when He was tempted by the devil and certainly, He overcame the devil as He always does. That was particularly to set an example for us to know that we cannot obtain spiritual victory, and for that matter physical success in a day, during the week, and in the year without battling with the word of God. We are therefore fragile before the attack of the devil because we are deficient of the word of God.

There is little or no deposit of the word of God in our minds to fetch us an answer to the devil any time we are approached by his agents. The sad thing is that we are the same people professing we are in Christ, and so eternal life is not far from our reach. What is so dangerous is that this character can lead us to lose eternal life together with all promises God has promised His children. All these promises and privileges for the child of God are hidden in the scriptures. So, if you don't search the scriptures, how are you going to be aware? Ignorance can enslave you under the manipulations of Satan till he leads you to your doom. You cannot access what you are ignorant of. Unless you get to know, you wouldn't even believe that it exists. How do we get to know; by searching thoroughly. This is the proper search that when we search, the heavens will open for us to find all we need to know to help us overcome the devil and to obtain eternal life.

A very important additive here is that a good prayer life enhances the urge to search the scriptures. **Prayer is the driving force for the desire to read the bible**. A prayerless person is without the appetite for the word of God. To obtain the desire to search the scriptures, we need to be prayerful. For all you know the devil would have shielded you from getting to know the hidden power of the knowledge of the word. You've got to pray yourself out of that shield so that you can access the power of the word of God. Do you know the surprising thing? As you read the bible, satanism and manipulations automatically get far from your dwelling. **Reading of the bible, in itself, is a weapon against Satan and his agents**. I believe that's the very reason the devil has weakened a lot of Christians towards that important opportunity. Let us therefore be enlightened as children of Light and claim what is ours through prayers and reading the word. When we are full of the word of God, we automatically become fully filled with Jesus, the Holy Spirit and the Heavenly Father. The Lord Jesus says it this way:

> If anyone loves Me, he will keep My word; and My Father will love him, and We will come to him and make Our home with him. (John 14:23)

Exactly confirmed, so when we keep His word by searching the scriptures to know and to obey, then God will love us. It is not that alone but the trinity would come and make their abode with us. The bible confirms that Jesus knocks at the door of our hearts to come in. As a result, the trinity comes to stay nowhere but in our hearts. If God is in your heart, eternal life is inside you, because inside God is eternal life. Don't just be any kind of giver, be among life-saving givers; those who seek eternal life not only by giving but also by searching the scriptures within which is the hidden life – Christ. I believe you are going to start any moment from now to search more into the word of God to know more of Christ Jesus more than you know. That we may know Him and the power of His resurrection that He would use to raise us from mortality into eternal living with Him forever and ever. Let's go on to the next characteristic of a life-saving giver.

Qualifies to be called a Neighbour

> And **who is my neighbour?** ...... So, **which of these three do you think was a neighbour** to him who fell among the thieves?

The need to spell out who a neighbour really is came as a result of the question the lawyer posed to the Lord after an interrogation about how to obtain eternal life. When this lawyer was asked to go and love his neighbour just as himself, he thought to justify himself by questioning back that, 'Who is my neighbour?'. The Lord Jesus therefore had to reveal the true identity of someone called a neighbour. In order to educate the educated and give understanding to the prudent who were around Him at that time, the Lord decided to redefine the term 'neighbour' differently from what is known by all the surrounding literates. By the dictionary definition of neighbour known generally, a neighbour is a person who lives or is located near another person.

The Lord's definition for a neighbour through the parable was different from this. There are many definitions of certain terminologies here on earth that have very different definitions from the divine point of view. When God Himself comes to the scene to explain some terms and processes, men would get to know that some of what they have concluded on them to be right are rather wrong. Men sometimes conclude without including God; hence, there results a lot of errors in our proposed hypothesis and hence our theories. When we talk of lawyers in those days, they were people who had studied the scriptures and knew a lot about other resources about life. The Lord had to disprove this definition by a true practical life example, the parable of the good Samaritan. So that the lawyers, Pharisees and other learned personalities around Him at that scene could draw the right definition of a neighbour out of the parable themselves.

The case study the Lord presented involved three personalities who all met the same condition of another man in trouble but acted differently. These three personalities were a priest, a Levite and a Samaritan. They all met a half dead man along their path and had to decide how to consider him. The Lord said the priest and Levite, having seen him, all passed on to the other side, forsook him and continued their journey for reasons known to themselves. Nevertheless, when the Samaritan reached the same spot where the other two reached and passed on to the other side, he came near the half-dead man and had compassion for him. All the three didn't know what had happened to this half-dead man; yet two decided not to go near him, let alone to touch him. Yet, the third man, a Samaritan, a stranger to the area, was touched at heart to help this man the moment he saw him.

The Lord took His time to consciously elaborate the scene to all the people who were listening to Him. These audiences were not illiterates; no, amongst them were highly learned Jews out of which came the lawyer who questioned the Lord. After the parable, the Lord asked them to answer themselves the question which they formally asked Him. This was the custom of the Lord, as He brought people to the point of knowledge by questioning them. Once the audience can come up with the proper answer from their own reasoning capacity, then effective teaching would have been achieved. The Lord is indeed a Rabbi, a divine teacher. The answer of His students at that point in time was not far from right, they answered correctly that the neighbour of the half-dead man is the man who had mercy on him. After enlightening their understanding by such a parable, the definition of neighbour changed from what they knew it was right from then.

A neighbour of a person, therefore, from divine definition, is someone who shows mercy on that person. Yes, he is a person who has compassion on the fellow needy nearby or along his path. A neighbour is not necessarily those we share walls and fences with. Neighbours are not church members; neither are they colleagues or friends at work or school. One can be a neighbour to some others very far from him depending on the conditions explained in the parable. People are neighbours to other peoples in different countries and different continents. As long as one can be touched with compassion that could produce an action of showing mercy on someone either near or far, the person can be considered a neighbour to those whom his mercifulness impacts. The fact that you see some people every day and exchange greetings does not make you neighbours. You only become divinely a neighbour when you are able to identify the need to go closer into the lives of those you meet to possibly help them out of the troubles which they find difficult overcoming on their own.

The man beaten by the thieves was helpless, but it took someone with compassion to come to his aid. He did not start his journey in that state but due to an unforeseen attack, he had then been rendered powerless and feeble such that only mercy could save him, but from where could he find it. He started his journey very rich; yet there he lay impoverished due to the attack by enemies. He was not strong enough to explain what had happened to him. Maybe those who passed by could come to his aid if they heard his story but there he was, lying speechless. He could have been a knowledgeable person, but who could identify that about him in that state. He might have been endowed with wisdom that could bring a positive change, but there was no measuring rod to identify the gifts that helpless man was made of. He might have been a prominent person among his own people, but how could he manifest his identity in that helpless state? Yes, if even the society where he stayed had no honour for him, at least he would have been highly revered by his family; but how could he explain to the passing strangers. He had a mouth but could not speak. He had an identity but could not prove it.

There was no way he could make evidence of his status. He was just helpless. The only thing he needed was mercy! He needed someone to show him compassion. In his thoughts, even if a little child could come his way, he would have been happy; but he was finding no help as he lay in the pool of blood due to his wounds. Virtue had left him due to the strike of his enemies. What he never expected had crossed his journey such that his vision of the day had been cut short. The only hope he had was the fact that he had life in him. Yet who would come to his aid so that the only breath of life he was existing on would also not leave him. 'Where would compassion come from? 'Wouldn't I get someone to show mercy?' 'Is no caring person going to come to my rescue?', he cried within himself as he lay helpless at the spot of need.

That is exactly the state of many others. They started their journey of life very strong and rich. They commanded respect and were highly honoured in their past life. Some even occupied positions such that they had control over properties and people. Yet, due to one reason or the other they have been stricken by an unforeseen blow along their journey of life. Life has turned upside down for them in their present state such that they have become helpless. They now have no one to speak for them nor to prove their identity. Many are loaded with talents and skills but are now helpless due to their current state. The attacks that come across people in the journey of life come in diverse ways. Someone wouldn't understand a particular attack another had encountered. Unless the victim is given a hearing ear, no one can really understand what he has been through. There were no CCTV cameras to capture the way the thieves brutally attacked the man in our case study. Whether it was his own mistake of travelling at that time or along that dangerous road, all that people came to see is a half-dead man. No one can really tell what really happened. Yet to save that helpless man from completely dying, a compassionate and merciful man was needed. A neighbour, for that matter, was needed to come on board.

The fact that you cannot understand the plight of someone must not deter you to restrain from offering a helping hand. There are different reasons why people end up in some situations as described here. It could be the victim's own mistake, that's possible. It could also be the outright opposite. But the issue at stake here is the importance of saving the life which is about to be lost. Only the compassionate and merciful can attain that level of understanding. The breath of life must not go off if there remains a slight opportunity to secure it. The gifts and talents in these victims must not die. The hope and aspirations in people in such a helpless state can be brought alive again with a helping hand. There is something that could be done to save the latent potentials of people whom we come across.

Sometimes they are not far. It is just that we pass to the 'other side' whenever divine waves bring them near to our attention. We come across them, but we decide to rather neglect them because of all sorts of fears that resound in our hearts concerning our personal safety. But if we could have some sense of compassion and if we could be moved by mercy, then we could possibly become neighbours to such people. Neighbours raise their fellow neighbours by a helping hand so that they who were lying helpless could rise onto their feet again to continue their journey of life. A true neighbour restarts the journey of his fellow neighbours. True neighbours strike on the play buttons of paused lives of their fellows such that those who had lost hope of continuity can progress to reach their target of life. Being a neighbour is far different from giving smiling gestures and greetings to those who are well and fit next to our doors. **True neighbouring is compassion and mercy in action**. True neighbours are compassionate in nature and merciful towards those they ought to show mercy to. They go near and lift the weak up!

Are you a neighbour? Do you qualify to be called a neighbour by divine standards? As much as this was part of the answer to obtaining eternal life, it implies that being a neighbour is not a choice for every child of God. Knowing that we all need to make it to heaven, let us not neglect this act desirable unto God. Generate compassion for others and show mercy unto those in need. That would qualify you to be a neighbour. A life-saving giver is a neighbour. That person gets nearer to people in need, identifies their needs and generates compassion to show mercy on them.

As much as possible, this is what depicts the episode of loving someone as yourself. All because anyone in the kind of condition as this beaten traveller would wish that someone could come to his aid. Everyone at one point or the other would desire to be shown compassion and mercy. So, showing compassion and mercy to the needy is an act that would allow God to remember you when you also are in need of compassion and mercy from Him along your path of life here on earth. And surely God would as well be compassionate to receive you into His eternal glory.

Is Spirit-led

To positively touch a life in need does not depend on physical calculations and emotions. It might not be a person who is generally known by people to be good that would be in such a position. It might not be an individual or group which is most expected. It takes someone who will be influenced by the Spirit of God who can execute that life-changing impact on persons in need. Those who yield to such influences of the

Spirit of God are few; they aren't common. We just found one out of three in this parable. It means percentage wise that one would get about only thirty percent of the people he comes across who might be willing to offer such a helping hand. Sometimes such a helper could be someone very strange; a person that is least expected. The other sixty to seventy percent group of persons who turn a blind eye are not people whom you would consider as bad people. They could be people that you most expect that they should have some empathy for your situation; yet you would be shocked by their reaction towards your destitution.

The people we know to be 'good' in society might not do good in such situations. This sometimes happens in accordance with the will of God so that a man would not rely on the strength of another expected man. For it is written 'Cursed is the man who trusts in man and makes flesh his strength' (Jeremiah 17:5). God has His own way of passing through some unexpected personalities to come to the aid of the needy who trusts in Him so that all the glory is given to God, and blessings to the vessel. The vessels through which God makes this impact of compassion and mercy are those who yield to the prompting of the Spirit of God at the said point of need. Such people could be complete strangers. The first two people who passed by the half-dead man were a priest and a Levite. All these two people are regarded as people very close to God because of their services in the sanctuary. If there was someone to be touched by the love of God to show pity, they are the very people who were expected to be in that position.

The priest was the first to encounter the beaten traveller. According to the descriptions of the functions of a priest, a priest is supposed to be someone with much compassion. All because he stands as an intercessor. He pleads for the forgiveness of the sins of his household and for all other people also. As such, his functions demand a heart of compassion. Yet the Lord declares that this priest, being the first to reach the scene, when he saw the half-dead man, just passed by the other side. He didn't even bother to get any closer to find out whether the man was still breathing or already dead. A whole priest looked completely indifferent about an incident that demanded someone with a heart of compassion.

Exactly so is the attitude of most potential helpers. They could be the very people supposed to feel the plight of some needy people, but they surprisingly act very indifferently. They act as if they have not even got the wind of the sufferings of their neighbours while they are much aware but have just ignored it. They would rather pass the other side when they see the needy. That isn't pleasant to the Lord. The Lord Jesus wanted to bring to the attention of all who listened to Him that there is a group of people who act like this priest in the parable. It is better to change if one finds himself among such groups because their indifferent character is not pleasant unto God. Their character disqualifies them to be called neighbours of such needy people they come across. Yet it might have been the desire of God for them to have taken some time to address the problem of the needy they encountered. Let's be cautioned.

The Levite, on the other hand, was the second person to witness the scene. A Levite is closely related to God because the Lord is his portion and inheritance such that all his life is spent in the sanctuary at the service of God. Therefore, in human perspective, the Levite is supposed to have a closer relationship to God than the other Jews and for that matter should have been in the position to exhibit the love of God. Apparently, the Levite is every day at the service of God; thus, a person who has sold out his lifetime unto the service of God. As a result, being influenced by the compassion and mercy of God to affect someone in need shouldn't be something strange for the Levite. Yet, the Lord said the Levite came and looked at the half-dead man and passed by the other side. As for him, at least he came closer, but that was not enough. He was just inquisitive; but not compassionate.

Such is the character of many potential helpers. After encountering the needy, they only want to know every bit about how and why the needy ended up so helpless. They would want to consider how hopeless and weak that needy is so that, should they be asked to report, they would get a better account. They just come to look and pass by. In a professing act of sympathising, they rather show an apathetic attitude in the long run. They are the people who request for the long-narrated stories of those in need but do nothing to support them. They are qualified in giving a chronological broadcast of other people's plight because they act as special investigators in people's matters. They conduct interrogations as 'How come? What happened? Why this?' and the others to really understand the whole problem from A to Z; yet they, at the end, leave the victims to suffer alone. They are the people Apostle James talked about and cautioned that:

> If a brother or sister is naked and destitute of daily food, and one of you says to them, 'Depart in peace, be warmed and filled,' but you do not give them the things which are needed for the body, what does it profit? (James 2:15, 16)

They show faith by word but are devoid of the works thereof. Such people identify the details of the problems of others but offer nothing of theirs to positively impact or solve the problems they identify. Their initial approach might seem that they understand how to feel weak and broken and therefore will do their best to help the weak, but they go no further. The Holy Spirit spoke through the Apostle here that it profits nothing to only get to know the problem of the needy and leave it just there without trying to contribute a factor of solution. There would be no need for giving the needy a hearing if you wouldn't be of any help to them. Sometimes it is not that such people cannot do anything about the problem of the needy due to lack, no. Should they decide to do something, they could do it. Yet, their inward calculations and suspicions become a barrier against their ability to extend a helping hand. Instead of responding to the prompting of the Holy Spirit they rather get moved by external signals from their surroundings.

Yet that shouldn't be the story of a child of God. A child of God must ask God what to do at the current scene he encounters. A Spirit-led person would get to know the mind of God on how to treat the needy whom he has just encountered. Even if not in haste, the communion of the Spirit, with time, must get a child of God with a true heart convicted enough to do the right thing about what he came across. There are instances where true children of God left the place of responsibility without acting in accordance with the will of the Spirit of God but eventually returned to do so because the Spirit of God pressed and drew them back there. The conscience of a Spirit-led child of God would never allow him to just neglect doing the right thing in accordance with the will of God about an incident he has been prompted about.

How would one know that the reason for coming into contact with a particular needy person at a particular time is because God desires that he should be of a particular help to that needy? Only the Spirit-led would obtain such a level of conviction from the prompting of the Holy Spirit. Conversely for some others, if they even hear a very loud audible voice asking them to help, they will neglect it. Some would even conclude that it is the devil's voice. All because, either they are not obedient to the Spirit of God, or they are spiritually insensitive to know which voice is or isn't from God. So, if it was really the desire of God for one to help the needy that he just met; but forsook it, what do you think would have happened. That would be forsaking divine responsibility. Any divine responsibility has also got its associated judgement for either obeying or disobeying in the divine perspective. Children of God would therefore need to be very careful how we treat such situations that we come across.

The qualification of the third personality who encountered the half-dead was not told; the Lord just left it commonly as a certain Samaritan. This person was from Samaria, but no one knew his further identity or position. For the other two people who led him, the Lord described their positions enough. They were all Jews in the first place; and not that alone, one was a priest and the other a Levite. Yet for the Samaritan, he was just described to be a common and an ordinary man journeying along. The Lord said, it is this common man that when he saw the half-dead man, had compassion for him, went to him and started working on him. It is witnessed that among the three who came across the half-dead man, this common Samaritan was the only one who was touched to be compassionate. I want to affirm that it was him, the Samaritan, who responded positively to the prompting of the Holy Spirit.

Though the others could have received this still voice through their conscience to stop by and do something, they decided not to. Upon physical calculations and assumptions, the priest as well as the Levite must have forsaken the prompting of the Holy Spirit. This common Samaritan was different. Going to the beaten man, bandaging his wounds, applying oil and wine, etc. showed how compassionate this Samaritan was to save the man who was about to die. His actions prove that he had determined to do his possible best to save the man from dying. That's a characteristic of a life-saving giver. He allowed himself to be moved by the Holy Spirit but not his flesh. How are you led in such circumstances? Do you listen to your fleshly inner voice by physical considerations of surrounding threats? Do you listen to the opinion of others less spiritual who dissuade and discourage you by faithless analysis of adverse conditions at stake?

It would be better to listen to the Holy Spirit than to listen to men. Thus, the Apostles questioned the Jewish leaders, 'Whether it is right in the sight of God to listen to you more than God, you judge' when they were confronted with a situation when they were being beguiled to obey human voice. The Holy Spirit will make you a vessel that saves lives if you allow Him to lead you. So, a life-saving giver allows himself to be driven by the Holy Spirit on the platform of love and compassion to do whatever possible to save the life which is about to perish prematurely.

Stands in the gap

God is still at the work of saving lives. Jesus is still at the business of positively transforming lives as it is day. Some lives need not be terminated at points where it is not divinely set for them to be terminated. All because it is not the will of God for some people to end their journey of life in some certain ways. Yet due to some circumstances beyond the control of certain victims whether through their own mistakes or other factors, they tend to come to that point of life where it seems they must just end it there. Yet that is not necessarily the mind of God concerning such people. At this point when they would want to give up prematurely is where some life-saviour needs to show up through divine order to come to their rescue. If no one shows up compassionate enough to be of help, these victims will just vanish off the scene; yet that might not be a planned way of exit with regards to the will of God concerning their lives.

Among these victims are divinely elected vessels who have significant missions to accomplish for God. Others too have inbuilt potential which has not yet been unveiled such that should they have had support to continue their journey of life, they would be much more productive to their families and continents. God desires vessels who would avail themselves so that He can save such lives from perishing prematurely. God is seeking for someone who can devote himself based on love and compassion to save such people from their plight so they can continue their life journeys to accomplish their life missions. In order that the very lives, visions, skills, etc. of such victims do not give up the ghost, God seeks for someone to stand in the gap.

Be aware that just like the traveller in the parable, many men started their journey very strong and sound. Many started very rich and heavily loaded but for the attack of an unforeseen storm of life, they are now empty. The traveller in this case study had prepared himself such that he would not have lacked any supply till he reached his destination. But the Lord said the thieves stripped off his clothing. Similarly, many have been stripped of their possessions and their current state seems as if they have never had any. Except for the adversity that came across some current needy people, they had a lot they could boast of. Some have been stripped of their loved ones who made life meaningful for them. Others have been rendered impoverished because all their wealth and possessions have been taken out of their hands.

For other people too, they are at the point where they cannot reach their own possessions and as such, they need some help so they can reach the place where they can lay their hands on their possessions. Some are even royals in disguise. This raided traveller was in the middle of Jerusalem and Jericho. Nobody knows whether he had properties in both cities that if he had had the opportunity to reach any of the cities, he could lay his hands on. Nevertheless, an unforeseen attack had kept him in the middle of the two cities at a point he needed help either to reach Jericho or return to Jerusalem. The only prayer of his heart was that someone would help him to get up so he could reach up to his own possessions. He might be having a lot of clothes elsewhere; yet there was he lying naked at the point of need. He could have had some money kept somewhere; yet he lay there with no money. All because, his adversaries had attacked and stripped off from him all that he had. Who would come to his rescue, if not the life-saving Samaritan, a person who can stand in the gap to ensure the continuity of life's journey.

A life-saving giver appears unexpectedly to ensure the incompleteness of death's authority on a victim at the boundary of life and death. The service of that person prevents death from taking over the life, potential, and capabilities of an individual put in need by circumstances of life. Life-saving givers stand in the gap. They step in to defend the one condemned to death by accusations that are beyond his appeals. They become the mouths of the victim who cannot speak for himself anymore. They offer support to a person who has been paralysed by life inconveniences such that there is almost no strength left in his bones. They are vessels of salvation in the hands of God. God uses them as tools in His mighty hands to execute His wonderful salvation that the victims least expect.

Life-saving givers are representatives of God, standing in the position of God to stop Satan for finalising his action on some potentially productive people. Satan might have stealth from a victim and would want to continue to kill and destroy him; yet life-saving givers appear, out of the blue, to stop the actions of the devil on the victims. They are means through which God denies death from implementing its last section of trial on victims. By the service of life-saving givers, a person who is at the point of death obtains a new hope of life. They are means by which God restores life to people. They are life-restoration media who stand in the gap according to the will of God. God always seeks to find a lot of such people; yet they are very scarce. Analyse God's search result when He sought to find any:

> So, I sought for a man among them who would make a wall and stand in the gap before Me on behalf of the land, that I should not destroy it; but I found no one. (Ezekiel 22:30)

In search of vessels who could stand in the gap so that some dear lives wouldn't be destroyed; sadly enough, the Lord found none. Sometimes it isn't only Satan who would want to destroy someone. It can be God Himself who would want to pour His wrath on some children of His because of their disobedience. Yet, God would still want to find someone to plead for the very people about to suffer from His wrath. God knows if He releases His wrath, no man can stand before it; and since it is not His desire to see lives perishing, He always wants someone to plead the cause of sinners.

The prophet of God, Moses did this for the Israelites at a point on their journey to the promised land. He stood in the gap; else, all Israel would have perished at that moment. When God decided to punish a city called Nineveh, He sent a prophet called Jonah to first caution them that they would plead for forgiveness and repent from their sins so that He would stop releasing His wrath on them. In fact, God does not fancy destroying His own people; yes, He takes no delight in seeing people perish. Nevertheless, the one to stand in the gap as a 'lawyer' to speak for some victims on trial before Him are very scarce per the search of God. God having a negative result for His search really means life-saving men to stand in the gap are very difficult to come by. It is not that some are hidden somewhere that He didn't find out because nothing can be hidden from God; it is just that they are almost nowhere to be found.

A life-saving giver who steps in the gap as the Samaritan in our case study does not necessarily plead for the sins of the victim but rather offers what he possesses to ensure that the victim survives. The needs of needy people at critical points varies depending on the type of need that needs to be met. Some needy men would require material support just as the raided traveller here. Other people would be requiring just a piece of exhortation to serve as a cushion of motivation to keep them ongoing. Just a single word or a sentence can lift someone up from his critical point where death would want to take over. It becomes difficult for such people to get someone to say that single word or sentence to them. Yes, some people have got whatever material wealth available but what they would need to survive for the next level of life is just a single word or sentence.

Men who stand in the gap to offer anything possible to help the needy cross over and overcome the action of death are very importantly needed at certain points as this. All because a little thing offered could be of great significance in the life of the afflicted. When death takes over, nothing else could be done again. It would therefore be better to do anything possible whether little or much to restrain death from taking over the lives, talents and potentials of victims at the point of need. When a man is able to stand in the gap that way, then the weak would now shout that he is strong, and the poor would say he is rich, due to what the Lord has done through that life-saving giver.

Do you know that these days people wait for people to die before they spend much for funeral services and expressing condolences? Meanwhile, they could have done something minimal that would have saved the life of the deceased. They don't give the little to save lives; yet they spend the lot to show that they care after the person is dead and gone. They write and read out lengthy touching condolences depicting that they cared for the deceased. That's hypocrisy and seeking human favour rather than being compassionate. If there is any compassion worthy to be shown to anyone, it should be demonstrated when that person is still alive; and not when the person is dead.

People cry for help till all their nerves have no strength anymore to shout; yet no one around them would come to their rescue. It is not that they are not heard and seen; they are really heard of their cries and seen of their plight; yet, forsaken by their listeners and observers. The scarcity of men to stand in the gap so that the about-to-die needy would survive is really a great concern for God. People have got what it takes to stand in the gap; yet to be willing to yield themselves has become a difficulty. This is the extra mile that a life-saving giver can go more than anyone else. Standing in the gap, a life-saving giver ensures the termination of the cries of the needy in order to stop the termination of their lives.

Overcomes all Barriers to Giving

The Lord was speaking to Jews, but He made them know that even a Samaritan whom they revile could be regarded as a neighbour. Jews and Samaritans were rivals during that time. As a result, the scene in the parable brought to light the fact that it doesn't matter the identity of a particular person when it comes to being a neighbour. Thus, when it comes to the instance when compassion must work out from the heart and mind to produce mercy towards someone in need, familiarity does not come in. Your own companion whom you have common characteristics through origin or association can ignore you at such points as this. Conversely, this was a lesson the Lord taught us to reveal that it isn't only those whom one is related to that he must give attention to help in situations when the need arises. The fact that you think you don't have anything in common with the needy does not mean you cannot be of help to him.

As a matter of fact, all human beings have one thing in common, we were all made from dust by one Maker, God. Thus, we are made up of the same composition -dust- and we are all the creation of God. All human beings on earth are the offspring of Adam, the first man God created; and that makes all of us brothers and sisters. Hence being touched by the Spirit of God for one to give at a particular instance should not be negatively influenced by origin or religion. As long as one responds to the prompting of the Holy Spirit to offer to an individual who is born of a woman, if the giver obeys, then it becomes a pleasant act unto God.

More importantly, believers in Christ Jesus are born anew by the Spirit of God and hence we are all offspring of God; and that makes it more obvious that we are more in common. The common characteristic of all children of God is the seal of God, which is the Spirit of God, He has given us. Life-saving givers possessing the Spirit of God would hardly discriminate in the act of offering a helping hand to the needy they come across no matter the calibre of that needy. All because we possess a Spirit that bears witness that we are children of God; and if so, then we are all siblings in Christ. Hardly often would a sibling refuse his other sibling of a need that is within his capability. Therefore, life-saving givers understand that we must be our brother's keeper in order to stand in the place of Christ in the lives of others.

The reason is because we understand that we are medium of salvation in the hands of God to do what Christ would have done if He was physically on earth. Departing to heaven and sending the Holy Spirit, Christ Jesus intends Christians to continue His mission of redemption even as we are driven by the Holy Spirit to execute divine missions He sets upon our hearts. We receive conviction from the Spirit to follow up with what is the will of God at a particular point in time. What we do is not under the influence of our might, neither is it by the ability of our power; but, by the leading of the Spirit of God. By this phenomenon the life-saving giver overcomes the barrier of discrimination that prevents others from stretching forth a helping hand for the safety of someone else in need. As long as the needy is a human being and the Spirit of God convinces them to give, life-saving givers do not excuse that divine task based on differences of personality or emotions that produces bias in consideration.

On top of that, life-saving givers develop a level of faith that gives them a strong conviction that God is their sufficiency. As a result, they never mind losing whole lots of resources from their coffers only for the survival of the needy. Sometimes, it is not that some givers have lots of reserves which they trust to resort to for their other personal needs. It is just that those people hope in the divine supply of God. They don't depend on what they have in store to give; but they believe in what God can provide to ensure the availability of enough resources first to meet the need of souls just about to perish and for their own needs also. Therefore, the internal fears that grips others and make them incapable of being of support to others do not have any influence on life-saving givers.

It is not because they are also not shot by the arrows of fear thinking about providing for themselves, family and maintaining the status of their businesses. Satan would never leave anyone who gets to that point of trying to accomplish a divine mission go scot-free. He tried and tested the Lord Jesus at the climax of His fasting before the Lord began His work; at which point the Lord Jesus won over him. Exactly the same, the devil struggles and battles any follower of Christ who is touched by the Holy Spirit to do something worthwhile that would reveal the glory of God in the lives of some people he (the devil) might have kept captives. These struggles come to the individual through dealing with thoughts in the mind. Satan would want to suggest all other alternate escape doors that would make 'good reasons' for the individual to forsake the divine task at hand.

So, life-saving givers have got to deal with those proposed opposing thoughts of the devil that are sent to scare them off from giving out to support the needy. They are able to overcome these internal fears by trusting in the divine provisions of God. Thus, they believe that if what they possess was provided by God, and they have come to a point that they must give some fraction of it to support the desire of God, and they obey, God is able to give them more. Trusting in the provision of the Good Shepherd, they do not get disappointed because God never lets them down.

Looking at the service of the life-saving Samaritan on the raided man, we get to know more about how compassionate, life-saving givers give. Touched at heart, he didn't begrudge spending his bandage, oil and wine right at the spot on the man as a first aid to keep the dying man alive and get his pains relieved. Those bandages, oil and wine were not intended to be spent on that man; yet, it had become necessary at that instance and hence the good Samaritan had no choice. He didn't care about spending all the quantity of those materials on the raided man. You can imagine how much quantity of bandage, oil and wine would be enough to dress a man wounded to the point of being half dead. Therefore, the Samaritan might have ended up using all the materials he had on the man; never having to be discouraged with the thought of 'What if I also get hurt along the way?'. If even that thought occurred to him, he overcame it and just ignored it because of the present necessity. **The necessity of the present situation and the urgency of action to be taken to save a life causes life-saving givers to let all other things wait**. They position the present need at the top of the scale of preference while all others can remain below.

The good Samaritan afterwards put this wounded traveller on his own animal to send him to where he could be catered for. That's one trait of a life-saving giver. This giver here had to give his own animal as a transporting medium for the half-dead person to make it somewhere safe. The animal here is equivalent to today's luxurious cars such as limousines, Rolls-Royce, land cruisers, etc. owned by some wealthy men of our time. Imagine how many of these men of our time will offer his car to help convey a bleeding wounded man to the hospital. It will be hard to find one, though a few would. Those few would be those who have the heart of a life-saving giver. So, the Samaritan had to lose his status by offering his own animal. The animal that classed him as wealthy or gave him a high status in his time needed to be offered to save a life; and he did not hesitate to give it out. He did not consider what class the animal placed him in life but how that animal can be used in such a case to save a life. He valued the human life at stake more than the animal he possessed. **Life-saving givers risk losing their status and resources to save the dying needy.**

The problem with many men today is that they cannot lose their status even for a second for the survival of another person. **Life-saving givers value life more than any material thing.** With the era we are in, many people value their possessions that place them in high status more than the lives they ought to have reached. Far it be from them to lose some costly classic material of theirs in the name of rescuing someone else. Nonetheless, no other thing under the sun and beyond could be so much more important and more precious than life. That's the reason, all angels in heaven rejoice when one life is saved, because one most valuable thing in the sight of God has been saved. This knowledge is not far-fetched from the reach of life-saving givers and hence they offer the perishables to save the non-perishables. Earthly status and resources are perishable; yet a soul saved for God continues into eternity.

As if it wasn't enough spending on the wounded man, the Samaritan went on to give money to the innkeeper to take care of the man. His readiness to provide both material and monetary support for the survival of the wounded man proved his genuine compassion. He had to pay for the cost of the living expenses of the raided man for the time he had to be kept by the innkeeper and promised to pay more if there arose further expenses. **This demonstrates the fact that a life-saving giver, as the Samaritan was, does not do incomplete service**. A life-saving giver does the best till he sees that the needy is completely redeemed from all hardships or problems. Until the needy becomes peaceful, a life-saving giver does not have peace of mind. He does not rest until the suffering of the needy comes to an end. Life-saving givers do not leave the needy whom they decide to help in the middle of the journey with the thought that they are done with their part.

A good work done is one that is successfully completed. A half-completed work does not deserve an optimum reward and sometimes such works would even not be rewarded at all. With regards to that, anyone who desires to help his neighbour must see to it that the menace that entangles the needy is dealt with to the end. Else, there is the possibility that a half-helped needy could revert back to point zero just as he was originally found. Yes, there is a very high probability of that happening. All because, in the first place, the needy was seen to be handicapped without the ability to help himself; that's what probably made the giver decide to offer up some help.

So, until the needy can be placed in a condition of sustenance or be restored and able to fend for himself or defend himself, he must not be left to be on his own. Else, all that has been done in part for a needy will easily be taken away again for the needy to go back to square zero; maybe because the needy might not yet have obtained the level of ability to keep himself safe. If that should happen, it would also mean that the initial help by the giver would have been wasted per the intention behind that help. Every support or help is intended to make the needy survive; so, if that which was provided could not make the needy survive as much as possible to the point where the needy wouldn't decline back to his destitution, it means it was not complete.

Most givers do not go to such an extent of ensuring, within their ability, the optimum survival of the needy they were led to help; but a life-saving giver would always do a complete service! This is the good thing that the good Samaritan did. He tried his best to put in proper place every condition that would ensure the complete recovery of the half-dead traveller for him to completely get his strength restored. Till they see that the needy is safe and fully restored, life-saving givers do not relent of their divine duty. It is a burden they carry that unless they fulfill it, they just feel uncomfortable. They don't do it because any man forces them to do it; their service is under no compulsion by any man. They do not do it because it is required of them as a responsibility by the systems of this world. Something beyond nature constraints them to that obligation and that keeps them consistent to it until they are completely through with it. A divine urge of responsibility is the driving force of life-saving givers which has a particular destination of accomplishment.

Despite ensuring the safety of the needy, notice here that the Samaritan did not waste all his time at the inn knowing that he himself was not doing much personally since the innkeeper had taken over. He thought it wise to also go and probably look for more money such that he could come and settle the further cost that might be incurred. This also informs that though the life-saving giver must ensure the complete survival of the needy, it doesn't necessarily mean he must be constrained not to manoeuvre around his own business that could even bring more resources to support the needy.

This is a very important notice to deter any needy from wrongly accusing a giver, should it become necessary that the giver must leave for a while. Yes, not to leave forever, but to go and come back again, all for the benefit of the giver himself and of the needy also. The compassion of a life-saving giver is akin to the care a mother has for her child. A mother who is away from her child, due to one reason or the other, always has concerns in her thoughts how well her child would or should be doing and yearns all the time to get back to the child no matter how life circumstances have separated them. Certainly, the same, every true life-saving giver would always look back and do whatever possible to come back to complete what was started in the life of the needy.

The Samaritan could stand properly at a position God desired him to be as a channel to save the dying traveller. When the need arose, he did not hold back his resources and even his status in order that a life could be saved. He did all these at the expense of having to battle the conflicting thoughts about fears of the lack he might face in the future on his own personal needs together with external fears. A point where robbers had attacked someone is never a safe place to spend even a minute. All because, other robbers could have also attacked this Samaritan while he was delayed at the place.

I'm sure this thought forms a greater fraction of the reason that the other two people never wasted time dealing with the half-dead man. They would have taught, 'What if the robbers are still around setting ambush to raid the next person?'. They therefore hastened on with their journey to save their lives from being attacked the same way. Nevertheless, so bold to save a life, the good Samaritan spent enough time at that very dangerous place spot to have all the wounds of the traveller dressed before sending him to the inner keeper. While others flee, life-saving personnel wait for any opportune chance to rescue the dying needy; also, they act within that fierce atmosphere having the lives to save as their priority thereby losing focus on the external fears.

At Gateway Church in Scotland, one Tuesday evening, I had an opportunity to listen to one of the front liners of the pending Ukraine-Russia war. One event of her narration that really challenged me was when one young man was able to take a van which could take a maximum of six people through the heat of the bombing zone just to rescue people who were stuck in there having no hope of escape. Putting his own life at risk, this person went around and got about twenty people rescued from that dangerous scene with that small van. This part of the narration caught my attention such that the Spirit of God began to minister to me on it.

That's a real trait of a life-saving giver. Bravery is a very important quality life-saving givers employ to overcome all adverse threats that would want to obstruct their service. All because, any life-saving giver should have overcome both internal and external fears before he/she even sets off to give. Else, even if one is peaceful on the inside, some external threats are bound to bump in to frighten the serene course of the saving service he has been touched to offer. Whoever that can pass through such fearful conditions to save a life, hence a life-saving giver, is a brave person.

The foremost source of such bravery is relying on the protection of the Spirit of God. Touched by the Spirit of God to offer some help to anyone, one must believe that God is with him through all what would happen in the saving process. Despite the unfavourable threats that could be speculated, with the presence of God, nothing is unsurmountable. 'If God be for us, who can be against us' (Roman 8:31), 'The Lord is on my side; I will not fear. What can man do to me?' (Psalm 118:6), 'So we may boldly say: 'The Lord is my helper; I will not fear. What can man do to me?' (Hebrews 13:6), etc. are quotations to ignite one's faith being led by the spirit to offer a helping hand to save someone. No matter the possible threats evaluated and proposed by 'concerned citizens', one must believe in God's word and the promptings of the Holy Spirit more than what he sees or hears. Being convicted of the presence of God, one must pursue his divine order of offering a helping hand with a genuine conscience; and everything shall be fine at the end.

Together with reliance on the Spirit of God, the second source of bravery for life-saving givers is the application of the golden rule which states that 'Love your neighbour as yourself.' (James 2:8). Apostle James quotes this from the Lord Jesus who said, 'And just as you want men to do to you, you also do to them likewise.' (Luke 6:31) No matter how fearsome the place where the raided man laid, the Samaritan had taught that if it were him lying at such a spot, he would have been grateful for someone to sacrifice to come to his rescue. After all, they all passed on the same road and if it had not happened to this traveller in particular, it is possible it could have happened to any other person.

That means this traveller, in other words, saved the others who came after him from the robbers' attack. All because, robbers hungry for attack wouldn't leave a spot if they do not get any victim to fall in their plot. As a result, the subsequent passers-by did not encounter any robbery because this dying man had already been sacrificed. Thinking that the situation of the attacked man could have been him because he is also coming along the same road, the Samaritan did what he would have wished someone did for him in case he was the one that had been attacked. Yet, how many men would obtain that second thought, if not a life-saving giver as this Samaritan.

What many people fail to do is to reason that they could be at the same spot where they now see some needy people; and to also think of how they would have expected other people to react to them if they were the victims. Therefore, the important question for one to ask himself now is 'If it were me, what would I expect a passer-by to do for me?' Take time to sincerely consider this question and obtain a reasonable answer; thus, the appropriate treatment you would wish that it be shown to you, were it you. If one has gotten an answer, then he should do the same for the needy nearby. It isn't what you would expect a relative, good person or friend to do for you; but what you would expect just a passer-by to do for you. All because one can get caught up in a net of trouble very far away from where there is a very low probability for those who are familiar to come along such a path. It could be in such a case that only unknown people would be available. So, in such a circumstance, what you would expect those unknown passers-by to do for you, go and do the same for the needy you have just caught a glimpse of. Thus says the golden rule of the scripture.

If all men could apply this rule and practically operate it on a daily basis, I believe almost every needy along the road of life would be attended to, if even not fully, up to a point that they would be comfortable to carry on and not to quit. Thus, every needy person would have some helping hand by any kind of passer-by because everyone would wish to be shown mercy if he finds himself in trouble. If not that we have forsaken the word of God that says, 'Blessed are the merciful, for they shall obtain mercy' (Matthew 5:7); then we would have reached the needy hands that are stretched towards us every day and fulfilled the golden rule.

It is sad that you could find someone who would wish to be shown mercy but denies showing mercy on another man at his doorstep. Some people wished they were helped; yet when they get to a point where they could be of help to others, they hesitate to respond positively. Just as the parable of the Lord Jesus concerning forgiveness portrayed. The servant who owed the master sought to be forgiven and was granted forgiveness by his master; but when this same person met some other person he had to forgive, he would never forgive the debtor for a lesser debt. How awful! That has been the character of many children of God; and that's against the golden rule. If it were them, mercy must be shown; but for others they see no reason to show mercy.

Life-saving givers are able to accomplish their divine task by employing the golden rule as a considered reason to help no matter the surrounding threats. If even someone is stuck in the middle of a place where bombing and shooting is ongoing, that person would still wish some saviour should manifest through the external fearsome conditions to come to his rescue. At that point, the victim would not think about what might happen to that saviour; all that he would desire is for such an imaginary saviour to emerge from anywhere possible and rescue him. Even amid a fire outbreak, victims stuck in the middle of intense heat of flaming fire would wish that someone would still bravely pass through the fire and come to their rescue. The problem is, would those very people do the same for others if they see other people in those conditions?'. Only life-saving givers can take such risks. As such, their selfless service is a delight unto the Lord Jesus who enacted the golden rule and hence He delivers them from all fearsome attacks that are associated to their service of rescuing others.

Is Godly but Not Religious

Being religious is to be concerned with sacred matters, religion or church. We kind of see this character in the first two personalities who came across the attacked man: that's the priest and the Levite. Their position caused them to be bound by sacred vows which they had to show themselves faithful for all to see. They were therefore more concerned with making sure they execute their responsibilities pertaining to the offices which they hold as clean as possible. As such, they would ignore anything that would cross their path that could cause their delay or stop them from meeting their religious requirement, no matter the circumstance. Such people are committed to properly delivering their religious obligations at the expense of any other thing. To ensure they are ceremonially clean, they are carefully selective of their associations and cases they would have to approach and others they should deny. Sometimes they would be compelled to ignore circumstances that concern their own relatives just to remain loyal to the religious vows.

Religion presents methods of approach to worship that should be chronologically and systematically followed, which is not bad because the believer gets to know the laid down principles that he must meet. Yet, since the process of worship is laid down, it becomes somewhat a compulsion to the believer just to ensure meeting what seems like written steps. That actually brings worship into the letter rather than into spiritual relationship with the one being worshipped. Letter worship reinstates the law of the old that had to be strictly observed just as it had been inscribed.

As said earlier, it isn't bad to know what is expressly required of a man to do and for him to do the same at particularly arranged times exactly. The problem generated here is when the spiritual communion and consent of God who is being worshipped is lost; yet the worshipper still believes to be pleasing Him with his properly followed and executed laid down chronological methods. Religious people are not touched or moved by a spiritual urge to do something; but they do things because it is supposed to be done that way and at that time. They hold up to propositions that are against amendment of the approach of worship whether physically or spiritually; hence it becomes hard for them to positively respond to current promptings of the Spirit of God.

Religious people tend to have difficulty in being led by the Spirit of God towards something that is different from what they are used to. Therefore, those who had issues with believing in the Lord Jesus Christ during His time on earth were especially religious people. Those that fought the Lord and eventually had Him sentenced to death on the cross were religious people. They couldn't understand how God could possibly do a new thing that is different from what they are acquainted with. Nevertheless, God is God and for that matter He chooses to do whatever He wants whether within or without the limit of knowledge of men. Yet, God does not deny men signals of His intentions and those signals are for those who have eyes and ears.

Though the prophecies about Christ were well recorded across their scrolls which they read day and night; yet they found it very hard comprehending how a son of man coming from a small city, Nazareth could be the Son of God. Forgetting and not acknowledging that the ways of God are far different from the ways of men, the religious leaders failed to give honour to Jesus as the Messiah sent from God to save all men including themselves. Though it was a prophecy that was bound to happen for them to hand Him over to the Romans, it came to pass through their religious way of thinking and approach to worship. Emmanuel, God with us, was Jesus Christ with them but they were too fleshy minded to notice Him. Hence, they accused Jesus of blasphemy that He made Himself equal God which is against their religious belief. Yet, that was how the prophecy declared it that God was now made flesh to dwell with men for the redemption and reconciliation of all men unto Himself.

Unfortunately, they beheld Jesus and the only thing they saw was a carpenter's son born in Nazareth. They couldn't recognize the God-factor of Jesus Christ because religious methods had blinded them. Together with that they saw Jesus' approach of worship which He taught His disciples as completely different from what they knew from old. That generated their hatred and envy which were the foundations for their accusations they rained on Jesus. If they could put aside their religious point of view and try to look at Jesus through the lens of the will of God for a particular season, they could have realised who Jesus Christ really is. They could have then known He is really a King not only of the Jews, but a King of all kings! Sadly, they saw all that they needed to be shown yet could not perceive; neither could they understand what they heard. All because their measuring rod was based on religious analysis.

I believe this Samaritan had something worthwhile to do that made him start his journey from Samaria. He would have got important tasks to accomplish among which there could be urgent ones. Yet seeing the situation at hand, he had to push all his targets to reach that day ahead of time in order to save a life. No matter how tight his schedule had been, he disrupted it because the circumstance of the half-dead man needed the most urgent attention as at that time. That is the lifestyle of a life-saving Giver. Sometimes they can't keep faithful to their own plans because other urgent matters that need their attention would creep in along the line. As the movement of those led by the Spirit is likened to how the wind moves, so are life-saving givers drawn to attend to critical situations which are sometimes outside their plans. Their readiness to adjust and attend to necessary calls in order to intervene in others' lives shows how compassionate they are towards what they do.

Religious people would not go away even a bit from what has been already planned or already known no matter the situation. Religious people keep the books clean while the practical grounds are not that clean. Religious people pretend even if what they are professing is not the same as what is in their heart, just to tell everyone they have followed the orderly ordered methods. Godly life-saving givers as the good Samaritan tackle the practical grounds to cause the cleansing of the heart and conscience before God. As a result, life-saving givers' actions touch the heart of God more than those who declare themselves clean by letter but not by Spirit-led necessary actions.

Gives not on Condition

Lying in a pool of blood was the traveller seeking for someone to come to his aid. In such a state as he was, one main question that could pop up in the mind of any passer-by would be about how beneficial it would be to sacrifice and help this man. All because I believe he was not able to speak enough to even give a promise to the one who passed by. With what economic benefit would the one going to help in such a case be moved. I mean what physical analytical benefit would compel one to come to the aid of a man in such a situation. None of such could be the basis of the Samaritan for going ahead to attend to someone strange to him such as this traveller. The action of the good Samaritan was based on no condition of expecting to gain something significant from the traveller. This is an important characteristic of life-saving givers. They do not set their eyes on specific returns they would gain from the needy and use them as their basis of jumping in to help. Life-saving givers approach their act of service in the ministry of giving with unconditional mindset and directing all their attention on how to restore life, strength and peace to the one in need.

The world today operates on the platform of give and take; thus quid pro quo, someone gives while simultaneously taking from whom he's giving to. If there is nothing to take from the receiver, it becomes unreasonable in the analysis of men in our days to commit to giving. The world would term it 'waste' if anyone is to go by the ideology of offering something without targeting to receive significant returns. Yes, to the world, it is a waste of time, waste of money, waste of strength, etc. to go all out with one's resources to ensure the establishment of something without targeting to get a significant reciprocation. It becomes economically unreasonable for anyone to take such a step in these days where hardship is rampant everywhere. Yet a life-saving giver will do exactly that if that is what needs to be done to save a life.

Though a life-saving giver would never go unrewarded due to how their work is desiring to God, the afterward reward is not the driving force for them to begin their service of giving. We have known previously about how life-saving givers obtain blessings here on earth and hereafter. Yet a life-saving giver would not want to know from analysis what sort of reward to receive from the needy or God before going all out to provide their services of giving. Their motivation is based on the love of God and the love and compassion they gain towards the needy. They do not go into terms of agreement with the needy before agreeing to help.

Giving on condition is like merchandise where you are telling the needy to buy your service. Yet, some of these needy do not have what it takes to buy some services else they would have purchased them and helped themselves out of their plight. A life-saving giver will surely receive a reward, but he does not sell his service to the needy by giving based on pre or post conditions. Giving based on condition limits the intensity of how one gets involved with his heart in the service of giving. When the analysis of inspecting to know what to receive afterwards proves less weighty, the conditional giver would then be discouraged to fully get involved with what he has. Yet the unconditional giver who is a life-saving giver does not get his focus on that and hence is able to fully concentrate on touching every needed aspect of the needy to ensure restoration and survival.

Points to note

➢ A life-saving giver is characteristically fond of having a longing desire to intercept the process of death on someone about to die because of need

➢ When all is said and done, worldly-riches-chasers find themselves wanting because they had no relationship with the eternal Lord

➢ Every action happening now has a reflection from what has already been written

➢ The knowledge of the word of God has the transforming power on the reader to empower him to obtain the gift of eternal life from God

➢ The word of God is the overcoming weapon against the deception of Satan

➢ Ignorance can enslave you under the manipulations of Satan till he leads you to your doom.

➢ Prayer is the driving force for the desire to read the bible. A prayerless person is without the appetite for the word of God

➢ Reading of the bible, in itself, is a weapon against Satan and his agents.

➢ A neighbour is a person who obtains compassion on the fellow needy nearby or along his path.

➢ Being a neighbour does not end at giving smiling gestures and greetings to people.

➢ True neighbouring is compassion and mercy in action

➢ The conscience of a Spirit-led child of God would never allow him to just neglect doing the right thing in accordance with the will of God about an incident

➢ Just a single word or a sentence can lift someone up from his critical point where death would want to take over.

➢ A little thing offered could be of great significance in the life of the afflicted

➤ Men who stand in the gap to offer anything possible to help the needy cross over and overcome the action of death are very importantly needed by God

➤ The scarcity of men to stand in the gap so that the about-to-die needy would survive is really a great concern for God.

➤ Life-saving givers believe that if what they possess was provided by God, and they have come to a point that they must give some fraction of it to support the desire of God, and they obey, God is able to give them more

➤ The necessity of the present situation and the urgency of action to be taken to save a life causes life-saving givers to let all other things wait

➤ Life-saving givers lose their status and resources to save the dying needy.

➤ Life-saving givers value life more than any material thing.

➤ They offer the perishables to save the non-perishables

➤ A life-saving giver, as the Samaritan was, does not do incomplete service

➤ A divine urge of responsibility is the driving force of life-saving givers which has a particular destination of accomplishment.

➤ While others flee, life-saving personnel wait for any opportune chance to rescue the dying needy. They act within that fierce atmosphere having the lives to save as their priority thereby losing focus on the external fears

➤ As the movement of those led by Spirit is likened to how the wind moves, so are life-saving givers drawn to attend to critical situations which are sometimes outside their plans.

➤ Religious people keep the books clean while the practical grounds are not that clean

➤ Godly life-saving givers as the good Samaritan tackle the practical grounds to cause the cleansing of the heart and conscience before God

➤ Giving on condition is like merchandise where you are telling the needy to buy your service

➤ Giving based on condition limits the intensity of how one gets involved with his heart in the service of giving

➤ Though a life-saving giver would never go unrewarded, the afterward reward is not the driving force for them to begin their service of giving

CHAPTER SEVEN

The Theme Centred on Jesus Christ

THE ULTIMATE LIFE-SAVIOUR

In as much as the Lord Jesus did present this parable as a lesson to teach His audience about how to positively affect the needy that one finds across his path, He also indirectly was presenting His own ministry as a Life-saving Giver through the parable of the good Samaritan. The role portrayed by the main character of this parable painted the exact portrait of the messianic ministry of the Lord Jesus. **There was always more to dig out from the parables the Lord Jesus gave out during His in-flesh crusade here on earth**. It was not easy for even the intellectuals among the Pharisees and Sadducees to comprehend and make total meaning out of what they heard from Him.

Unless it is given from above, no man holds divine authentication into the divine mysteries of the kingdom of God. For hearing, it is easy to hear but to understand is far different. Understanding a single word from God takes more than physical intellect and experience. The Pharisees and Sadducees had a good record of book knowledge and experience; yet they were found wanting in the act of trying to comprehend what Christ meant in all His words. Understanding Jesus throughout the whole bible, takes the Spirit of God. With even those who are possessed with the Spirit of God, there are different measures of understanding that they are divinely authorised to access with regards to their maturity in the Lord.

It is needless to make the secrets that are made available to grown men accessible to babies. All because very deep important matters will seem as playing instrumental platforms to babies for them to entertain themselves. Babies always seek for opportunities to play and as such yearn for playing gadgets. They would either play with their available playing gadgets or use what they are given, no matter what it is, in place of that to entertain themselves. Secrets of God are accessed through divine authentication as to the level and discipline a man is positioned in the will and mission of God. There were therefore more padlocks of knowledge that were needful to be unlocked in the parable of the good Samaritan in order to obtain the full package of the knowledge behind Jesus' presentation.

As a result, though it was good for the audience of Jesus to learn how to be kind to strangers and even relatives from the parable of the good Samaritan, there was yet another revelation of the ministry of the Christ Himself who was presenting the parable. Yes, He spoke about Himself. So, in the following section we have made a comparison of the good Samaritan and the character of Jesus, the part of the Godhead, beheld by the world as the Son of God full of grace and truth during His practical mission of redemption on earth. He presented Himself through the parable of the good Samaritan and His presentation will be discovered through the following sections.

JESUS EQUATED TO THE GOOD SAMARITAN

Jesus was Eternal-life Conscious

Jesus' constant parables about the Kingdom of God well demonstrated how He was eternal life conscious and how He wanted men to be more concerned with eternity beyond mortality. He spoke more of heaven and hell, especially hell where men should never desire to end up after this life. Making His audience know clearly that there is life after this present life, the Lord Jesus directed the conscience of men more on the reality of the existence of eternity after mortality through His parables. His encounter with Zacchaeus shows how willing He is to go so far to help bring eternal life into the home of wordly men who have been condemned by themselves and by others not to be deserving to receive eternal life in their hearts .

Zacchaeus himself testified from the happiness he had obtained, in which he had to do all necessary restitutions which also demonstrated the unspeakable joy he had received for having Jesus come into his home. Hence it was confirmed by Jesus: "And Jesus said to him, "Today salvation has come to this house, because he also is a son of Abraham; for the Son of Man has come to seek and to save that which was lost (Luke 19:9,10). The Lord is very much concerned with our lives in Him after mortality; so the basis of His mission was to seek the lost so they would obtain eternal life through being saved.

He himself rejected being enthroned as king by the men who admired his teachings and demonstration of signs and wonders. Not to show that accepting kingship is wrong but to demonstrate that accepting an offer against the divine will of God for your life is an error. All because **the offer of the world that's not divinely aligned to the mission of a man will automatically prevent that man from accomplishing his divine assignment**. Therefore, putting eternity above all other things, Jesus demonstrated that our acceptance of offers must be in relation to our divine missions that would help us accomplish our divine purpose within which lies eternal life for our souls.

Jesus is the real example and role model for the world. Although having life in himself, he lived as orderly as required by divinity just as a person who wants to attain eternal life from God would. He did this all in the purpose of setting for us the example which is the way to attain eternal life. For that reason, He said I am the way, the truth and the life. Through His well lived life and His words, we find the truth which shows us the way to eternal life. The totality of the life of Jesus is the true way to eternal life.

Jesus was a True Neighbour

He had shown His followers how to give to their fellow who has an empty bowl when they (His followers) notice that they have more than enough. In order to show them how to be compassionate and to have the eyes to see when people are suffering, he fed the hungry thousands in the wilderness. It takes the compassionate eyes to witness that someone close is really in pain. Sometimes the victims might not have the strength and desire to voice their plight; yet a compassionate companion would always notice that something is wrong. The power to sense that people around us are not in the right mood necessitates the correct action to be taken to dig out and solve the root problem causing the change of state and mood of the victims.

Jesus Christ saw it straight away that the people who had followed Him all day needed to be strengthened. Leaving them to go for their own food might not be the best choice because some being so weary might fall along their way, not being able to reach the source of food. Working all that out through His compassionate heart, He saw that food must be provided for them there and then. Twice on different accounts at different places he fed thousands of people who were weak and weary for lack of food by commanding food from heaven. In each of these settings the people ate and gathered superfluous food. Meaning that what He offers in His intervention to solve the problem of the needy is always more than sufficient. This manner of His character proved that Jesus is a real neighbour. He identifies the need of the close neighbour by compassion and takes an action sufficient within His ability to solve the need at stake.

Jesus, seeing that a widow's only son was dead, and the corpse being sent to burial, felt very sorry for the lady who was wailing because her only source of human companionship is being taken away by death.

Jesus went there without being called to raise the son in order to solve the broken-hearted need of that lady. Yes, He was not invited; yet He saw the need to act through compassion. As said earlier, sometimes the need at stake takes the whole breath of the needy such that either they cannot even ask for help from others, or they do not know how to ask for the help. It takes a true neighbour, just as Jesus demonstrated, to approach them and help them even if they have not requested. A help provided from true compassion from the heart whether requested or not does a great deal in a great way in the lives of the needy involved. This character of Jesus was portrayed by the good Samaritan having compassion and approaching to attend to the raided man without invitation.

Jesus was Spirit-led

The Lord Jesus Christ demonstrated the need of being Spirit-led right from the start of His ministry to the end. The Spirit of God led Him right from baptism to wait while fasting in the wilderness before coming to face men. That's really a great example needed to be explored by Christians; why the Son of God who is the Word of God and who could have started preaching His word, already in Him, right away; yet, needed to go for isolation all by the leading of the Spirit. His first Sermon at the synagogue revealed His acknowledgment of the Spirit leading when He began by reading from the prophesied words, "The Spirit of the Lord is upon Me…". When it comes to reaching people's needs, we find Him being led by the Spirit of God on the platform of compassion to go and raise Lazarus up from the dead. This decision of going to Judea where Lazarus had died particularly was opposed by His disciples. Let's have a look:

Then after this He said to the disciples, "Let us go to Judea again." The disciples said to Him "Rabbi, lately the Jews sought to stone You, and are You going there again?" … He said to them "Our friend Lazarus sleeps, but I go that I may wake him up." (John 11:8,9)

The disciples trying to spell out the external dangers that could befall Jesus for taking that step to Judea, intended to dissuade Him from that decision but they could not succeed. It isn't that what the disciples were putting across was not factual; the potential dangers they were spelling out were all intact, but that could not stop Jesus. All because that was the next agenda on the Spirit's rota. Amidst the dangerous atmosphere, Jesus stuck to being obedient to the leading of the Spirit in order to accomplish the desire of God by meeting the need of the family of Lazarus which in turn brought glory to God.

This character of Jesus is portrayed by the good Samaritan staying alone at a dangerous zone to attend to the half-dead man at the expense of his own life. He just did not give in to the voice of people around Him about the external fears in relation to what God had placed on His heart to do at that moment. Looking at where the Spirit of God is looking at a particular time to act accordingly is termed the will of God at that said time. External fears couldn't dissuade the Lord from reaching out to some people who were in dire need of His presence. That has always been the character of the Lord Jesus; He reveals Himself at any place where there is enormous hunger for His presence.

The risk a normal person wouldn't take for fear of his life, a life-saving giver as Jesus, portrayed in the parable of the good Samaritan, will do it being led by the Spirit on the platform of compassion. What do you think made Jesus follow up till Golgotha to be stripped off naked and crucified, if not because He was steered by the Spirit of God to accomplish His divine mission, for which He came to the earth? He laid down His life for the whole world because that was the agenda of the Spirit of God per the timely divine assignment that had been enacted even before the foundation of the earth. There He was to accomplish what had been written in the books about Him.

Jesus had no choice because all His choice had been yielded into the plan of the Spirit of God who had filled Him to the full. His desire was therefore driven to be in line with the desire of the Spirit of God so that it might not be the will of His flesh that would be done but the will of God that would be accomplished. The Spirit of God was looking to the cross and hence He had to yield to be driven to follow accordingly because that was the will of God that had caught all the attention of Heaven at that time. Jesus wouldn't have desired to fail the kingdom of God whose dignitaries were all interested to get the updates of the outcome of the ongoing mission targeted to unlock the prisons of hell and death where men had been captivated by the influence of Satan. The Lord Jesus wouldn't have desired to fail His Father by denying consent to be used as the sacrificial lamb because both had agreed by covenant of oneness of the Godhead to execute this mission under the leading of Spirit; hence He gave in. He walked on earth as a fully Spirit-led Man.

Jesus stood in the gap

For all have sin and come short of the glory of God (Romans 3:23). Separated from God due to our sins and sentenced to death, men had no opportune way to obtain back the life and glory God gave to us. There were the souls of men wandering about being bound by the chains of sin and doomed to suffer eternal death. Our flesh was in rebellion to God due to deception of Satan yet deep down within us, our souls cried for a saviour. Men needed an intercessor to plead our cause before God and speak on our behalf. A voice that will not accuse us but will look beyond our sins and guilt. All because men realised we are indeed getting drowned in the pool of sin; how to get out of sin and gain our grounds with God was the problem. If another man was righteous enough to plead for us before God, that would have been helpful. Yet when God checked if He could find one to plead for the others, He didn't find any.

Good looks down from heaven upon the children of men, to see if there are any who understand, who seek God. Every one of them has turned aside; they have together become corrupt; there is none who does good; no, not one. (Psalm 53:2,3)

Sin had become a worldwide pandemic and all men tested positive for it. Since the unrighteous could not stand in for other unrighteous, men needed someone righteous yet not among men because all men had sinned. Men dearly needed someone to stand in the gap so that the final verdict of our case before God will go in our favour. The accusations raised by Satan on all men implied all men had to make their way to eternal doom if we had no one to speak for us. Men had to elect one among us who was worthy to stand for us to present our appeal before God. Men needed a lawyer, a righteous one for that matter, and hence that figure was scarce per the search results on people on the earth. How then could man gain victory over sin and death? How could men be liberated from the manipulation of Satan and his devices? These were the unanswered questions the souls of men kept struggling with.

God, knowing all things, had made provision for the redemption of men even before that point was reached. Foreordained before the foundation of the world, God had made a plan for the remission of the sins of fallen men through the sacrifice of the divine lamb. In due time, Christ Jesus the word of God manifested in flesh to accomplish this mission which no man could do due to our state of unrighteousness. God came into flesh as Jesus Christ so He could be the voice of plea for men; so that He could be our sin offering to pacify God; and so that He could be the bridge to restore men back to their place and position with God.

The righteous therefore had to die for the unrighteous in order to set men free. Since men had no man righteous among us, and the divine requirement for our salvation also demanded the sacrifice of a righteous man, it necessitated God to become man, in the nature of Christ. God's love for men is thus demonstrated in His willingness to offer Himself to meet the requirements of men's salvation. These requirements are spiritual codes that are employed in the spiritual law courts. God, bringing every spiritual legal requirement checked, offered Christ, God who has become man, who is righteous to stand for all men.

The souls of men then rejoiced at the revelation of Christ, a man not from our descent of unrighteousness, to represent us. All the accusations laid on men before God were nullified because the Messiah had died on the cross in the place of all men. When the Lamb of God had been slain, the chains of sin and death were broken such that men now have the opportunity to make their way to be in relationship with God almighty. Other than that, the destinies for the sinful men were to end up in doom. All men were at the verge of eternal destruction when the ultimate Life-saviour Jesus manifested out of the blue to stand in the gap.

Jesus stood in the gap to take upon Himself all our suffering. He was bruised, buffeted and disgraced for the sake of men. All this He did, so that men would not end up in eternal death. That's the characteristics of a true life-saving giver. The Lord Jesus terminated the action of death on men the moment he had offered Himself as a sacrifice for sin. Then was there a shout 'O Death, where is your sting? O Hades, where is your victory?' (1 Corinthians 15:55) The Lord Jesus had taken the authority over Death and Hades and had issued the way to Salvation to all men through believing in Him. A life-saviour indeed He was to lead all who were even captivate in Hades into His glory. He stood in the gap and stopped Satan from completing his cycle of stealing, killing and destroying on all men.

Without Jesus, Satan would have led all the souls of men into destruction. Satan begins by deceiving men to sin, and when he has succeeded in that, he raises accusations even based on the word of God for the sinful men to be destroyed. Thanks to Jesus, the light of the world who drives out the darkness of deception employed by Satan from the eyes of men. The word of God lets us know in as much that Satan comes to steal, kill and destroy, Jesus came that men may have life and have it in abundance.

Jesus Christ is seated on the right hand of God still interceding for those who believe in Him. His character of desiring to stand in for men didn't end while He was on earth. Now seated as the Lord of lords, He still pleads through His blood for whoever believes in Him and for that matter calls on His name. What a heart of compassion and determination to save men the Christ has! Jesus is He who is and who was and is to come, the Almighty. As a High Priest who has been tested as a human being and hence knows our weakness, Jesus is ever ready to stand in the gap for whoever calls upon His name. He is a ready life-saviour who is omnipresent and hence appears everywhere through His Spirit to stand in the gap and intervene for anyone who asks for His help. Be aware, Jesus is ready to come to you now, not to condemn you but to intercede for you, when you call for Him.

Jesus was Godly but not religious

He had already told them that He came to seek and find the lost. He added that He did not come for the sake of the righteous but for the sake of sinners for them to receive salvation. His attention was different from that of the Levites, the Priests and the devout Jews who sought to please God in their daily execution of what is inscribed in the Law barring humane expressions of pity for those who were in dire need. The Priest in this case, as presented by the parable, might have left the poor wounded man to attend to other righteous active men in the temple waiting for his service. Yet, Jesus (portrayed in the action of the good Samaritan) would always have His eyes turned to the weak men and attend to them. The attention of Jesus while on earth was searching, day and night, for the ones in bondage; in order to deliver them. Think of the woman Jesus found bent over by a disabling spirit for eighteen years, check this out below:

Now He was teaching in one of the synagogues on the Sabbath. And behold, there was a woman who had a spirit of infirmity eighteen years, and was bent over and could in no way raise herself up. But when Jesus saw her, He called her to Him and said to her, "Woman, you are loosed from your infirmity." And He laid His hands on her, and immediately she was made straight, and glorified God. But the ruler of the synagogue answered with indignation, because Jesus had healed on the Sabbath; and he said to the crowd, "There are six days on which men ought to work; therefore come and be healed on them, and not on the Sabbath day." The Lord then answered him and said, "Hypocrite! Does not each one of you on the Sabbath loose his ox and donkey from the stall, and lead it away to water it? So ought not this woman, being a daughter of Abraham, whom Satan has bound for eighteen years, be loosed from this bond on the Sabbath?" And when He said these things, all His adversaries were put to shame; and all the multitude rejoiced for the glorious things that were done by Him. (Luke 13:10-17)

The priests and Levites saw this defect as legally normal and hence had a problem with Jesus who attached urgency in granting her deliverance there and then at the spot in the temple on the Sabbath day. The then leaders of the synagogue saw no problem for the lady suffering. Their only care was that the Sabbath be observed and observed keenly without breaking protocols per the ordinance of the law. So, no matter the conditions of the celebrants of the Sabbath, these rulers of Synagogue had no concern. Whether troubled, in pain or in bondage, just come and keep the law and go and suffer alone in your house. Fortunately for the woman, the Lord of the Sabbath came to church that day and He did contrary to the expectations of the Scribes and Priests; Jesus broke the protocol of the Sabbath to set a captive free.

The Lord Jesus couldn't fathom how uncaring these leaders were with regards to the spiritual condition of the congregants. If they all did not care, Jesus cared, just as He always does! No matter how occupied He was with preaching in the temple, He halted to attend to the deliverance of this woman. Though the others were being blessed by His message, He had to put a pause to them and attend to someone who was more in need. Jesus could have ignored the woman and continued His sermon to gain a nice applause for a sermon well preached; yet His compassion wouldn't allow Him to go on while some innocent daughter of Abraham was still suffering in bondage. He attended to the longing needy whose life was in jeopardy due to the burden Satan had put on her even if that meant to break boundaries of the religious law. This demonstrates that the Lord Jesus Christ was godly and compassionate but not religious which is a characteristic of a life-saving giver as described above.

Jesus gave His life unconditionally

There was no pre or post conditional agreement between the Lord Jesus and men before He accepted to offer Himself as a ransom for us. For the men who had already died and known their fate, their souls were craving for mercy that could be shown beyond their guilt. They had no opportunity to establish a conditional agreement. For the other men who were still living, due to the deception of Satan, their hearts were hardened towards perceiving the will of God that would benefit their souls. Their eyes were blindfolded with different forms of sin to the point that there was the absence of crystal-clear vision of their state with regards to the doom set before them. Hence, they would reject what is good for them and opt for what will destroy them.

The Lord Jesus accepting to die for men therefore was not based on any established condition but based on pure love and compassion. It is written that while we were still sinners, Christ died for us. (Romans 5:8) This shows that men were yet not in one mind with God, yet the Messiah still decided to work out the salvation of men through His compassion. If Christ had looked at the returns He was receiving even when He was with men, He would not have completed His mission. He overcame all barriers to giving and eventually finished His missions. How could He do that? Unconditional love for the souls of men was the driving force for His heart.

Men cannot pay for the service the Lord rendered for us. The cost for redeeming our souls which demanded that Jesus lay down His life and shed His blood is beyond our reciprocating ability. No amount of resources put together can reciprocate such an amount of love that cost Him His very life. As a result, Jesus too died out of unconditional love and compassion. The only thing a man can do to appreciate this love of God is hold fast the salvation that is won for him so that he loses it not again. The devil held men captives; Jesus broke the chains of captivity by the power of His blood when He had nullified all accusations on men by His death on the cross.

The only call of Jesus to the delivered man is to remain in the right position with God so that the devil gets no chance to ensnare him again. The commandments of Jesus therefore are the benefits to the soul who believes that the saved would not get trapped into the chains of devil any longer. The unconditional sacrifice has already been made. Serving God through the words of Jesus is for the benefits of our souls. Jesus is the revelation of the love of God towards men. Jesus is the Light thrown from God unto the darkened world to lead men safely to God. He is the unconditional lover of our souls.

Jesus is Coming Back Again

On the next day, when he departed, he took out two denarii, gave them to the innkeeper, and said to him, 'Take care of him; and whatever more you spend when I come again, I will pay you

These were the words of the good Samaritan after rescuing the traveller and conveying him to the innkeeper safely. The Samaritan gave an assurance that he will surely be coming back again. To the point of getting the half-dead man to the innkeeper, he had done his best that was enough on his part to sustain the traveller. Now that the traveller was in safe hands, there was no need for the Samaritan to spend the rest of his time there. Note he made provision for the traveller's health care before leaving and promised to come back in due time. What was he going away for? To prepare and to come back again. Coming back again the good Samaritan would ensure the safe home return of the traveller and also render payment. For paying the innkeeper, he expressly made it clear that when he had come back, he would pay whatever he needed to pay. That's he would justly render the payment that is due the innkeeper for his service of taking care of the traveller.

There are a few things to notice from this part of the parable which relate to Jesus, the Messiah. During the time He was making assurance to come back again, He also made His audience aware of what would occur while He is away and at His coming, what He would be coming to do. Let's look at four of them which are all reflected in the parable of the good Samaritan:

➢ The Assurance of the company of the Holy Spirit

> And I will pray the Father, and He will give you another Helper, that He may abide with you forever; the Spirit of Truth, whom the world cannot receive… (John 14:16,17)

Having given them assurance that He would not leave them as orphans but would come back again, He promised the disciples that He would make provision for a companion who would be with believers while He is away. The companion He promised was the Holy Spirit who descended upon the apostles on the day of Pentecost and from then has been dwelling in whoever believes in Jesus Christ. Meaning just as the good Samaritan, the Lord made provision for His believers whom He came to save while He is away for a while. He had shouted 'It is finished' on the cross and He needed not to delay any longer on earth. He had overcome Satan, death and Hades so the captivated men were at liberty. Better was He to go and prepare and come back again; yet He committed His believers to the Holy Spirit who would assist, comfort and remind the children of God of the words of Jesus.

All because the newly rescued sinner is still with a lot of wounds which needs continuous treatment by the word of God.

Revealing the current Ministry of Jesus from the Good Samaritan Parable

Jesus Christ is still at work today but through His elected people who are filled with the Holy Spirit whom He promised unto all who believed in Him. Right from the point of meeting the sinner till the time that this sinner is fully prepared to meet the Lord, there are divine assignments worked out by the elects of God who are filled with the Spirit of God. The Holy Spirit serves as a medium for the ministers to transport Christ and His love to the spiritually raided soul.

The Work of the Evangelist/Apostle

Just as the good Samaritan met the wounded man who was in need of help, so are the works of the Evangelists and Apostles. A sinner is full of wounds and hurts that are a threat to the salvation of his soul. A sinner, therefore, is in dire need of help from a life saviour. Some of them who realise such a state of their lives due to lack of internal peace always yearn for a breakthrough but do not know how to go about it; they just go through cycles of being in bondage and addicted to all sorts of things. Some of them who also do not realise their state of destitution continue on to endanger their souls except if they meet some light greater enough to bring them to the point of realisation of their state. The enemy who had set an ambush with his devices has entrapped such people, inflicted wounds on their souls as a result of encapsulating them into different forms of sins, and finally stolen all their divine destinies from them.

A lot of wounded souls in such an episode are just helplessly lying down on the road of life not knowing their fate. Just like the bleeding wounded traveller, the souls of sinners today are yearning for a saviour.

These souls are looking for someone who would not ignore nor condemn them but would compassionately realise their poor states and have mercy on them. The only life-saviour with such compassion and love is the Lord Jesus who is ever willing to get close to them and save them. He is not physically on earth now as He was during His earthly ministry; yet omnipresently appearing to everyone who believes. The presence of the Holy Spirit is to make known the love of Christ to the sinner so that the sinner will have a continuous relationship with Christ. So, Jesus has commissioned such a ministry of salvation for which He came to the earth to His co-workers who are His elect so He, the Lord will continuously be changing lives for the better. This means that He is doing such work of salvation through the ministers whom He has chosen for Himself and empowered with His Spirit.

The divine assignment committed to the Evangelist and Apostles then is to search for these categories of sinners who are all wounded on the road of life. With the preaching of the word of God which is powerful to illuminate the blindfolded eyes and also to bring assurance of hope to the sinner, the evangelist is able to win the attention of the sinner who is in dire need of the help of God knowingly or ignorantly. The word of God is filled with the power of God unto salvation to all who believe. But listen to how Apostle Paul asks the questions that came from the divine inner circle of God when God had met with the dignitaries of Heaven.

For "whoever calls on the name of the Lord shall be saved." How then shall they call on Him whom they have not believed? And how shall they believe in Him of whom they have not heard? And how shall they hear without a preacher? And how shall they preach unless they are sent? As it is written: "How beautiful are the feet of those who preach the gospel of peace, who bring glad tidings of good things! (Romans 10:13-15)

Answering these questions back to front means, a preacher needs to be sent so that the gospel will be preached, then would sinners hear, then would sinners believe, then would sinners call on the name of the Lord, and then would sinners finally be saved. The gospel of peace serves as a powerful headlight aimed to find out the lost soul in the midst of this dark world. The preachers are the carriers of this powerful tool of salvation. So they are sent by the Lord and are empowered by the Spirit of God to embark on such a search. Jesus Christ is the central theme of their message! The accompanying love and compassion of this message is able to get closer to the lost soul more than even the clothes they wear. This divine contact between the sinner and the Lord is achieved through the delivery of the message of the cross by the evangelist under the influence of the Holy Spirit. Every divine contact achieved like this causes joy in the holy chambers of Heaven because a soul has been found by the great light, Jesus.

After the evangelist has found the wounded soul, it does not end there. The evangelist would then assist the soul to a safe place where all the wounds incurred can be well treated and cured. The evangelist goes to deliver the found but wounded soul to the Pastors, Teachers and Prophets. This is exactly what the good Samaritan did. After giving the attacked man first aid, he transported this wounded man to the innkeeper to receive further treatment. The message of the cross serves as the first aid to help sinners encounter Christ, which then gives them hope of survival. Yet for them to fully survive with regards to their salvation, just as the Samaritan wisely did, they ought to be sent under the canopies where continuous nourishment or treatment which would yield full recovery can be attained. Else leaving them after just a one-shot message would render the greater percentage to easily backslide into their formal vices because the world is so slippery with lots of attracting delights of sin. Such a canopy for the newly saved Christian is under the pastors, teachers and prophets.

The work of Pastors, Teachers and Prophets

Just as the innkeeper was committed to ensuring that the wounded man become fully restored, so are pastors, teachers and prophets committed by the Lord to ensure that newly saved Christians are well nourished by the word of faith. For one to have an encounter with Christ means the person is, from that point, born again not of blood nor by the will of flesh but by the will of God as the bible says. (John 1:13) For that matter, as it is fitting for every newly born child to be fed with the right food so as to ensure proper maturity, so does it apply to those who are born again in the Lord.

Improper feeding would lead to malnourishment which leads to improper growth and which would shorten the life of a person. Right food as well as balanced diet is paramount when it comes to taking care of a newly born child. The survival and well-being of a child mainly depends on how right, how often and the quality of food given to the child. There are lots of records of increasing children mortality rate in areas in the world where children are poorly fed. Salvation is no different, if newbies in the Lord are not given attention and are not fed with the right food from the word of God, their survival with regards to retaining their salvation becomes at stake.

The pastor is therefore a significant joint partner of the great commission, together with the evangelists and apostles who go on the streets. As the innkeeper was supposed to do, the pastor also holds a commissioned responsibility to gently tend the sheep (newly saved) brought to his care. The teacher is required, by the authority of his gift, to open the minds of the newly saved into the word of God by the help of the Holy Spirit. Exactly the same, the prophets with edifying, cautioning and correcting revelations from God, ought to uphold the faith of the new child of God. Whether it is the encouragement from the pastor, enlightenment from the teacher or the prophecy of the prophet, they all come together as a balanced feed that is able to help the new believer to build up faith hence yielding maturity. The word of the Lord serves as divine medicine to heal all the broken heart and the bruises of wounds that the world through Satan might have inflicted on the newly saved.

This commission of the pastors, teachers and prophets, whom I refer to as innkeepers continues till the believer matures into the nature of Christ as the Holy Spirit that through the food they provide the believer. So are the assignments of these innkeepers in the inn (church) on the souls as commissioned by the Lord who called the shepherds into their offices of ministry.

➤ Back Again with his Reward

> And behold, I am coming quickly, and My reward is with Me, to give to everyone according to his work. (Revelation 22:12)

At His coming, Jesus is coming with His reward He would give unto all accordingly. The good Samaritan promised to come and pay the innkeeper. Therefore, just as at his return, the good Samaritan would be coming with a pay; so is the Lord coming with a pay (reward). The word from Him to the Apostle John implies the reward would be given exactly in accordance with the work done. The representative of the innkeeper in our time, as enumerated in the section above, are Pastors, teachers and prophets who stay with converted sinners to nourish them with the word of God till they are fully healed from the torture of Satan. Apostles as well as evangelists go out as fishermen to throw their net (which is the word of God) into the sea (the world). Men who are fished out through believing in the word they heard and develop faith which comes by hearing the word of God are sent to the service of the pastors for further nourishment. The strike of the devil through sin leaves lots of bruises and pain on victims such that for the newly converted to be fully fit needs continuous nourishment and medication through the word of God.

Pastors, teachers and prophets who are commissioned to such services are given the mandate by God to do so with full commitment. This is to ensure that the one who was at the verge of dying in sin but was delivered through his encounter with God's word would not turn back to lose his life again. Hence, when all is said and done, the Lord is coming with a reward at His second appearance for all these ministers who worked on sinners in order to save their lives.

At the mention of reward or pay, there is a good feeling in expectation of something good. Certainly, it would be good news for some people but for others it would not. At His coming "...we must all appear before the judgement seat of Christ, so that each may receive what is due us for the things done while in the body, whether good or bad (2 Corinthians 5:10 NIV). What this means is that the reward would be in twofold: one as a response to good deeds and the other as a response to bad deeds. Good deeds rewards are good indeed, yet bad deeds reward equal punishments.

The living man must therefore be aware that whoever a man is, he would not be exempted from the reward the Lord Jesus is coming with irrespective of his status. No man can escape from this time of payments. The only better escape one can do is to escape from the bad rewards which are akin to punishments. Believing in the Lord Jesus and relying on the Holy Spirit who is our help to keep us in line with the word of God would help us escape from the bad wages or payments the Lord is carrying with Him at His coming. All because it would not be easy; that time shall be dangerous.

Remember, the Samaritan initially gave the innkeeper two dinarii to enable him to start his job of taking care of the wounded traveller. This could be attributed in our time as the provisions the Lord make available for pastors, teachers and prophets to enable them to execute their ministerial responsibilities. So, a minister of God must note that he has received part of pay which represents the blessing that should enable him to accomplish the divine task the Lord has commissioned to him. So, the abundant grace and provisions one enjoys as far as being in the office of ministry are what God has made as a medium of working ability for the minister of God. Evangelists, Apostles, Pastors, Teachers and Prophets are blessed with such initial medium of assistance to help them start and embark on their mission. Those who use them proficiently for the work assigned to them would doubtlessly receive good rewards at the return of the Lord. The vice versa is also very valid, let the one has an ear listen, hear, and put into practice what the Spirit of God says to His church.

➤ Back Again to take God's children Home

> And if I go and prepare a place for you, I will come again and receive you to Myself; that where I am, there you may be also. (John 14:3)

The good Samaritan had to go away to make preparation and come back for the traveller. The traveller would have to continue his journey of life but he cannot remain with the innkeeper forever, so the going away of the Samaritan was good to get things sorted so that right from the innkeeper the traveller would have somewhere to go and rest. Every child of God is on a journey which is divinely allotted to him by God. The ultimate end which is desired by the soul is to end up in the presence of the Elohim to worship Him for-evermore. When the Samaritan would have returned, the two things to do were to pay the innkeeper and take the traveller home. Though taking the traveller home is not expressly shown in the parable, the good Samaritan could never leave the traveller without ensuring he arrives home. Due to how sympathetic he had proven from the beginning; he would surely provide conditions of ensuring the traveller gets home, a place of rest. If he had been able to offer his donkey and other materials for the well-being of this traveller, it would not be surprising if he was going to make sure this traveller makes his way to a place of peace and harmony devoid of the threat he had earlier encountered.

Just as the good Samaritan, after going to make necessary preparations, the Lord promised that He would come back and receive His children unto Himself. Where He is, there His children too would be. This Home is the perfect abode of the righteous where peace and love abounds. Though the children of God are liberated from the chains of Satan, yet there is a better dwelling than this world. So, saving us through His death on the cross, He made us a promise that He would come back and take us to the prepared abode once the time is due. What makes the believer well assured of this truth and promise is that the Lord did not deny giving us His own life. It was prophesied of His coming to die for us. At the appointed time, He accepted willingly to accomplish all protocols that would meet our redemption through His death on the cross. Why won't He come the second time if He has promised? The first coming that was full of disgrace, torture and pains, He came for our sake; much more will He come the second time in power and glory to evacuate us from this defiled world into His rest. One thing to take note is that at birth, every soul starts his journey of life meandering through many uncertainties to find his final abode. So, along the road of life if a soul responds positively to his encounter with the life-saviour, Jesus, He leads him safely home; if not, the soul gets lost forever. Watch out!!!

➤ Uncertainty of His coming

The good Samaritan did not specify the day and time he would come back. He just gave the assurance that he would come back. Be it the next day, week or month, the parable does not disclose that. Yet I believe the traveller surely believed what the good Samaritan promised. All because there is a reasonable cause for him to believe someone who stooped low to pick him from the point of death and helped him to survive to that level. So, though the Samaritan did not specify the time of his coming back, the wounded man believed that he would return. The same was the promise that Jesus made to His followers. Jesus Christ did not specify when He was coming. At a point where He was confronted by questions directed specifically to when He would come, His answer was:

'...no one knows the day or hour when these things will happen, not even the angels in heaven or the Son himself. Only the Father knows.' (Matthew 24:36)

So, He left the time of His coming uncertain or unspecified; yet we believe that faithful is He who has promised and surely He would accomplish His word. All because, coming with love and compassion for the first time to work out our redemption by His death on the cross, He fulfilled all the prophecies written about Him. As a result, we are very sure that His words are yea and amen and for that matter He would come in due time just as He has promised. The living saved are therefore not hopeless but have assurance in the faithful words of one compassionate and loving Saviour, Jesus Christ, who keeps His word.

A call to become a Life-saving Giver

With the above characteristics of Jesus Christ paralleled to the character of the good Samaritan, it is obvious that Jesus spoke about Himself in the parable. Hence the practical life of a life-saving giver has already been lived so that men can emulate to become just as He was. Jesus is the ultimate life-saviour to the world. Walking in His already set steps, it becomes possible by the help of the Spirit of God for one to exhibit the same characteristics of offering what he possesses to be of help to others.

Due to scarcity of workers on the field, and because the harvest is already due, there is the need to pray that the Father grants a lot of workers to join the field. There are few who accept the call into true service that glorifies God. There are many givers; yet there are few life-saving givers. As a result, there is a gap that needs to be filled so that the available needy would be served to save their lives to the glory of God.

God is seeking for people who are willing and would opt to be at service whenever they are needed. People who can yield to the leading of the Spirit of God to offer what is in their possession to save the about-to-die needy are being sought for. The Lord is ready to employ whoever is ready to be built up with the characteristics of a life-saving giver.

To be a life-saving giver is to be joining the mission of Christ and to act in place of Him to continue what He started. The totality of this mission is being eternal life conscious, a neighbour, spirit-led person, being able to stand in the gap, overcoming any barriers to giving and reflecting the unconditional love of God unto other lives by giving whatever is in one's ability. Yet all service here is done on the platform of compassion and love through the help of the Holy Spirit.

God is calling, let the willing heart respond and yield, because such a heart would duly be rewarded.

Notable bullets

➤ There was always more to extricate from the parables the Lord Jesus gave out during His in-flesh crusade here on earth.

➤ There are different measures of understanding that they are divinely authorised to access with regards to their maturity in the Lord

➤ Secrets of God are accessed through divine authentication according to the level and discipline a man is positioned in the will and mission of God.

➤ The offer of the world that's not divinely alienated to the mission of a man will automatically prevent that man from accomplishing his divine assignment.

➤ Jesus is a real example and role model for the world.

➤ The totality of the life of Jesus is the true way to eternal life.

➤ It takes the compassionate eyes to witness that someone close is really in pain.

➤ Looking at where the Spirit of God is looking at a particular time to act accordingly is termed the will of God at that said time.

➤ The Lord Jesus reveals Himself at any place there is enormous hunger for His presence.